"Joel presents a fascinating overview of how Biblical and Islamic viewpoints on eschatology overlap, making a convincing case that reading this book and studying what the Old and New Testaments have to say about the "end times" are imperative for Christians today. This book is a wakeup call for Christians to learn how the future of the church, the future of Islam, and the future of the entire world are divinely and directly interconnected. The reader will also gain significant insight into the nature of the last days and the course on which the world is heading at ever increasing speeds."

—*Dr. Tom White, executive director, The Voice of the Martyrs*

"A fascinating and provocative work. Joel has broken fresh ground in the ongoing exploration of the relationship between Islam and the rest of the world. A must-read for priests and pastors, students and lay readers everywhere. Bravo!"

—*Robert Spencer, director of Jihadwatch, author of* Islam Unveiled *and* Onward Muslim Soldiers

"This book definitely provides a fresh look at Bible prophecy in light of current affairs with the global rise of Islamic fundamentalism. Not only does Joel accurately analyze those Islamic doctrines and practices that are relevant to biblical end-time prophecy, but his interpretation of biblical prophecy is also solid—soundly adhering to the accepted rules of hermeneutics."

—*Walid Shoebat, former Palestinian terrorist and author of* Why I Left Jihad

"Joel Richardson provides a weighty analysis of Islam and its messianic figure. This book is central to recognizing the fulfillment of biblical end times prophecy in our day and understanding the role Islam plays in it."

—*Pastor Reza F. Safa, former radical Muslim, author of* Inside Islam

"Joel Richardson serves both the Christian and Muslim communities well. He thoroughly explores the source documents of early Islam and later Muslim theologians and the New Testament. He summarizes them admirably without being too technical. This book clarifies the differences between Christianity and Islam. It is a must-read for Christians and Muslims alike."

—*James M. Arlandson (Ph.D.) teaches at a college in southern California and regularly writes for AmericanThinker.com and Answering-Islam.org.*

"Joel Richardson has posited a scholarly, thoughtful, compassionate, and scriptural concept regarding the astounding theological anti-parallels between the eschatologies of radical Islam and biblical faith. He makes a strong case that this is no mere humanistic coincidence. However, Joel is neither a knee-jerk reactionary nor a paranoid radical. He is, rather, a seeker and lover of truth who has the love and courage to simply lay the historical and theological evidences for his convictions out before us and then grants us the dignity of examining the facts for ourselves so that we can draw our own conclusions. Joel Richardson is a humble servant of Jesus Christ whom I personally know to be a faithful and devoted husband, father, and friend to all the people that God has brought his way. May God grant us all the same courage to open our eyes to the ever-intensifying spiritual warfare we face in this fallen age and also to the beauties of Christ's work in the earth so that we will be able to navigate well in this world until we see our Lord Jesus face to face."

—*Michael Sullivant, pastor, conference speaker, author of* Your Kingdom Come *and* Prophetic Etiquette

"With the mind of a scholar and the heart of an intercessor, Joel Richardson has brought forth an intriguing *exposé* on the coming "battle of the ages." As militant Islam arises in fury fueled by a raging anti-Semitic spirit, another body of people shall arise at the same time, willing to give their lives for the Gospel of Jesus Christ. Stirring...insightful...and a wakeup call to all sincere believers."

—*James W. Goll, cofounder of Encounters Network, author of* The Seer, The Lost Art of Intercession, *and* Praying for Israel's Destiny

"This is *the* must-read book for anyone interested in end times Bible prophecy! Joel Richardson has broken fresh ground in the emerging consensus of Islam's vital role in Antichrist's kingdom. Joel's evidences come straight from the Islamic traditions of the *hadith*, a very important source of Muslim doctrine, well-known to Muslims, but unknown to most Westerners. Any open-minded reader will be unable to dismiss the uncanny parallels between the Islamic traditions and the biblically described agenda of Antichrist. His clear and insightful presentation on the role of beheading in Islamic law is gripping. His scenario for how the earth will fall into line behind Antichrist is entirely credible. Jesus exhorted us to pray and be alert for the time of testing that is coming on the earth. You will find yourself doing just that. For the reader unsatisfied with anything but the truth, this is a book that absolutely must be added to your library."

—*Robert Livingston, missionary to the Middle East, author of* Christianity and Islam: The Final Clash

"Joel Richardson's thorough knowledge of Islam provides Christians with much helpful information on the traditions and teachings of Islam, revealing the striking affinities between Christian end times prophecy and Islamic expectations of world domination. His balanced use of Islamic texts and the Bible is so convincing that after reading the book, one is hardly able to imagine how Antichrist could be any other than a Muslim *caliph*. But what I appreciate most is that he argues his point not with venom but with tact, even love, as he urges Christians to love their Muslim neighbors and to win them for Christ. This book is an important read for Christians who wish to learn more about the world's fastest growing religion or who want to be better prepared to dialogue with and witness to Muslims."

—*Steve Alt, assistant professor of theology, F.I.R.E. School of Ministry, Concord, NC*

"After many years of reflection, I shy away from detailed specifics in end-time scenarios. However, while this book does contain some such specific details, I nevertheless believe that the basic thrust, that Islam is the Antichrist system of the last days, is persuasively presented as a very possible scenario. In addition, the information in this book about Islam and Antichrist is very important and is not, to my knowledge, accessible elsewhere. In these days of Islamic terror, an understanding of the information presented in this book, particularly regarding Islamic eschatology, I believe is crucial. Hence, this book definitely makes an important contribution. I highly recommend a thoughtful examination of the information contained in these pages."

—*Dr. Daniel C. Juster, author of* Jewish Roots *and* Israel, the Church, and the Last Days, *executive director of Tikkun Ministries International*

"Sound, responsible scholarship. A timely breakthrough in Biblical eschatology, *The Islamic Antichrist* presents a captivating paradigm that will profoundly change your perspective on the end times."

—*Jeremy Ray, Sr. pastor, Old Washington United Methodist Church, Old Washington, Ohio*

"This volume will immerse you in end times, Islamic style—head, heart and soul! It will also get you off the couch and on your feet to share the Gospel with Muslims. Finally, it will drive you to your knees to pray for the followers of Mohammad to come to faith in the true Messiah—Jesus."

—*Dr. R. Philip Roberts, president, Midwestern Baptist Theological Seminary*

"This book absolutely revolutionized my end-times theology! On almost every page I had an "ah-ha!" moment as I saw the eschatological puzzle pieces neatly fitting to reveal a prophetic picture of the coming Antichrist that made perfect Biblical and logical sense—a picture that is being brought sharper into focus daily by breaking news and world events! After reading *The Islamic Antichrist* I sent an e-mail to all my ministry colleagues urging them to get and read this book. Joel Richardson's book is an absolute must-read for anyone who wants to understand how current events are rapidly coming together to propel the nations toward their Biblically predicted futures!"

—*David A. Crisp, senior. pastor of Hanover Evangelical Friends Church, Mechanicsville, VA, author of* The View From Here—Seeing Christ in the Everyday

"This book could spark a paradigm shift in the world of eschatological interpretation. Joel makes an excellent case for both an Islamic Antichrist and Islamic beast empire as the likely fulfillment of the the biblical prophecies regarding the last days. The research involved in the production of this book is impressive and the evidence provided for the Islamic eschatological interpetation is compelling. Whether you are a serious student of the Scriptures or just getting started, this book will be a treasured reference. This book is a must-read for any serious student of Bible prophecy!"

· —*Chris Zeller, senior pastor, Golden Shores Community Baptist Church, Arizona*

"Joel's research and information is presented well and gives us a compelling look at the times in which we live. This is a book I ask every believer I know to read, regardless of their denominational leanings—it is that important for this information to be released to the body of Messiah. The time you invest in reading this book will pay huge dividends for the Kingdom of God, as it will give you insight to the motivations of those who are working to establish Islam as the world's dominant religion, and probably help focus your own eschatology, as well."

—*Randall Westfall, pastor, Forerunner Ministries, Mew Mexico*

"Joel Richardson is a MUST READ author. While many teachers have taught us to look to the West for the fulfillment of Bible prophecy, Richardson's perspective and his documentation is spot on. Joel reminds us that Gods throne is not draped in the flag of the U.S., Britain, or the EU. Joel reorients the reader to the fact that the Bible is a thoroughly Israel-centric/Middle Eastern book and it is to the East where we need to look for the fulfillment of Bible prophecy and not toward the West."

—*Ray Gano, director of Prophezine.com*

"Many Bible prophecy students and scholars have come to the realization that Islam is the system that will bring forth the Antichrist and his kingdom. Joel Richardson has done an excellent job through his extensive research of comparing the Biblical Antichrist with Islam's awaited Messiah known as Imam Al Mahdi. I highly recommend this book to all serious and honest students of end-time prophecy."

—*Rodrigo Silva, director, Bible Prophecy in the News.com*

"After many years of studying Bible prophecy from a Western perspective only to be left with more questions than answers, I found Mr. Richardson's *The Islamic Antichrist* both refreshing and insightful. Joel has a thorough knowledge of the Middle Eastern history and Islamic ideology that are necessary when examining the Antichrist's kingdom. This book is a must-read for any teacher or student that wishes to delve deeper into the eschatological studies within Islam, given events of yesterday, today, and tomorrow from the world's fastest growing religion."

—*Christine Marie Hobson, Director of Discerning the Times Online.net and Prophecy Chat.com*

THE ISLAMIC ANTICHRIST

THE ISLAMIC ANTICHRIST

THE SHOCKING TRUTH
ABOUT THE REAL NATURE OF THE BEAST

By Joel Richardson

WND Books

THE ISLAMIC ANTICHRIST
A WND Books book
Published by WorldNetDaily
Los Angeles, CA
Copyright © 2009 by Joel Richardson

Jacket design by Genesis Group

WND Books are distributed to the trade by:
Midpoint Trade Books
27 West 20th Street, Suite 1102
New York, NY 10011

WND Books are available at special discounts for bulk purchases. WND Books, Inc. also publishes books in electronic formats. For more information call (310) 961-4170 or visit www.wndbooks.com.

First edition published 2006, originally published as *Antichrist: Islam's Awaited Messiah*. Second edition 2009

ISBN 13-Digit: 9781935071129
ISBN 10-Digit: 1935071122
E-Book ISBN 13-Digit: 9781935071662
E-Book ISBN 10-Digit: 1935071661
Library of Congress Control Number: 2009925812

Printed in the United States of America

10 9 8 7 6 5 4 3 2

I dedicate this book to my father. I couldn't ask for a better dad—
a humble servant and a true follower of Jesus.

TABLE OF CONTENTS

ACKNOWLEDGMENTS

I most especially want to thank my beautiful and beloved wife. I simply could not have done this without you—you already know that—but I wanted everyone else to know as well. You are an amazing woman. I love you.

I want to thank my good friend Adam for his courageous Luther-like refusal to accept the status quo. *You've emboldened and inspired me to dig where few others tread. I want to thank Wes and Jane for their encouragement and help. You two are an awesome couple. Thank you to Robert Livingston for your friendship and encouragement during this whole process. Also to that conservative professor from Chicago, the first one to give me the time of day on this whole project—you're a true forerunner in your field and most generous as well. Thanks for your time and your honest input. A dual-pronged thank you/sorry goes out to J. Hall for being the first to read and comment on the early and exceedingly chaotic version. My deepest and most heartfelt thanks go to those of you who have given your endorsements to this book. The number and the qualifications of those of you who have done so have humbled me. Also, thanks go out to my business partner Bob for being a godly friend and daily companion and for listening to me endlessly ramble on about such dark topics. And to everyone else who has supported me and affirmed me, may it all be returned back unto you tenfold.*

In writing this book, I have found myself in a difficult position for more than one reason. On one hand, I would like to share with you the reader a little bit about myself—my experience with Christian/Muslim interfaith dialogue and the story of how I came to write this book. On the other hand, I have, with good reason, determined not only to use a pen name but also to share as little personal information as possible.

On any given day, I receive one or perhaps several e-mails from Muslim friends from all over the world. Most of these e-mails are very nice and include personal information as well as portions of ongoing theological discussions that we are usually having. This is a delight for me and I truly enjoy and value these friendships. Unfortunately, not all of the e-mails that I receive are pleasant or friendly. While the following e-mail was not the only death threat that I have received, it was this one in particular that caused me to begin practicing quite a bit more discretion in my interactions with Muslims in the context of interfaith dialogue. (The portions in parentheses I have added for clarity):

> …*Allahu Akhbar*!! (Allah is the greatest!) *Yaaaa Allah*!! (Oh, Allah!) I will chop off your head! May Allah damn you and your whole family. May you and your whole family all rot in hell forever. I want you to know that all Muslims call upon Allah to damn you and put you in hell. I will personally kill you. I will personally kill your family. You will die a very slow and painful death *inshallah* (by the will of Allah). *Ameen, Ameen, Ameen* (Amen, Amen…). *Allahu Akhbar*!! *Allahu Akhbar*!! *Yaaaa Allah*!

It was not only the nature and the intensity of this threat that caused me to take it seriously, but also the perfect punctuation, spelling, and sentence structure. There were no indicators that this threat came from outside of the country.

Now I have to admit I have no idea specifically what motivated this particular threat. I am not sure specifically what I said or did that incurred such a strong reaction. Of course, when speaking with Muslims, my normal practice is to speak equally straightforwardly about everyone's need for a savior, as most of my Muslim friends likewise speak very straightforwardly about our lack of a need for a savior. Seems reasonable to me. But apparently for this great sin I received this threat to my life and to the life of my family. While threats of this sort are certainly not uncommon in many parts of the world, it still amazes me that merely sharing my beliefs could incur such a strong reaction. In any case, for obvious reasons, for the safety of myself and my family, I have chosen to remain anonymous with regard to this book. I trust that you understand.

Nevertheless, in order to establish a measure of credibility with the readership, I will simply say that the information in this book comes from a person who is not only well versed in the Islamic source materials and the sacred literature that is quoted throughout this book, but who also, as noted above, has extensive experience in interfaith religious dialogue with Muslims. The information that you will read has been researched in an exhaustive fashion. To convey an accurate and complete picture of Islamic doctrine and belief, I have utilized not only nearly every book available in English on the subject of Islamic eschatology, but also articles beyond counting and interviews with hundreds of Muslims on their specific beliefs about the last days. My purpose here was not merely to present a book which would educate Christians; I also wanted to write a book that Muslims—even if they disagree with my conclusions—would appreciate for both its honesty and its use of quality references. While I'm quite sure that due to the nature of this book, very little will go unchallenged by Muslim apologists, I have written this work knowing that any readers who look up the sources can see for themselves that what I have written is an accurate representation and overview of Islamic teaching and belief. I have also striven to be as unsensational as the subject matter allows. I have personally read many overly sensational works on the subject of prophecy and I do not personally value this approach.

The other primary reason that I had a hard time writing this book is that it is, to some degree, a polemical work. While I am not above writing a book of this nature, if at all possible I would far rather avoid it altogether. While I do believe that polemics have a completely valid place within the landscape of Christian/Muslim interfaith dialogue, I am also aware that love will win far more souls into God's Kingdom than a hundred intellectual reasons. Samuel M. Zwemer, Christian missionary to the Muslims of a century ago, put it well: "After forty years' experience—sometimes heartbreaking experience, of sowing on rocks and of watching the birds pick away the seed to the last grain—I am convinced that the nearest way to the Muslim heart is the way of God's love, the way of the Cross."[1] I fully agree. I would far rather be involved in the type of relationship with Muslims that consists of mutually beneficial dialogue and genuine friendships than engage in polemics which are by their very nature negative. Indeed, this book contains information about Islam that is negative, much of it outright disturbing. Nevertheless, I felt a very strong mandate from the Lord that this book needed to be written and this information made known. The primary purpose of this book is to warn—both those within and those outside of the church walls.

I also want to stress very strongly that my purpose is by no means to "bash" Muslims in any way. While the premise and the points of this book are indeed a strong charge against the religion of Islam, this should not be interpreted in any way as an attack against Muslim individuals. Like any other religion, Islam is not monolithic and not all Muslims believe or agree with every article of faith attributed to them in this book. This point cannot be stressed enough. Many Muslims are wonderful, peaceful people. We must never categorize people according to the group to which they belong but rather we need to get to know them personally, one individual at a time. As such, because of the frightening and rather disturbing information about Islam that this book contains, I strongly encourage you at the outset to spend some time in prayer and ask God to protect you from any negative feelings, fears, or prejudices that the human heart is so prone to, and instead to touch your heart with His heart for Muslims. Perhaps you, as I did, will fall in love with these whom God so eagerly desires to adorn with redemption, transformation, and His beautiful garments of salvation. And, if you are a Muslim, I pray that through the ancient prophecies analyzed in these pages truth will become manifest and God will guide you to the straight path.

CHAPTER ONE

WHY THIS BOOK?
WAKING UP TO THE ISLAMIC REVIVAL

"Blow the trumpet in Zion; sound the alarm on my holy hill. Let all who live in the land tremble, for the day of the LORD is coming. It is close at hand—a day of darkness and gloom, a day of clouds and blackness. Like dawn spreading across the mountains a large and mighty army comes, such as never was of old nor ever will be in ages to come."

—Joel 2:1-2

In the days in which we are now living, I believe that there are a handful of issues that God is trying to highlight to the West and specifically to the Western Christian church. Yet sadly, even among those few who seem to hear the trumpet blasts from heaven, there are even fewer who seem to discern what they mean. The signs are now emblazoned across the front page almost daily, yet few seem to understand where these signs point. It is my hope that this book will contribute to opening the eyes of many to the times quickly approaching. Beyond this, my prayer is that this book will add understanding to those whose spirits are already both watchful and discerning.

MORE END TIMES NONSENSE?

Before we begin, we need to identify what type of attitude yours is toward the study of eschatology, that is, end times issues. If you are someone who is cynical regarding this type of study, then I want to ask you to do something before you continue. I want you to read the appendix first. The appendix explains why I believe that eschatology is a necessary aspect of the normative Christian life. If you are unsure of the necessity of fully embracing biblical eschatology, then please read the appendix first and come back here. If you are already interested in the study of eschatology, then please proceed from this point.

THE PREVAILING IGNORANCE

This book is first and foremost a study of Islamic eschatology (end time belief) and those specific Islamic doctrines and practices that seem to correlate—in quite an astonishing way—to the biblical descriptions and prophecies of the last days. As a result, I find myself presented with the interesting challenge of introducing much of my readership to more than one subject about which most people are largely uninformed. Certainly most people have some vague ideas about what the Bible says about the "last days"—the difficult times that will encompass the earth, the plagues, the ecological disasters, the eventual return of Jesus. But even many Christians—those who read the Bible regularly—are not exactly sure what they believe about many of the specifics of the last days. And if it can be said that ignorance of biblical eschatology is common, then consider how many people—particularly in the West—have any knowledge at all about what Islam teaches about the last days.

Some Christians are aware of the fact that in Islam, as in Christianity, there is an expectation that Jesus will return to the earth from heaven. This excites most Christians, who see this as an opportunity to build bridges of dialogue between Christians and Muslims. Indeed, the return of Jesus can be a good starting point for such interfaith dialogue. Unfortunately, though, beyond this one point, most Christians generally understand very little about the Islamic end-time perspective, or Jesus' return, or indeed the nature of who the "Islamic Jesus" really is. Certainly many Christians who live or minister among Muslims have some understanding of these issues, but this understanding certainly has not been conveyed to the church on a broader scale. It is time to release this startling information to the non-Muslim world. This book represents the first comprehensive popular study of Islamic eschatology as it relates to biblical eschatology. But beyond a mere academic or theological study, this book is also a wakeup call. It is a call for many to realize the degree to which the future of the Christian church—indeed the future of the entire world—and the future of Islam are divinely and directly interconnected.

Through this study, which presents an introductory overview of both biblical and Islamic eschatology, a much clearer picture of the future will emerge. The overlapping of beliefs in the two systems, and the ways that Islamic eschatology reinforces Christian eschatology, are astonishing and downright eerie. I believe that this study will help the reader gain significant insight into the nature of the last days and help many to begin to see and understand the direction that the world is heading at ever increasing speeds. This leads us to the most obvious reason to take notice of Islam: its dramatic and rapid growth and present worldwide revival.

THE ISLAMIC REVIVAL

The clearest reason to study and understand Islam and specifically Islamic eschatology is quite simply because Islam is the future. Yes, you read that correctly: Islam *is* the future. If present trends do not change *dramatically*, Islam will bypass Christianity for the title of the world's largest religion very shortly. In fact, according to most statistics, this may take place in less than twenty years. A majority who read this book will live to see this. Islam is the fastest growing religion in the world, growing at a rate four times faster than Christianity.[1] Presently, those who practice Islam make up approximately one-fifth of the world's population. One seasoned Bible teacher from England after reviewing the statistics recently commented that, "if present trends continue, half of all global births will be in Muslim families by the year 2055."[2] Something dramatic and revolutionary is happening right before our eyes, and most Western Christians are oblivious to it. The purpose of this chapter is to inform the reader about the rapid growth of Islam. The picture I am about to paint may surprise some people. Some may be confused. Some may even deny it, but it is the truth and it needs to be told. Even by itself, the growth and spread of Islam is a powerful wakeup call to all Christians.

Islam is the fasting growing religion, not only in the world, but also in the United States, Canada, and Europe.[3] The annual growth rate of Islam in the U.S. is approximately 4 percent, but there are strong reasons to believe that it may have risen to as high as 8 percent over the past few years. Every year, tens of thousands of Americans convert to Islam. Prior to 2001 most reports have the number at roughly twenty-five thousand American converts to Islam per year.[4] This may not sound like much, but this yearly figure, according to some Muslim American clerics, has *quadrupled* since 9/11.[5] That's right: since 9/11 the number of American converts to Islam has skyrocketed. As early as one month after the World Trade Center attacks, the reports began flowing in from mosques all over America. Ala Bayumi, the director of Arab affairs at the Council for American Islamic Relations (CAIR), on November 11, 2001, in the London daily newspaper *Al-Hayat* said this:

> Non-Muslim Americans are now interested in getting to know Islam. There are a number of signs... Libraries have run out of books on Islam... English translations of the Qur'an head the American bestseller list... The Americans are showing increasing willingness to convert to Islam since September 11... Thousands of non-Muslim Americans have responded to invitations to visit mosques, resembling the waves of the sea crashing on the shore one after another...[6]

After testifying to the dramatic strides that Islam had taken as a result of the 9/11 attacks, Bayumi went on to say that:

> Proselytizing in the name of Allah has not been undermined,
> and has not been set back fifty years, as we thought in the
> first days after September 11. On the contrary, the eleven
> days that have passed are like eleven years in the history of
> proselytizing in the name of Allah.[7]

In an article from the British newspaper the *Times of London*,
January 7, 2002, just four months after 9/11, we read:

> There is compelling anecdotal evidence of a surge in
> conversions to Islam since September 11, not just in Britain, but
> across Europe and America. One Dutch Islamic centre claims a
> tenfold increase, while the New Muslims Project, based in
> Leicester [England], and run by a former Irish Roman Catholic
> housewife, reports a "steady stream" of new converts.[8]

I recently asked a Muslim acquaintance how many Americans
he has witnessed convert to Islam in just the past year. He
explained that he has personally participated in at least one
hundred conversion ceremonies in the past year alone. I have
similarly asked dozens of American Muslims if they have
witnessed a dramatic increase in conversions to Islam since
9/11, and the answer every time has been a resounding *yes*.
Newer official data is difficult to come by and analyze for more
than one reason. First of all, very few comprehensive studies
have been done since 9/11; most studies seem to have been
done just prior to 2001. Also, since 9/11, many American
Muslims are very hesitant to give information away to pollsters
who come to the mosques. There is a widespread suspicion
among the Muslim community that pollsters are gathering
information for the United States Department of Homeland
Security (DHS) or the FBI. Most converts wish to remain
relatively anonymous. But in my own personal, albeit
anecdotal, experience, I have talked to many American converts
to Islam who have converted since 9/11.

But here's the other sad aspect of these figures: Over 80
percent of these American converts to Islam were raised in
Christian churches.[9] If the higher figures of conversion are

accurate, that would mean that as many as sixty thousand Americans raised in Christian homes convert to Islam annually. I have one acquaintance who, although he was a pastor's son raised in a deeply religious and traditional Christian family, nevertheless converted to Islam in college. I have read numerous testimonies of bishops, priests, missionaries, and divinity students, not to mention members of the Christian laity, who have converted to Islam. Among them are even self-described former "spirit-filled Christians." If you are a Christian, you may object that this is impossible. If this is the case, you might ask, then why aren't these statistics more widely known? You may be wondering why you do not personally know anyone who has converted. There are easy answers to these questions. One of the primary reasons that these trends have gone largely unnoticed is that most American Muslims are concentrated in the larger metropolitan centers. The greater Chicago metropolitan area for instance is home to well over 350,000 Muslims. Greater New York City has twice that number with over seven hundred thousand Muslims.[10] The other important statistic that sheds light on why this issue isn't more commonly discussed in many white American churches is that 85 percent of American converts to Islam are African-American. White Christian America has not been as impacted by this phenomenon nearly as much as black Christian America has. Islam is absolutely sweeping through the inner cities, a very sad commentary on the discontinuity and disunity of the American church. One Muslim authority estimates that by the year 2020 most American urban centers will be predominantly Muslim.[11] But as the number of conversions increases, the face of the Muslim convert is changing as well. Shortly after 9/11, National Public Radio did a special on Islam and those who had converted after 9/11:

> One of the most important topics [in an NPR broadcast] was an interview with several young women at American universities who recently converted to Islam through the

Islamic Society of Boston. They hold advanced degrees from universities in Boston, such as Harvard, and they spoke of the power and the greatness of Islam, of the elevated status of women in Islam, and of why they converted to Islam. The program was broadcast several times across the entire U.S....[12]

From an article in the *New York Times*, October 22, 2001, we read a portion of Jim Hacking's story:

Nine years ago, Jim Hacking was in training to be a Jesuit priest. Now, he is an admiralty lawyer in St. Louis who has spent much of the last month explaining Islam at interfaith gatherings... He made the *Shahadah* [Muslim conversion ceremony] on June 6, 1998. *"The thing I've always latched to is that there's one God, he doesn't have equals, he doesn't need a son to come do his work"* (emphasis mine).[13]

A typical testimony of a former Christian convert reads:

As a child, Jennifer Harrell attended church and Sunday school. In high school, she was on the drill team and dated a football player. After college, she became a Methodist youth minister. At age 23, she became a single parent. At age 26, she became a Muslim. "I grew up in Plano doing all the things I thought I was supposed to do," said Ms. Harrell, 29, of Dallas. "I went to church. I went to parties. But I wasn't concerned about heaven or hell. I took it all for granted." Eventually, she took a job in sales, where she was introduced to Islam by Muslim co-workers. One of them loved to debate religion, which stirred Ms. Harrell to rethink her Christian faith. She studied the Bible, but also Islam, in order to do a better job of defending her faith. Instead, she became intrigued that Muslims prayed five times a day, fasted, and gave alms as a way of life. "I wasn't the type of Christian who prayed every morning," she said. She said Muslim beliefs about Jesus made more sense to her because they revere him as a prophet and not God's son. "When I was a Christian, I never understood why Jesus had to die for my sins," Ms. Harrell said. "I mean, they're my sins." Before becoming a Muslim, she visited a Christian minister. She said she asked why Christians ate pork, why women didn't cover their heads in church, and why

Christians dated. "I wanted him to defend the Bible," she said. "I gave him everything that I had found wrong with Christian interpretation." His answers didn't satisfy her.[14]

Stories like Jim Hacking's and Jennifer Harrell's are legion. I have probably read a hundred such stories.

A NEW MONOTHEISTIC OPTION

In the past, whenever Westerners came to believe in a personal God and decided to make this new faith a primary aspect of their lives, they usually have found the expression for their faith in a Christian church. But now, as Islam spreads in the West, many are realizing that Christianity is not the only monotheistic option available to them. Sadly, many are choosing Islam instead of Christianity. David Pawson, a prominent Bible teacher and author from England, recalls the experience of one of his friends:

> A Christian friend of mine is a counselor in a state school. He was delighted when a boy he was trying to help find a purpose in life told him he had become convinced that there was a personal God in whom he could believe. To his surprise and disappointment this English boy told him some weeks later that he had become a Muslim. He was one of many thousands who had made the same choice.[15]

As Islam grows in the West, this story is sure to be repeated many times.

A WARNING FOR ENGLAND

In his book, *Islam's Challenge to Christians*, Pawson sounds what may very well be a genuine prophetic warning, not only to England but also to the entire Western church. Pawson, a well-seasoned and well-respected leader in the church in England, recounts a recent experience he had while listening to well-known authority on Islam Patrick Sookhedo give a lecture. If a leader of less distinction had made the following statement we might justifiably let it pass, but instead, we should all be very sobered by what David experienced:

> In the middle of his talk, both unexpected and unrelated to its contents, I was suddenly overwhelmed with what could be described as a premonition that Islam will take over this country [England]. I recall sitting there stunned and even shaking. We were not just listening to an interesting lecture about a religion and culture which others believed and practiced. We were hearing about our future![16]

In the rest of the book, Pawson walks through what he feels are some proper Christian responses to his prediction. His recommended course of action includes three primary components: reality, relationship, and righteousness. I will not endeavor to expound on these three issues, as Pawson has already done so with conviction. Of course, Pawson's warning has proven to be highly controversial throughout the church in England. The real question, however, in the opinion of this author, is not whether or not Pawson's warning will come to pass, but rather: Will the church in England choose to implement Pawson's recommended plan of response? This remains to be seen.

BALANCING THE FACTS

Now the point here is not to paint an overly dismal picture. I also need to point out that Muslims are converting to Christianity all over the world. Many Muslims repeatedly make the claim that no Muslim ever leaves Islam. This claim is refuted without much effort. One Muslim *sheikh* recently claimed that in Africa alone, there are over six million Muslim converts to Christianity annually. That would break down to about 667 an hour, or sixteen thousand a day. From January of 2003 to the middle of 2004, the ministry of German evangelist Reinhardt Bonnke saw over ten million Africans make decisions to follow Jesus. A large percentage of those who made these decisions were Muslims. In fact, Muslims from all over the world are making decisions to become followers of Jesus.[17] Many of these decisions come following a spiritual dream or a vision.[18] There are many wonderful and powerful testimonies of the goodness of God in the lives of Muslims coming to know Jesus. I believe with all my heart that the Middle East will see a revival of Muslims coming to a biblical faith in Jesus. Christianity in Latin America, Asia, and Africa is now experiencing what we can only call a revival. But this does not negate the fact that the growth of Islam is still much faster than that of Christianity, not only in America, Canada, England, and Europe, but worldwide. Now, I must state here that much of the reason for the faster growth of Islam is simply higher birth rates among Muslims. Muslims are just having far more children than Christians. The growth of Islam does not find its primary source from conversions, but, nevertheless, it is growing—and spreading faster than Christianity. The simple fact of the matter is that we as the Western church have completely missed the undeniable worldwide significance of Islam.

For now, the point that needs to be emphasized is that *the beliefs of the world's second largest and fastest growing religion should matter to us.* This is especially true in light of Islam's potential to soon become the world's largest religion. A fair prediction is that if the time comes when Islam indeed does bypass Christianity as the world's largest religion, or even as it merely begins to draw closer to that point, a tipping point will come whereby the rate of growth will increase exponentially. Bandwagon conversions and confusion among faithful Christians will rule the day. We cannot underestimate the power of a worldwide trend. Indeed one of the primary aspects of the last days is what the Bible calls the "great apostasy," a significant global falling away from the Christian faith. While Islam now exists as an insecure religion wrestling with why Allah has allowed Islam to remain an inferior presence on the earth compared to Christianity, the day will likewise come for Christians when they too will have to wrestle will why God has allowed Islam to bypass Christianity in terms of both growth and influence. This could begin to happen as soon as fifteen years from now. It could be sooner. I sincerely hope that this is not the case, but at present, there are very few indicators to suggest otherwise. The only hope for a turnaround in this trend is a significant, full-scale worldwide revival; the kind of revival that until now has never been seen. But for now, as the trend is just beginning in America, it is time to become informed and prepared for what promises to be the church's greatest challenge ever. As I said earlier, Islam is the future (albeit only temporarily so). It is time for the church to face reality. As Brother Andrew, the man who became so well known for smuggling Bibles past the Iron Curtain as told in the modern Christian classic, *God's Smuggler*, said as early as 1994, "What Communism was to the twentieth century, Islam will be for the next one hundred years."[19]

CONCLUSION

So maybe you now agree that it is important to become informed regarding Islam, but you may wonder why it is important to understand Islamic *eschatology* specifically. That's a good question. Please think through some of these points carefully: The Bible makes it clear that the Devil's primary plan for the last days has been, for the past few thousand years, to raise up two men, *the Antichrist* and the *False Prophet*, as his primary instruments to deceive the inhabitants of the earth. How do you suppose that Satan has planned to include the world's 1.5 billion Muslims in his grand end-time deception? Did Satan fail to foresee and strategize regarding the global spread of Islam? Or has Satan included the Muslims of the world in his end-time strategy? Will Islam, the world's third monotheistic religion, also undergo the persecution of Satan along with Christians and Jews as they all resist the Antichrist together? Or will Islam—the religion that prides itself on resisting any form of idolatry—simply submit to a demonic and false religious leader without putting up any real fight? For years, I questioned the Lord about these issues. In time, as my

11

knowledge of Islam deepened, the answers to my questions became very clear. This book is my attempt to share with you what I have learned. I understand that this may sound like a strong statement to make, but I believe that the information presented in this book will establish the fact that Islam is indeed the primary vehicle that will be used by Satan to fulfill the prophecies of the Bible about the future political/religious/military system of the Antichrist that will overwhelm the entire world just prior to the second coming of Jesus Christ.

THE SACRED TEXTS OF ISLAM

A*s we begin our study,* we first turn to a brief introduction to the sacred texts of Islam. The purpose here is to acquaint the reader with the sacred texts of Islam and their places within the authority structure of Islam. Many of the references in this book will come from these various sacred texts.

THE QUR'AN

The first and most well known of Islam's sacred books is the Qur'an. The Qur'an is the foundational holy book of Islam, conveyed entirely by Muhammad, the founder and "prophet" of Islam. "*Qur'an*" literally means "recitation" or "reading" in Arabic. The Qur'an is comprised of 114 chapters called *surahs.* Throughout this book, whenever a portion of the Qur'an is cited, following the citation it will say "surah" followed by the chapter, verse, and translation.

The Qur'an may somewhat be viewed as the Bible of Islam in that it is the primary holy book of Islam. The Qur'an, however, is not the only source of sacred or even *inspired* traditions in Islam. While the Qur'an is the only text within Islam that is said to record the literal words of Allah, of equal importance to all Muslims is the Sunna.

THE SUNNA

"Sunna" in Arabic literally means *"a clear or well-trodden path."* It refers to whatever Muhammad said, did, condoned, or condemned. It is the record of Muhammad's sayings, customs, teachings, and the example that he left for all Muslims to follow. Muslims view Muhammad as the perfect example for all human beings—a doctrine spelled out quite clearly in the Qur'an:

> If you love Allah, then follow me. (Muhammad) -Sura 3:31 (Shakir)
>
> Ye have indeed in the Apostle of Allah a beautiful pattern of (conduct) for anyone whose hope is in Allah and the Final Day. -Sura 33:21 (Yusuf Ali)

Whatever Muhammad did or said, therefore, becomes the basis from which to model all life and belief. What non-Muslims must understand regarding the Sunna is that it is equally important to the Muslim as the Qur'an. The Sunna interprets the Qur'an. *Without the Sunna, the Qur'an cannot be properly understood.* In fact, many aspects and practices of the Islamic religion are not even mentioned in the Qur'an but are found only in the Sunna. So the Qur'an and the Sunna together form the basis for the beliefs and practices of Muslims everywhere.[1] In this sense, Muslims believe both the Qur'an and the Sunna to be inspired and authoritative.

SOURCES OF THE SUNNA

The Sunna is mined primarily out of two different types of Islamic literature. The first and most important of the two types of traditions is *hadith* literature. *Hadith* literature specifically records the sayings of Muhammad. Second, there is *sirat* or *sirah* literature. *"Sirat"* literally means *"biography."* So the *sirat-rasul* is a biography of the "apostle" or "prophet" Muhammad. There are many ancient and modern biographies of Muhammad's life.

The most popular English translation of an ancient *sirat* is Ibn Ishaq's *Sirat Rasul* (*The Life of Muhammad*), translated by noted orientalist A. Guillaume. Besides these two types of literature are histories of Islam and commentaries on the Qur'an by early scholars called *tafsir*. When I speak of these types of literature collectively in this book, I will simply use the general term "Islamic traditions."

HADITH LITERATURE

For the purpose of this study, the *hadith* literature will probably be the most crucial of the various Islamic traditions to understand. This is because so much of Islamic belief and practice, particularly the Islamic beliefs about the end times, comes from the *hadith* literature.

As mentioned above, a *hadith* is a record of the sayings and deeds of Muhammad. According to Muslim scholars, during the lifetime of Muhammad and after he died, his followers began to orally relay their memories of all of the things that Muhammad said or did.

THE *ISNAD* AND THE *MATN*

Each *hadith* consists of two parts—the *isnad* and the *matn*. At the beginning of any *hadith* is the *isnad*, or the chain of transmission. The *isnad* is essentially the "he said, she said, he said" chain of people who relay a memory of something Muhammad said or did. In English, an *isnad* might read, "John said he overheard Mary say that Muhammad used to say such and such." To complicate this further for those unfamiliar with Islamic literature, of course all the names are Arabic. Many of the names are therefore long and possibly compounded. So here is a real example of an *isnad* from a *hadith* taken from *Malik's Muwatta*:

> Yahya related to me from Malik from Amr ibn Yahya al-Mazini from Abu'l-Hubab Said ibn Yasar that Abdullah ibn Umar said…[2]

Sometimes there will be, however, only one name listed in the *isnad*, which is usually an indicator that the person relating the *hadith* was a direct companion or family member of Muhammad. An example might be: "Ayesha related that Muhammad (peace be upon him) said…"

The other part of the *hadith* contains the actual text. It is the portion that records the sayings or deeds of Muhammad. This part of the *hadith* is called the *matn*.

So every *hadith* consists of the *isnad* (chain of transmitters) and the *matn* (the sayings or actions of Muhammad). Throughout this book, in order to simplify things, we will generally quote the *matn* only. The *isnad* will appear with the references in the endnotes.

CHAPTER THREE

ISLAMIC ESCHATOLOGY

Most books on Islamic eschatology primarily consist of the author's best attempts to gather, compile, and relay the most reliable hadiths and various traditions relating to the end times. Beyond this, of course, most Islamic eschatology books also contain commentary from the author. Because I am not a hadith scholar (nor do I aspire to ever become one), and because I do not want to merely present my own interpretation of what Islam teaches regarding the end times, I have strictly utilized either Islamic traditions or commentary from Islamic scholars and authors who have already written extensively on these subjects. Therefore, this book will be heavy with such quotations and references.

The majority of Islamic studies of eschatology are divided into two categories, the Minor Signs and the Major Signs. The Minor Signs are sometimes thought of as the equivalent of what Jesus referred to as "the birth pangs," which is to say that they are those signs that precede the Major Signs. To a degree this is true. The difference, however, is that many of the Minor Signs actually take place concurrently with the Major Signs. Thus the Minor Signs should not necessarily be thought of as the *first signs*, but rather the *lesser signs*. Some of the Minor Signs are quite interesting, but for the purpose of this study we will not delve into them. Instead we will move directly into the Major Signs.

THE MAJOR SIGNS

Crucial to this study is a clear understanding of just what Islam teaches regarding the Major Signs. The Major Signs or the Greater Signs obviously speak of far more significant events than the Minor Signs. These signs relate to issues such as the coming of the Muslim Antichrist (Ad-Dajjal), or the return of the Muslim Jesus (Isa Al-Maseeh), or most importantly, the coming of the Muslim Savior/Messiah figure (Al-Mahdi). They do not relate to, for instance, the increase in immorality, or religious ignorance, or other such general signs. While some of the Minor Signs are fairly vague and debatable as to their legitimacy, the Major Signs are absolutely a non-negotiable entity to the Muslim mind. In order to understand the importance of the Major Signs to Muslims, one must first understand the importance of end-time belief among Muslims.

PRIORITY OF THE LAST DAYS IN ISLAMIC BELIEF

The Qur'an mentions five things that a Muslim must believe in order to be a Muslim. These five things have, as a result, become a creed of sorts within Islam. From the Qur'an we read:

> It is not righteousness that ye turn your faces to the East and the West; but righteous is he who believeth in Allah and the Last Day and the angels and the Scripture and the prophets... -Surah 2:177 (Pickthall)

Notice the order of the five tenets of belief:

1. Belief in Allah.
2. Belief in the last day.
3. Belief in angels.
4. Belief in the scripture.
5. Belief in the prophets.

This is very different than in Christianity. Unfortunately, while end-time belief plays a prominent role in the New Testament and in the life of the early church, today belief in the last days has become essentially optional or generally ignored by most. But not so with Islam: There are no true Muslims who do not believe in the last day and the events which precede it. Understanding the Islamic perspective regarding the last days and specifically the Major Signs, therefore, is crucial if we wish to understand the central religious anticipations of the 1.5 billion Muslims worldwide. It is to these core beliefs that we now turn.

CHAPTER FOUR

THE MAHDI: ISLAM'S AWAITED MESSIAH

A *mong the Major Signs*, the most anticipated and central sign that Muslims await is the coming of a man known as "The Mahdi." In Arabic, "*al-Mahdi*" means "the Guided One."[1] He is also sometimes referred to by Shi'a Muslims as *Sahib Al-Zaman* or *Al-Mahdi al-Muntadhar*, which translated mean "the Lord of the Age" and "the Awaited Savior." The Mahdi is the first of the Major Signs. This is confirmed by Ibn Kathir, a renowned Muslim scholar from the fourteenth century:

> After the lesser signs of the Hour appear and increase, mankind will have reached a stage of great suffering. Then the awaited Mahdi will appear; He is the first of the greater clear, signs of the Hour.[2]

The coming of the Mahdi is the central crowning element of all Islamic end-time narratives. So central to Islamic eschatological expectations is the coming of the Mahdi that some Muslim scholars do not even refer to "the Minor Signs" as such, but instead refer to them as "the signs accompanying the Mahdi."[3] While there are some variations of belief between the Sunni and Shi'a sects of Islam, and while certain quarters of Sunnis reject him altogether, general belief in the Mahdi is not a sectarian issue within Islam, but is universal among most Muslims. According to Shaykh Muhammad Hisham Kabbani, chairman of the Islamic Supreme Council of America: "The coming of the Mahdi is established doctrine for both Sunni and Shi'a Muslims, and indeed for all humanity."[4]

Ayatullah Baqir al-Sadr and Ayatullah Murtada Mutahhari, both Shi'a Muslim scholars, in their book, *The Awaited Savior*, describe the Mahdi this way:

> A figure more legendary than that of the Mahdi, the Awaited Saviour, has not been seen in the history of mankind. The threads of the world events have woven many a fine design in human life but the pattern of the Mahdi stands high above every other pattern. He has been the vision of the visionaries in history. He has been the dream of all the dreamers of the world. For the ultimate salvation of mankind he is the Pole Star of hope on which the gaze of humanity is fixed.... In this quest for the truth about the Mahdi there is no distinction of any caste, creed, or country. The quest is universal, exactly in the same way as the Mahdi himself is universal. He stands resplendent high above the narrow walls in which humanity is cut up and divided. He belongs to everybody. For all that and much more, what exactly is the Mahdi? Surely that is the big question which the thinking people all over the world would like to ask.[5]

Indeed, just who is this "awaited one" that the Islamic world longs for, and what will he do that has Muslims in such a state of anticipation? This chapter will attempt to thoroughly answer this question primarily by citing various Islamic traditions and the interpretations of Muslim scholars that study them. I would like to encourage you to take the time to read each and every quote. It is in these references that we find an articulation of one of the central beliefs and passions of many of the 1.5 billion Muslims with whom we presently share the earth. Those of us who desire a greater understanding of one of the primary underlying spiritual factors affecting the world today should pay very close attention.

ISLAM'S MESSIAH

In the simplest of terms, the Mahdi is Islam's *messiah* or savior. While the actual terms *messiah* and *messianism* have very clearly Judeo-Christian roots, University of Virginia Professor Abdulaziz Abdulhussein Sachedina agrees that these terms are appropriately used in an Islamic context when referring to the Mahdi. In his scholarly work on the subject, *Islamic Messianism*, Sachedina elaborates thusly:

> The term "messianism" in the Islamic context is frequently used to translate the important concept of an eschatological figure, the Mahdi, who as the foreordained leader "will rise" to launch a great social transformation in order to restore and adjust all things under divine guidance. The Islamic messiah, thus, embodies the aspirations of his followers in the restoration of the purity of the Faith which will bring true and uncorrupted guidance to all mankind, creating a just social order and a world free from oppression in which the Islamic revelation will be the norm for all nations.[6]

Thus it is fair to say that the "rising" of the Mahdi is to the majority of Muslims what the return of Jesus is to Christians. While Christians await the return of Jesus the Messiah to fulfill all of God's prophetic promises to the people of God, Muslims await the appearance of the Mahdi to fulfill these purposes. Sheikh Kabbani likewise identifies the Mahdi as Islam's primary messiah figure: "Jews are waiting for the Messiah, Christians are waiting for Jesus, and Muslims are waiting for both the Mahdi and Jesus. All religions describe them as men coming to save the world."[7]

A MAN FROM THE FAMILY OF MUHAMMAD

The first and most often cited Islamic belief with regard to the Mahdi is the tradition which states that the Mahdi will descend from the family of Muhammad and will bear Muhammad's name:

The world will not come to pass until a man from among my family, whose name will be my name, rules over the Arabs.[8]

The Prophet said: The Mahdi will be of my family, of the descendants of Fatimah [Muhammad's daughter].[9]

A UNIVERSAL LEADER FOR ALL MUSLIMS

Throughout the Islamic world today there is a call for the restoration of the Islamic *caliphate*. The *caliph* (*khalifa*) in Islam may be viewed somewhat as the Pope of the Muslims. Muslims view the *caliph* as the vice regent for Allah on the earth. It is important to understand that when Muslims call for the restoration of the *caliphate*, it is ultimately the Mahdi that they call for, for the Mahdi is the awaited final *caliph* of Islam. Muslims everywhere will be obligated to follow the Mahdi:

> If you see him, go and give him your allegiance, even if you have to crawl over ice, because he is the Vice-regent [*Khalifa*] of Allah, the Mahdi.[10]

> He will pave the way for and establish the government of the family [or community] of Muhammad... *Every believer will be obligated to support him* (emphasis mine).[11]

THE RULER OF THE WORLD

The Mahdi is believed to be a future Muslim world leader who will not only rule over the Islamic world, but the non-Muslim world as well. The Mahdi is said to lead a world revolution that will establish a new Islamic world order throughout the entire earth:

> The Mahdi will establish right and justice in the world and eliminate evil and corruption. He will fight against the enemies of the Muslims who would be victorious.[12]

> He will reappear on the appointed day, and then he will fight against the forces of evil, lead a world revolution, and set up a new world order based on justice, righteousness, and virtue...ultimately the righteous will

24

take the world administration in their hands and Islam will be victorious over all the religions.[13]

He is the precursor of the victory of the Truth and the fall of all tyrants. He heralds the end of injustice and oppression and the beginning of the final rising of the sun of Islam which will never again set and which will ensure happiness and the elevation of mankind.... The Mahdi is one of Allah's clear signs which will soon be made evident to everyone.[14]

The Mahdi's means and method of accomplishing this world revolution will include multiple military campaigns or holy wars (*jihad*). While some Muslims believe that most of the non-Muslims of the world will convert to Islam peaceably during the reign of the Mahdi, most traditions picture the non-Muslim world coming to Islam as a result of conquest by the Mahdi. Abduallrahman Kelani, author of *The Last Apocalypse*, describes the many battles of the Mahdi:

[A]l-Mahdi will receive a pledge of allegiance as a *caliph* for Muslims. He will lead Muslims in many battles of *jihad*. His reign will be a *caliphate* that follows the guidance of the Prophet. Many battles will ensue between Muslims and the disbelievers during the Mahdi's reign...[15]

Even Harun Yahya, a moderate and very popular Muslim author, refers to the Mahdi's invasion of numerous non-Muslim lands: "The Mahdi will invade all the places between East and West."[16]

THE ARMY OF BLACK FLAGS

The Mahdi's ascendancy to power is said to be preceded by an army from the East carrying black flags or banners of war. Sheikh Kabbani states:

Hadith indicate that black flags coming from the area of Khorasan will signify the appearance of the Mahdi is nigh. Khorasan is in today's Iran, and some scholars have said that this *hadith* means when the black flags appear from

Central Asia, i.e. in the direction of Khorasan, then the appearance of the Mahdi is imminent.[17]

Another tradition states that:

The Messenger of Allah said: The black banners will come from the East and their hearts will be as firm as iron. Whoever hears of them should join them and give allegiance, even if it means crawling across snow.[18]

Islam waves two flags. One is white and one is black. Written across both flags in Arabic are the words, "There is no God but Allah and Muhammad is his Messenger." The white flag is called *Al-Liwaa* and serves as the sign for the leader of the Muslim army and is the flag of the Islamic state. The black flag is called *Ar-Raya* and is used by the Muslim army. It is also called the flag of *jihad*, and is carried into battle. One flag is governmental and the other is military.[19] When Muhammad returned to his home city of Mecca after eight years of exile, he returned as a conqueror. With him marched ten thousand Muslim soldiers. They carried with them black flags. On the flags was one word written in Arabic: *punishment*.[20]

I was once talking to a group of young Muslim men and asking them some questions. I asked them if the obvious superior militaries of America and Israel compared to the militaries of any Islamic nations were a source of difficulty for Muslims. One of these men grew very angry at my question and snapped out, "You Americans and Zionists better get ready, because the black flags are coming!" At the time, I had no idea what he was talking about. Later I learned the meaning.

THE CONQUERING OF ISRAEL

Islamic tradition pictures the Mahdi as joining the army of Muslim warriors carrying black flags. The Mahdi will lead this army to Israel and re-conquer it for Islam. The Muslims will slaughter Jews until very few remain and Jerusalem will serve as the location of the Mahdi's rule over the earth:

> Rasulullah [Muhammad] said: "Armies carrying black flags will come from Khurasan. No power will be able to stop them and they will finally reach Eela [Baitul Maqdas in Jerusalem] where they will erect their flags."[21]

It is important to note here the reference above to "*Baitul Maqdas.*" In Arabic this means "the holy house." This is referring to the Dome of the Rock Mosque located on the Temple Mount in Jerusalem.

In a particularly venomous manner, Egyptian authors Muhammad ibn Izzat and Muhammad 'Arif comment on the above tradition:

> The Mahdi will be victorious and eradicate those pigs and dogs and the idols of this time so that there will once more be a *caliphate* based on prophethood as the *hadith* states.... *Jerusalem will be the location of the rightly guided caliphate and the center of Islamic rule, which will be headed by Imam al-Mahdi....* That will abolish the leadership of the Jews...and put an end to the domination of the Satans who spit evil into people and cause corruption in the earth, making them slaves of false idols and ruling the world by laws other than the *Shari'a* [Islamic Law] of the Lord of the worlds (emphasis mine).[22]

A very famous tradition often quoted throughout the Islamic world speaks of the Mahdi's military campaign against Israel. The tradition is both sickening and very sobering:

> The Prophet said...the last hour would not come unless the Muslims will fight against the Jews and the Muslims would kill them until the Jews would hide themselves behind a stone or a tree and a stone or a tree would say: Muslim, or the servant of Allah, there is a Jew behind me; come and kill him.[23]

THE MIRACULOUS PROVIDER WHO WILL BE LOVED BY ALL

It is said that the Mahdi will have control over the wind and the rain and the crops. Under the Mahdi's rule, the world will live in prosperity. Islamic tradition relates that Muhammad once said:

> In the last days of my *ummah* [universal Islamic community], the Mahdi will appear. Allah will give him power over the wind and the rain and the earth will bring forth its foliage. He will give away wealth profusely, flocks will be in abundance, and the *ummah* will be large and honored…[24]

> In those years my community will enjoy a time of happiness such as they have never experienced before. Heaven will send rain upon them in torrents, the earth will not withhold any of its plants, and wealth will be available to all. A man will stand and say, "Give to me, Mahdi!" and he will say, "Take."[25]

As a result of the numerous benefits that the Mahdi brings, it is said that all the inhabitants of the earth will deeply love him:

> Allah will sow love of him in the hearts of all people.[26]

> Al Mahdi appears; everyone only talks about Him, drinks the love of Him, and never talks about anything other than Him.[27]

THE TIMING OF THE MAHDI'S REIGN

While there is more than one tradition regarding the nature and timing of the Mahdi's ascendancy to power, one particular *hadith* places this event at the time of a final peace agreement between the Arabs and the Romans. ("Romans" referrs to Christians, or more generally, the West.) Although this peace agreement is made with the "Romans," it is presumably mediated through a Jew from the priestly lineage of Aaron. The peace agreement will be made for a period of seven years.

> Rasulullah [Muhammad] said: "There will be four peace agreements between you and the Romans [Christians].

> The fourth agreement will be mediated through a person who will be from the progeny of Hadrat Haroon [Honorable Aaron—Moses's brother] *and will be upheld for seven years* (emphasis mine).[28]

It appears that the period of this seven-year peace agreement will likewise be the period of the Mahdi's reign. While a few traditions specify that the Mahdi will reign on the earth for as much as eight or possibly even nine years, most traditions state that his reign will last seven years:

> The Prophet said…He will divide the property, and will govern the people by the Sunnah of their Prophet and establish Islam on Earth. *He will remain seven years,* then die, and the Muslims will pray over him (emphasis mine).[29]

> The Prophet said: The Mahdi…will fill the earth will equity and justice as it was filled with oppression and tyranny, and *he will rule for seven years* (emphasis mine).[30]

AL-MAHDI, THE RIDER ON A WHITE HORSE

The Mahdi is believed to ride on a white horse. Whether or not this is symbolic or literal is hard to say. Quite interestingly, this tradition comes from the Muslim interpretation of Christian Scriptures. Despite the fact that Muslims view the Bible as changed and corrupted by Jews and Christians, they claim to believe that some portions of the "original" inspired books remain within the "corrupted" Bible. A tradition within Islamic scholarship seeks to extract those portions of the Bible that Muslims feel may be untainted by the corrupting influence of Jews and Christians. Muslims call these Judeo-Christian traditions *isra'iliyyat.* One such transmitter of biblical traditions is Muslim scholar Ka'b al-Ahbar, viewed among Muslims as a trustworthy transmitter of *hadith* as well as *isra'iliyyat.*[31] Ka'b al-Ahbar's view, that this description of the rider on the white horse as found in the Book of Revelation is indeed the Mahdi, is supported by two well-known Egyptian authors, Muhammad Ibn 'Izzat and Muhammad

'Arif. In their book, *Al Mahdi and the End of Time,* they quote Ka'b al Ahbar as saying:

> I find the Mahdi recorded in the books of the Prophets.... For instance, the Book of Revelation says: "And I saw and beheld a white horse. He that sat on him...went forth conquering and to conquer."[32]

'Izzat and 'Arif then go on to say:

> It is clear that this man is the Mahdi who will ride the white horse and judge by the Qur'an [with justice] and with whom will be men with marks of prostration on their foreheads [marks on their foreheads from bowing in prayer with their head to the ground five times daily].[33]

Some claim this is the reason Saddam Hussein painted numerous murals all over Baghdad portraying himself as a Muslim knight on a white horse with sword drawn doing valiant battle against the infidels.[34]

AL-MAHDI THE MIRACULOUS ARCHAEOLOGIST

In one final very interesting series of traditions regarding the Mahdi we find that he is said to produce some previously undiscovered Bible scrolls—even the Ark of the Covenant itself:

> Ka'b al-Ahbar says, "He will be called 'Mahdi' because he will guide [*yahdi*] to something hidden and will bring out the Torah and Gospel from a town called Antioch."[35]

> As-Suyuti mentioned in *al-Hawi* that the messenger of Allah, may Allah bless him and grant him peace, said, "He is called the Mahdi because he will guide the people to a mountain in Syria from which he will bring out the volumes of the Torah to refute the Jews. At the hands of the Mahdi the Ark of the Covenant will be brought forth from the Lake of Tiberias and taken and placed in Jerusalem."[36]

> Ad-Dani said that he is called the Mahdi because he will be guided to a mountain in Syria from which he will bring forth the volumes of the Torah with which to argue

against the Jews and at his hands a group of them will become Muslim.[37]

Apparently, the purpose of finding these "lost" portions of the Old and New Testaments as well as the Ark of the Covenant is to help the Mahdi win converts from both Christianity and Judaism prior to "eradicating" the remainder who do not convert to Islam. We will discuss this aspect of Islamic tradition further in later chapters.

SUMMARY

After reviewing the various Islamic traditions and opinions of the Muslim scholars, let's now review and walk through a list of what we have learned about the person and the mission of the Mahdi as he exists in the minds of the 1.5 billion Muslims worldwide. Remember, this is the man that the Muslims of the world eagerly await:

1. The Mahdi is Islam's primary messiah figure.

2. He will be a descendant of Muhammad and will bear Muhammad's name (Muhammad bin Abdullah).

3. He will be a very devout Muslim.

4. He will be an unparalleled spiritual, political, and military world leader.

5. He will emerge after a period of great turmoil and suffering upon the earth.

6. He will establish justice and righteousness throughout the world and eradicate tyranny and oppression.

7. He will be the *caliph* and *imam* (vice regent and leader) of Muslims worldwide.

8. He will lead a world revolution and establish a new world order.

9. He will lead military action against all those who oppose him.

10. He will invade many countries.

11. He will make a seven-year peace treaty with a Jew of priestly lineage.

12. He will conquer Israel for Islam and lead the "faithful Muslims" in a final slaughter/battle against Jews.

13. He will establish the new Islamic world headquarters from Jerusalem.

14. He will rule for seven years (possibly as much as eight or nine).

15. He will cause Islam to be the only religion practiced on the earth.

16. He will appear riding a white horse (possibly symbolic).

17. He will discover some previously undiscovered biblical manuscripts that he will use to argue with the Jews and cause some Jews to convert to Islam.

18. He will also re-discover the Ark of the Covenant from the Sea of Galilee, which he will bring to Jerusalem.

19. He will have supernatural power from Allah over the wind and the rain and crops.

20. He will posses and distribute enormous amounts of wealth.

21. He will be loved by all the people of the earth.

CHAPTER FIVE

COMPARING THE BIBLICAL
ANTICHRIST AND THE MAHDI

M*ost people who haven't even read the Bible* have heard of the man known popularly as "the Antichrist." Simply put, according to the Bible, the Antichrist will be Satan's primary human agent on the earth in the last days. Interestingly, the Bible refers to him only once by that specific name (1 John 2:18). Using other names, however, there are numerous references to the Antichrist found throughout the Bible. Some of the various names that Scripture assigns to him are "the Beast" (Revelation 13:4), "the abomination that causes desolation" (Matthew 24:15), "the desolator" (Daniel 9:27), "the man of sin," "the man of lawlessness," "the son of destruction" (2 Thessalonians 2), "the little horn" (Daniel 7:8), "the Assyrian" (Micah 5:5, Isaiah 10:5, 14:25), "the oppressor," "the king of Babylon" (Isaiah 14), and even the mysterious "Gog" (Ezekiel 38:1, Revelation 20:7). There are several other names that Scripture uses to refer to the Antichrist as well.

But beyond all of his unusual names, who exactly is the Antichrist? In this chapter we will review a few of the primary descriptions and actions that define just who the Antichrist is according to the Bible. Our examination will also focus on several very specific similarities between the Antichrist and the Mahdi.

A POWERFUL POLITICAL AND MILITARY WORLD LEADER

From the Bible, we learn that, in the last days, the Antichrist will emerge as a man who will lead a very powerful world empire, the likes of which history has yet to produce. This powerful leadership role of the Antichrist is first described clearly in the Bible by the Prophet Daniel. In the Book of Daniel, in the seventh chapter, we find Daniel describing a vision of four very bizarre and gruesome "beasts." After describing the first three beasts, Daniel says this of the fourth:

> After that, in my vision at night I looked, and there before me was a fourth beast—terrifying and frightening and very powerful. It had large iron teeth; it crushed and devoured its victims and trampled underfoot whatever was left. It was different from all the former beasts, and it had ten horns. While I was thinking about the horns, there before me was another horn, a little one, which came up among them; and three of the first horns were uprooted before it. This horn had eyes like the eyes of a man and a mouth that spoke boastfully (Daniel 7:7-8).

Then, in verses 15-16, Daniel asks an angel in his vision to explain the interpretation of the vision of the four beasts. The angel explains that the four beasts represent four very great kingdoms or empires:

> I, Daniel, was troubled in spirit, and the visions that passed through my mind disturbed me. I approached one of those standing there and asked him the true meaning of all this. So he told me and gave me the interpretation of these things: The four great beasts are four kingdoms that will rise from the earth (Daniel 7:15-17).

It's actually pretty straightforward. Daniel again asks the angel specifically about the fourth beast and in particular about the "little horn" that uprooted three horns. The angel again responds with a very direct and clear explanation:

> He gave me this explanation: The fourth beast is a fourth kingdom that will appear on earth. It will be different from all the other kingdoms and will devour the whole earth, trampling it down and crushing it. The ten horns are ten kings who will come from this kingdom. After

them another king will arise, different from the earlier
ones; he will subdue three kings (Daniel 7: 23-24).

Essentially, the angel explains that the fourth kingdom causes
great destruction to the whole earth. Initially, this kingdom will
consist of ten kings. Then another king, an eleventh, will arise
and displace three of the previous kings. This eleventh king is
the Antichrist, first referred to as "the little horn." Thus we see
that, based on the vision that Daniel saw, the Antichrist is a
future king who will first gain control over three other
kingdoms or nations, and eventually over ten, thus forming his
future ten-nation "beast" empire—an empire of unparalleled
power and ferocity which will "devour the whole earth,
trampling it down and crushing it."

In the last part of Daniel chapter seven, the angel describes
to Daniel the actions of this king as well as his end:

> He will speak against the Most High and oppress his saints
> and try to change the set times and the laws. The saints will
> be handed over to him for a time, times and half a time. But
> the court will sit, and his power will be taken away and
> completely destroyed forever (Daniel 7:25-27).

The king is said to oppress the saints of God for a period of time
that most Bible scholars agree is three and a half years (a time,
times and half a time). But eventually his dominion will be taken
away, and replaced by the Kingdom of "The Most High" God.

Three hundred years later, in the Book of Revelation, the
Apostle John likewise describes the Antichrist and his "beast"
empire in very similar terms:

> And I saw a beast coming out of the sea. He had ten horns
> and seven heads, with ten crowns on his horns, and on
> each head a blasphemous name. The beast I saw
> resembled a leopard, but had feet like those of a bear and
> a mouth like that of a lion. The dragon gave the beast his
> power and his throne and great authority.... Men
> worshiped the dragon because he had given authority to
> the beast, and they also worshiped the beast and asked,

"Who is like the beast? Who can make war against him?"
The beast was given a mouth to utter proud words and
blasphemies and to exercise his authority for forty-two
months. He opened his mouth to blaspheme God, and to
slander His name and His dwelling place and those who
live in heaven. He was given power to make war against
the saints and to conquer them. And he was given
authority over every tribe, people, language, and nation.
All inhabitants of the earth will worship the beast—all
whose names have not been written in the Book of Life
belonging to the Lamb that was slain from the creation of
the world (Revelation 13:2, 4-8).

While the symbolic language here is fairly thick, if we
understand the biblical usage of particular symbolic terms, then
the picture is actually quite clear. The "beast" again refers to the
Antichrist, king over a ten-nation empire. The horns represent
authority and power. Ten horns speak of an extremely high
degree of authority as well as the number of nations and their
kings that will unite to form the beast's kingdom. The "dragon"
who gives the beast his authority is Satan. Satan is often spoken
of in the Bible as a dragon or a serpent. The global impact of this
beast-like empire is made clear by the phrase: "And he was given
authority over every tribe, people, language, and nation." We see
the specific question that the people of the earth ask is, *"Who is
like the beast? Who can make war against him?"* It appears to those
on the earth that the beast is absolutely beyond challenge. And
again, we see the same specific period of time that was given to
the beast to persecute God's people as forty-two months. Forty-
two months is three and a half years. This same timeframe
appears in the previously cited passage of Daniel 7:25.

Thus, we have seen that the Bible prophesies that the
Antichrist will be a political and military leader with power
unparalleled by any other world leader throughout history.

THE MAHDI AS WORLD RULER

As we have seen from the Islamic traditions and Muslim scholars, the Mahdi, like the Antichrist, is also prophesied to be a political and military world leader unparalleled by any other throughout world history. The Mahdi is said to "fight against the forces of evil, lead a world revolution, and set up a new world order based on justice, righteousness, and virtue."[1] At this time, according to Islamic tradition, the Mahdi is said to preside over the entire earth as the final *caliph* of Islam. And of course as we saw in the last chapter, the Muslims will "take the world administration in their hands and Islam will be victorious over all the religions." Without question, Islam views the Mahdi as one whose rule will extend over all of the earth. Clearly then, we see that the Antichrist and the Mahdi are both described as political and military leaders the likes of which the world has never before seen. While many powerful leaders have arisen throughout world history, the descriptions given concerning both the Antichrist and the Mahdi surpass any that have yet arisen. But the Mahdi and the Antichrist are both described as more than merely political and military leaders. They are both viewed as supreme religious leaders as well.

THE ANTICHRIST AS A SPIRITUAL WORLD LEADER

The Bible establishes the fact that the Antichrist will be a spiritual leader whose authority will be acknowledged worldwide. After examining the Antichrist's role as a universal religious leader, many Bible prophecy teachers have talked about the coming of the "One World Religion" or "the false church" which the Antichrist will both create and enforce upon the entire earth. This concept of a coming dominant and demonically inspired world religion is partly arrived at due to the frequent references to worship associated with the Antichrist throughout Scripture. In the Book of Revelation we read that the Antichrist will both inspire and demand worship. This worship will be directed at both Satan, referred to as "the dragon," and the Antichrist, referred to as "the beast":

> Men worshiped the dragon because he had given authority to the beast, and they also worshiped the beast and asked, "Who is like the beast? Who can make war against him?".... All inhabitants of the earth will worship the beast—all whose names have not been written in the Book of Life belonging to the Lamb that was slain from the creation of the world (Revelation 13:4, 8).

Beyond the fact that the Antichrist establishes a worldwide worship movement, another reason to see him as a spiritual world leader is because the Bible says a man whom it refers to as "The False Prophet will assist him. Of course, the very title False *Prophet* assumes the religious nature of this man. One of the primary roles of the False Prophet is to perform deceptive "signs and wonders" that will help persuade the inhabitants of the earth to worship the Antichrist/Beast:

> But the beast was captured, and with him the false prophet who had performed the miraculous signs on his behalf (Revelation 19:20).

It is clear then, that the Bible teaches that the Antichrist will lead a worldwide religious worship movement that will attempt to displace and usurp worship from the God of the Bible. This worship will then be directed toward both himself and to Satan—the invisible spirit—the provocateur and puppet master that motivates, empowers, and gives authority to the Antichrist to accomplish his worldwide task.

THE MAHDI AS A SPIRITUAL WORLD LEADER

Likewise, it almost goes without saying, the Mahdi of Islam will be the leader of a worldwide worship movement, a worship movement that will seek to cause anyone who practices any religion other than Islam to renounce his faith and worship

Allah, the god of Islam. As we saw in the last chapter, the Mahdi "will govern the people by the Sunnah of their Prophet and establish Islam on Earth."[2] And "Islam will be victorious over all the religions."[3]

Thus we see that the Mahdi leads a world revolution that will institute a "new world order" based on the religion of Islam. Islam will be the only religion allowed. Both the Antichrist and the Mahdi are said to be the unqualified leaders of a global religious movement that will draw worship away from the God of the Bible and His Son Jesus Christ. As we will see clearly in later chapters, inherent in the worship of Allah within the context of Islam is a direct denial of the God of the Bible and His Son Jesus Christ. In fact, this is the reason that some Muslims feel so strongly as to say that the Mahdi will "eradicate those pigs and dogs"—the Christians and the Jews who refuse to convert to Islam. Which leads us to the next obvious similarity between the Antichrist and the Mahdi.

THE ANTICHRIST'S TARGETED CAMPAIGN AGAINST JEWS AND CHRISTIANS

The Bible is very clear that Satan, through the Antichrist, will specifically target first Jews and then Christians for death. In the Book of Revelation, chapters twelve and thirteen, we read another prophetic passage of Scripture rich with symbolic language. Initially it is slightly difficult to understand, but after the symbols are explained, it becomes very clear:

> A great and wondrous sign appeared in heaven: a woman clothed with the sun, with the moon under her feet and a crown of twelve stars on her head (Revelation 12:1).

The "woman" symbolically pictured here is the family or nation of Israel, the Jewish people. We see that she is crowned with twelve stars. This represents the twelve sons of Israel who became the twelve tribes that make up the family or the nation of Israel (Genesis 35:23-26).

> She was pregnant and cried out in pain as she was about
> to give birth. Then another sign appeared in heaven: an
> enormous red dragon with seven heads and ten horns and
> seven crowns on his heads. The dragon stood in front of
> the woman who was about to give birth, so that he might
> devour her child the moment it was born. She gave birth
> to a son, a male child, who will rule all the nations with an
> iron scepter. And her child was snatched up to God and to
> His throne (Revelation 12:2-5).

The woman—Israel—becomes pregnant and gives birth to a
"male child, who will rule all the nations with an iron
scepter." This is a clear reference to Jesus, the Jewish Messiah
(see Psalm 2:9). The dragon mentioned here is identified in
verse 9 as "that ancient serpent called the devil or Satan, who
leads the whole world astray." We see that Satan desires to kill
Jesus, but instead Jesus is "snatched up to God and to His
throne." This is a reference to Jesus' ascension to heaven after
the Resurrection (Acts 1:8). After this:

> The great dragon was hurled down—that ancient serpent
> called the devil or Satan, who leads the whole world astray.
> He was hurled to the earth, and his angels with him…. He
> [the dragon] pursued the woman who had given birth to
> the male child…. The woman was given the two wings of a
> great eagle, so that she might fly to the place prepared for
> her in the desert, where she would be taken care of for a
> time, times and half a time, out of the serpent's reach. Then
> the dragon was enraged at the woman and went off to
> make war against the rest of her offspring—those who obey
> God's commandments and hold to the testimony of Jesus
> (Revelation 12:1-6, 9, 13, 14, 17).

We see that Satan is "enraged at the woman (Israel) and "went
off to make war against the rest of her offspring—those who
obey God's commandments and hold to the testimony of Jesus."
Israel's "other offspring" are those Christians who indeed "obey
God's commandments and hold to the testimony of Jesus." This
is the only passage that makes specific reference to Satan making
a direct target of both Jews and Christians. And we know that

this passage speaks specifically of the end times, because it mentions twice the three and a half year period (1260 days and "a time, times and half a time") that the Antichrist will have authority to war against the saints:

> The beast was given a mouth to utter proud words and blasphemies and to exercise his authority for forty-two months. He opened his mouth to blaspheme God, and to slander His name and His dwelling place and those who live in heaven. He was given power to make war against the saints and to conquer them. And he was given authority over every tribe, people, language, and nation (Revelation 13:5-7).

The Prophet Daniel also saw that the Antichrist would have this authority to wage a successful war against "the saints." *Saints* is also translated as "holy ones" in some translations. It speaks primarily of the true followers of Jesus who know and serve the One True God.

> He will speak against the Most High and oppress his saints and try to change the set times and the laws. The saints will be handed over to him for a time, times and half a time (Daniel 7:25).

Again here we see the reference to the three and a half year period that the Antichrist will persecute those who resist him.

The Bible is clear then, the Antichrist will specifically target those who resist his attempts to establish his religion all over the earth. From the Book of Revelation as well as the Prophet Daniel, we see that the two groups that most enrage Satan are the Jews and the Christians.

THE MAHDI'S TARGETED CAMPAIGN AGAINST JEWS AND CHRISTIANS

Interestingly enough, Islamic tradition speaks much of the Mahdi's special calling to convert Christians and Jews to Islam, yet speaks very little specifically of conversions from other faiths. It seems as though converting Christians and Jews to Islam will be the primary evangelistic thrust of the Mahdi. The following quote from Ayatollah Ibrahim Amini clearly articulates this vision:

> The Mahdi will offer the religion of Islam to the Jews and Christians; if they accept it they will be spared, otherwise they will be killed.[4]

And of course we cannot forget the infamous *hadith* that has become a favorite of many Muslim anti-Semites. Again, note that it is speaking specifically about "the last hour":

> The last hour would not come unless the Muslims will fight against the Jews and the Muslims would kill them until the Jews would hide themselves behind a stone or a tree and a stone or a tree would say: Muslim, or the servant of Allah, there is a Jew behind me; come and kill him; but the tree Gharqad would not say, for it is the tree of the Jews.[5]

After commenting on this particular *hadith*, several Muslim authors will quickly point out the very "interesting" fact that this particular tree, "the Gharqad" (apparently the boxwood tree), is presently being planted in abundance by Jews in Israel. The point is that Muslims expect this final holocaust to take place within the present state of Israel. This of course corresponds to another very specific similarity between the biblical Antichrist and the Mahdi.

A MILITARY ATTACK AGAINST ISRAEL AND THE ESTABLISHMENT OF THE TEMPLE MOUNT AS THE SEAT OF AUTHORITY

The Bible teaches that the Antichrist, with his multi-nation coalition, will attack Israel, and specifically Jerusalem, to conquer it:

> I will gather all the nations to Jerusalem to fight against it; the city will be captured, the houses ransacked, and the women raped. Half of the city will go into exile, but the

rest of the people [who submit to Antichrist's rule] will not be taken from the city (Zechariah 14:2).

You [Gog—Ezekiel's name for the Antichrist] will go up, you will come like a storm; you will be like a cloud covering the land, you and all your troops, and many peoples with you. Thus says the Lord GOD, "It will come about on that day, that thoughts will come into your mind and you will devise an evil plan, and you will say, 'I will go up against the land of unwalled villages. I will go against those who are at rest, that live securely, all of them living without walls and having no bars or gates, to capture spoil and to seize plunder, to turn your hand against the waste places which are now inhabited, and against the people [Israelites] who are gathered from the nations, who have acquired cattle and goods, who live at the center of the world'" (Ezekiel 38:9-12, NASB).

According to the Bible, after this attack, the Antichrist will specifically set up his "throne" in "God's Temple." The Apostle Paul lays this out quite clearly:

He will oppose and will exalt himself over everything that is called God or is worshiped, so that he sets himself up in God's temple, proclaiming himself to be God (2 Thessalonians 2:4).

The location of the Jewish Temple has always been on Mount Moriah in Jerusalem. Today, the Temple that once stood on Mount Moriah does not exist; it was destroyed by the Roman emperor Titus in AD 70 according to the prophecy of Jesus:

Jesus left the temple and was walking away when his disciples came up to him to call his attention to its buildings. "Do you see all these things?" he asked. "I tell you the truth, not one stone here will be left on another; every one will be thrown down" (Matthew 24:1, 2).

Today, Mount Moriah, sometimes known as the Temple Mount or in Arabic as *Haram Ash-Sharif*, is the location of two mosques and the third holiest site of Islam. There is endless speculation about the Temple Mount regarding issues such as exactly where the Jewish Temple once stood on the Mount or whether or not a rebuilt Jewish Temple will rise there in the future. The above verse from the Apostle Paul certainly seems to indicate that a rebuilt Jewish Temple will indeed appear in Jerusalem. The Apostle Paul says that the Antichrist will "set himself up in God's Temple," or more literally, "he takes his seat in the temple of God." This speaks not so much of a literal sitting down as it does of a taking a position of authority. Thus we see that the Antichrist will make Mount Moriah and, more specifically, the rebuilt Jewish Temple, the specific location of his rule. Jesus warned of this event two thousand years ago. Referring to the Antichrist having set himself up in the Jewish Temple, and the events that will immediately follow, Jesus said:

> So when you see standing in the holy place "the abomination that causes desolation," spoken of through the Prophet Daniel—let the reader understand—then let those who are in Judea flee to the mountains. Let no one on the roof of his house go down to take anything out of the house. Let no one in the field go back to get his cloak. How dreadful it will be in those days for pregnant women and nursing mothers! Pray that your flight will not take place in winter or on the Sabbath. For then there will be great distress unequaled from the beginning of the world until now—and never to be equaled again. If those days had not been cut short, no one would survive, but for the sake of the elect those days will be shortened (Matthew 24:16-22).

Here we see Jesus referring to the Antichrist's occupancy of the Temple as "the abomination that causes desolation." The "desolation" refers to the chaos and severe persecution against the Jews and Christians that will immediately follow when the Antichrist's true identity is revealed. After his military campaign against Jerusalem, the Antichrist will make his base of authority the Temple Mount itself. At this time, it is clear that the Antichrist's malevolent feelings toward Israel will become fully manifest, so much so that Jesus warns the inhabitants of Jerusalem to straightaway flee to the mountains.

THE MAHDI'S ATTACK OF JERUSALEM AND THE ESTABLISHMENT OF THE ISLAMIC *CALIPHATE* FROM JERUSALEM

Likewise the Mahdi is said to attack Jerusalem and re-conquer it for Islam in order to establish Islamic rule over the earth from Jerusalem:

> [Armies carrying] black flags will come from Khurasan [Iran]. No power will be able to stop them and they will finally reach Eela [the Dome of the Rock in Jerusalem] where they will erect their flags.[6]

> Jerusalem will be the location of the rightly guided *caliphate* and the center of Islamic rule, which will be headed by Imam al-Mahdi[7]

Also, as we just saw in the section above, the Mahdi will not end his campaign against Jerusalem in a peaceful way. For the Jews, the Islamic version of the last days ends with the last few surviving Jews hiding behind rocks or trees from the sword of Islam. The military campaign against Jerusalem and the establishment of the Islamic *caliphate* there likewise will not result in a benevolent rule over the Jews by the Mahdi, for as we have already seen, the last quote above continues:

> ...that will abolish the leadership of the Jews...and put an end to the domination of the Satans who spit evil into people and cause corruption in the earth.[8]

In relation to the above attack against the inhabitants of Israel, there is, quite interestingly, another very specific correlation between the actions of the Mahdi and the actions of the biblical Antichrist. While the similarities between the Antichrist and the Mahdi that we have already discussed are astonishing, I believe that the specificity of this next parallel is simply incredible.

THE ANTICHRIST'S SEVEN-YEAR TREATY WITH ISRAEL

After rising to power, and as a prelude to his invasion of Israel, the Antichrist is said to initiate a treaty with the nation of Israel for seven years:

> He will confirm a covenant with many for one "seven." In the middle of the "seven" he will put an end to sacrifice and offering. And on a wing of the temple he will set up an abomination that causes desolation, until the end that is decreed is poured out on him (Daniel 9:27).

In context, this verse shows us that the Antichrist will establish a "covenant" with Israel for seven years, giving the Israelis a false sense of security.

The specific Hebrew word used in this verse translated as "seven" is *shabuwa*. It means a week, but can mean either a "week" of days or years. In Hebrew thought, a seven year period is similar to our decade. We in the West tend to measure years through a decimal system based on increments of tens, while we measure days in terms of seven (a week). The Hebrews measured both days and years in increments of seven. The word translated as "seven" in Daniel 9:27 refers to seven years. This is the specific amount of time that the Antichrist will set for his peace treaty with Israel. Then, in the middle of the seven years, the Antichrist will renege on his treaty and stop the offerings and sacrifices in the Jewish Temple and then he will proclaim himself not only the ruler of the world, but God himself. Isaiah the Prophet makes mention of this "covenant" and rebukes Israel for making it: He actually refers to it as a "covenant with death" (Isaiah 28: 14-15).

THE MAHDI'S SEVEN-YEAR TREATY

Again, similarly, the Mahdi is said to initiate Islam's fourth and final treaty between "the Romans" and the Muslims. (Again, "Romans" should be interpreted as Christians or the West in general—the executioners of Nicholas Berg in their pre-execution statement addressed President Bush as "You, O dog of the Romans.") Interestingly enough, this fourth treaty is said to be made with a descendant of Moses's brother, Aaron the Priest. Such a descendant would be a *cohen*. That is to say, he would be a priest. Only *cohanim* among Jews can officiate the priestly duties of the Temple. This is important in light of the fact that many Christian prophecy teachers and theologians have speculated that the treaty that the Antichrist will initiate with Israel will include an agreement to allow the Jews to rebuild their Temple. But probably the most amazing aspect of this treaty that the Mahdi makes with this Jew of priestly lineage is its timeframe. The specific timeframe given for the treaty is exactly the same as the Antichrist's peace treaty—seven years! Citing *hadiths* which speak of the Mahdi's emergence and rule, Muhammad Ali ibn Zubair relates this amazing tradition:

> The Prophet said: There will be four peace agreements between you and the Romans. The fourth will be mediated through a person who will be *from the progeny of Hadrat Aaron* [Honorable Aaron—the brother of Moses] and will be upheld *for seven years*. The people asked, "O Prophet Muhammad, who will be the *imam* [leader] of the people at that time?" The Prophet said: He will be from my progeny and will be exactly forty years of age. His face will shine like a star… (emphasis mine).[9]

CHANGING THE LAWS AND THE TIMES

Another of the Antichrist's goals according to the Book of Daniel is to "change the set times and the laws":

> He will speak against the Most High and oppress his saints and try to change the set times and the laws. The saints will be handed over to him for a time, times and half a time (Daniel 7:25).

This is actually quite a big hint into the person of the Antichrist. For by his actions, we see a hint of his origin. It is said that he will desire to change two things—times and laws.

Now we have already seen that the Mahdi will change the law by instituting Islamic *shariah* law all over the earth, but we have not seen any evidence in Islamic apocalyptic literature of him changing the "times." The simple question, however, is, who else other than a Muslim would desire to change the "times and the laws"? Besides the Gregorian calendar used by the West, there is also a Jewish, a Hindu, and a Muslim calendar, among others. Jews and Hindus, however, would not desire to impose their religious laws or calendars onto the rest of the world. Islam however, does have both its own laws and its own calendar, both of which it *would* desire to impose onto the entire world. The Islamic calendar is based on the career of Muhammad. It begins at the migration (*hijra*) of Muhammad from Mecca to Medina. The Muslim calendar is mandatory for all Muslims to observe. Dr. Waleed Mahanna articulates the Islamic position regarding the Islamic *hijra* calendar:

> It is considered a divine command to use a [*hijra*] calendar
> with twelve [purely] lunar months without intercalation,
> as evident from…the Holy Qur'an.[10]

Not only does Islam view as a divine imperative the use of a unique religious calendar, it also has its own week. Unlike the Western rhythm of a week; Monday through Friday being the body of the workweek followed by Saturday and Sunday as the weekend, with Judaism and Christianity using these two days for their respective days of worship, Islam holds Friday as its sacred day of prayer. This is the day that Muslims meet at the mosque to pray and listen to a sermon.

Thus it quite plausible that the biblical reference to the Antichrist who will "try to change the set times and the laws" describes a Muslim. As we look at the full picture, only Islam fits the bill of a system that has its own unique calendar, a week based on its own religious history, and a clear system of law that it wishes to impose onto the entire earth. Surely if a Muslim ever emerges as powerful as the Mahdi, he will attempt to institute Islamic law worldwide—and the Islamic calendar and week as well.

THE RIDER ON A WHITE HORSE

The final similarity between the Antichrist and the Mahdi that we will discuss in this chapter is the fact that both the Antichrist and the Mahdi are identified with a biblical passage that describes a rider on a white horse. While this could be literal, it is most probably a symbolic picture of the two men. The amazing thing is that the origin of the biblical tradition of the Antichrist on a white horse and the origin of the Islamic tradition of the Mahdi on a white horse come from the same passage in the Bible.

The basis for the symbolic picture of both the Antichrist and the Mahdi on a white horse is the sixth chapter of the Book of Revelation. Here the Apostle John describes his vision of the release of the events that mark the beginning of the end times. The picture is of Jesus holding a scroll—on the outside of the scroll are seven wax seals. The breaking of each seal releases a specific and distinct end-time event:

> I watched as the Lamb [Jesus] opened the first of the seven seals. Then I heard one of the four living creatures say in a voice like thunder, "Come!" I looked, and there before me was a white horse! Its rider held a bow, and he was given a crown, and he rode out as a conqueror bent on conquest (Revelation 6:1-2).

The seals that follow this rider are:

1. Peace is taken from the earth.

2. Famine.

3. Plagues and death.

4. Persecution and martyrdom of God's people.

5. A great earthquake.

6. The wrath of God.

So we see that after the rider appears on the scene, the world essentially freefalls into the chaos that defines the last hour. The interpretation that many Bible scholars apply to this passage is thus: The white horse is an imitation of the white horse that Jesus will ride when He returns (Revelation 19:11). Thus the rider is an imitation Christ, an imposter—an Antichrist. The bow without arrows that the rider carries represents a false peace. The rider carries with his rise to power a false promise of peace. This is in alignment with and may be a direct reference to the false peace treaty that the Antichrist makes with Israel at the start of the seven year period of his rule. The crown on his head obviously refers to his position of authority and leadership. And we see that the true motivation and bent of the rider is to conquer. In light of the identity and activity of the rider, then, we are not surprised to find out that the events that follow his emergence onto the world scene do not bring an age of peace, but rather an age of apocalyptic chaos. Apparently this is not a problem for Islamic scholars, who generally adopt a very arbitrary pick-and-choose approach to the Bible. For in seeing the Antichrist on the white horse with a crown and conquering, Muslim scholars see a clear picture of the Mahdi. As mentioned in the earlier chapter on the Mahdi, the early Muslim transmitter of *hadiths*, Ka'b al Ahbar is quoted as saying:

> I find the Mahdi recorded in the books of the Prophets...
> For instance, the Book of Revelation says: "And I saw and
> behold a white horse. He that sat on him...went forth
> conquering and to conquer."[11]

So in conclusion, we see that several of the most unique and distinguishing aspects of the biblical Antichrist's person, mission, and actions are matched to quite an amazing degree by the descriptions of the Mahdi as found in the Islamic traditions. And now, even further, we see that Muslim scholars actually apply Bible verses about the Antichrist to their awaited savior, the Mahdi. This must be seen as quite ironic, if not entirely prophetic.

CHAPTER SIX

THE MUSLIM JESUS

A*fter the emergence* or the "rising" of the Mahdi, the second most important event among the Major Signs is the return of Jesus Christ. Christians who love Jesus understandably get quite excited by the prospect that Muslims look for and long for His return. Unfortunately, the Islamic belief of just who this Jesus is that is coming, and what He does once He has arrived, is drastically different than what Christians believe about Jesus.

The first thing that Christians need to understand regarding the Islamic belief about Jesus is that Muslims of course reject the idea that Jesus was or is the Son of God. According to Islam, Jesus is not as the Bible articulates, God in the flesh. Second, in Islamic belief, Jesus never died on a cross for the sins of mankind. The Qur'an specifically denies that Jesus was ever crucified or that He ever experienced death. Muslims believe that after Allah miraculously delivered Jesus from death, He ascended into heaven alive in a similar fashion to the biblical narrative regarding Elijah. Since then, Muslims believe, Jesus has remained with Allah, awaiting His opportunity to return to the earth to finish His ministry and complete His life. As such, to the Islamic mind, Jesus was not in any way a "savior." To Muslims, Jesus was merely another prophet in the long line of prophets that Allah has sent to mankind. The special title of Messiah, although retained in the Islamic tradition, is essentially stripped of any truly biblically defined messianic characteristics. According to the sacred texts of Islam, as we are about to see, when Jesus returns, it most certainly will *not* be to restore the nation of Israel to the Jewish people. Nor will Jesus' purpose be to save and deliver His faithful followers from the ongoing persecution of the Antichrist. In order to understand the Islamic concept of Jesus' return, the first thing that needs to be realized is that when Jesus comes back, *He comes back as a radical Muslim!*

This chapter will outline the Islamic traditions regarding the return of Jesus. Many of the *hadiths* below that refer to Jesus do not call Him by the name Jesus, but rather Isa. Muslims occasionally will refer to Jesus by His English name for our sake, but the name that the Qur'an gives Him, and which most Muslims use, is Isa (or Eesa) al-Maseeh (the Messiah). Other common titles that Islam uses when referring to Jesus are Hadrat Isa (Honorable Jesus), Isa bin Maryam (Jesus son of Mary), or Nabi Isa (Prophet Jesus). Some of these titles may be used below.

THE RETURN OF THE MUSLIM JESUS

According to Islam's sacred traditions, Jesus' return is usually described as taking place just outside Damascus:

> At this very time Allah would send Christ, son of Mary, and he will descend at the white *minaret* in the eastern side of Damascus wearing two garments lightly dyed with saffron and placing his hands on the wings of two angels. When he would lower his head, there would fall beads of perspiration from his head, and when he would raise it up, beads like pearls would scatter from it.[1]

THE SUBORDINATE OF THE MAHDI

At this time, Jesus descends to meet the army of the Mahdi, which will be preparing for battle. It will be just before the time of prayer:

> Muslims will still be preparing themselves for the battle drawing up the ranks. Certainly, the time of prayer shall come and then Jesus, son of Mary would descend.[2]

Based on the relevant *hadith*, Islamic scholars seem to be in universal agreement that the Mahdi will ask Jesus to lead the prayers. Jesus will then refuse this request and will defer instead to the Mahdi to lead the prayer:

> The Messenger of Allah said: A section of my people will not cease fighting for the truth and will prevail until the day of resurrection. He said: Jesus son of Mary would then descend and their [Muslims'] commander [the Mahdi] would invite him to come and lead them in prayer, but he would say: No, some amongst you are commanders over some.[3]

The important element to stress here is that Jesus will then pray behind the Mahdi as a direct statement regarding Jesus' inferiority of rank to the Mahdi:

> Jesus Christ will decline the offer and invitation of Imam Mahdi to come and lead the Muslims in prayer, and say his prayer behind Imam Mahdi.[4]

> Jesus (peace be upon him) will come and will perform the obligatory prayers behind the Mahdi and follow him.[5]

> [Jesus] will be following the Mahdi, the master of the time, and that is why he will be offering his prayers behind him.[6]

JESUS THE FAITHFUL MUSLIM

After Jesus returns, in keeping with His identity as a faithful Muslim, He will perform the ritual pilgrimage to Mecca called *hajj*:

> The Prophet said: Verily Isa ibn Maryam shall descend as an equitable judge and fair ruler. He shall tread his path on the way to *hajj* [pilgrimage] and come to my grave to greet me, and I shall certainly answer him![7]

JESUS WILL INSTITUTE ISLAMIC LAW

While the Mahdi, as the *caliph* (vice regent) and *imam* (leader) of the Muslims is clearly superior to Jesus in Islam, Jesus remains a leader of the Muslim community. According to the

Islamic traditions, Jesus' primary purpose will be to oversee the institution and the enforcement of Islamic *shariah* law all over the world:

> Ibn Qayyim mentioned in *Manar al-munif* that the leader...is the Mahdi who will request Jesus to lead the Muslims in prayer. Jesus will remain on the earth, not as a prophet, but as one of the community (*ummah*) of Prophet Muhammad. Muslims will follow him as their leader. According to Shalabi, the Mahdi will lead the Muslims in prayer, and Jesus will rule the Muslims according to the divine law (*shariah*).[8]

> Jesus, the son of Mary will descend and will lead them judging amongst them according to the holy Qur'an and the Sunnah of the Prophet Muhammad.[9]

JESUS: THE GREATEST MUSLIM EVANGELIST

Islamic tradition teaches that because Jesus will declare Himself to be a Muslim, He will lead many Christians to convert to Islam. Regarding those who do not convert to Islam, the Qur'an states that Jesus will be a witness against them on the Day of Judgment:

> There is not one of the People of the Scripture [Christians and Jews] but will believe in him before his death, and on the Day of Resurrection he will be a witness against them (Surah 4:159).

Commenting on the above verse, Mufti Muhammad Shafi and Mufti Mohammad Rafi Usmani in their book, *Signs of the Qiyama* [the final judgement] *and the Arrival of the Maseeh* [the Messiah], explain that the phrase "will believe in him before his death" means that Christians and Jews will:

> ...confirm that he is alive and has not died and he is not God or the Son of God but [merely] His [Allah's] slave and Messenger, and Isa [Jesus] will testify against those who had called him son of God, the Christians, and those who had belied him, the Jews.[10]

Sheikh Kabbani, chairman of the Islamic Supreme Council of America, clearly articulates the Islamic perspective regarding Jesus' evangelistic role when He returns:

> Like all prophets, Prophet Jesus came with the divine message of surrender to God Almighty, which is Islam. This verse shows that when Jesus returns he will personally correct the misrepresentations and misinterpretations about himself. He will affirm the true message that he brought in his time as a prophet, and that he never claimed to be the Son of God. Furthermore, he will reaffirm in his second coming what he prophesied in his first coming bearing witness to the seal of the Messenger, Prophet Muhammad. In his second coming many non-Muslims will accept Jesus as a servant of Allah Almighty, as a Muslim and a member of the community of Muhammad.[11]

Al-Sadr and Mutahhari likewise articulate this same expectation:

> Jesus will descend from heaven and espouse the cause of the Mahdi. The Christians and the Jews will see him and recognize his true status. The Christians will abandon their faith in his godhead [sic].[12]

JESUS WILL ABOLISH CHRISTIANITY

It is crucial to understand that according to Islamic tradition and belief, when Jesus returns, He does not come to convert *most* Christians to Islam but to abolish Christianity entirely. This fact is understood when we analyze a very well-known and oft-quoted tradition that refers to four specific things that Jesus will do when He returns. Jesus is said to:

1. Break crosses.

2. Kill all swine.

3. Abolish the *jizyah* tax (a Muslim tax on non-Muslims).

4. Kill the Muslim antichrist and his followers.

> The Prophet said: There is no prophet between me and
> him, that is, Jesus. He will descent [*sic*] (to the earth)... He
> will break the cross, kill swine, and abolish *jizyah*. Allah
> will perish all religions except Islam.[13]

The three actions of breaking the cross, killing pigs, and
abolishing the *jizyah* tax are based on the notion that Jesus will
eliminate all other religions on the earth other than Islam. Shafi
and Usmani explain that to "break the cross" means to "abolish
worship of the cross." Several Muslim friends that I've spoken
with have expressed their understanding of this tradition: Jesus
will break or remove all crosses from the rooftops and steeples of
churches throughout the earth. This action will thus indicate that
Jesus will be making a clear statement regarding His disapproval
of the false notion that He was ever crucified on a cross. The
killing of the swine is so that the "Christian belief of its
lawfulness is belied."[14] The reason for abolishing the *jizyah* tax
(the compulsory poll tax that non-Muslims must pay in order to
live in a Muslim land) is based on the idea that when Jesus
returns, the *jizyah* tax will no longer be accepted. The only choice
that Christians will have is to accept Islam or die. As Sideeque
M.A. Veliankode states in *Doomsday Portents and Prophecies*:

> Jesus, the son of Mary will soon descend among the Muslims
> as a just judge.... Jesus will, therefore, judge according to the
> law of Islam...*all people will be required to embrace Islam and
> there will be no other alternative* (emphasis mine).[15]

Even Harun Yahya likewise affirms this belief in his book, *Jesus
Will Return*, when he says, "Jesus will remove all systems of
disbelief in that period."[16]

Muslim jurists also confirm these interpretations: consider,
for example, the ruling of Ahmad ibn Naqib al-Misri (d. 1368)
from *The Reliance of the Traveller*, the classic Shafi manual of
Islamic jurisprudence:

> [T]he time and the place for [the poll tax] is before the final
> descent of Jesus (upon whom be peace). *After his final*

coming, nothing but Islam will be accepted from them, for taking the poll tax is only effective until Jesus' descent (upon him and our Prophet be peace)..." (emphasis mine).[17]

JESUS THE SLAYER OF JEWS

Beyond the "accomplishment" of abolishing Christianity on a worldwide scale, another of Jesus' primary jobs is to kill a figure known as the Dajjal, or the Muslim version of the Antichrist. Jesus will kill not only the Dajjal but also all of the Dajjal's followers, most of whom will be Jews. Muhammad Ali Ibn Zubair in an article entitled "Who is the evil Dajjal?" elaborates:

> The Yahudis [Jews] of Isfahaan will be his [the Dajjal's] main followers. Apart from having mainly Yahudi followers, he will have a great number of women followers as well.[18]

Veliankode explains that one of the main reasons for Jesus' return is "to refute the Jews over the controversial issue that they killed Jesus.... However Jesus will kill them including their leader, the Antichrist."[19] Listing the events of the last days as they occur, Muhammad Ali Ibn Zubair, author of *The Signs of Qiyama* (Judgement Day), begins:

> His followers the Yahudis, will number seventy thousand.... [Then] Hadrat Isa [honorable Jesus] kills the Dajjal at the Gate of Hudd, near an Israeli airport, in the valley of "Ifiq." The final war between the Yahudis will ensue, and the Muslims will be victorious.[20]

We will discuss this "final war" between the Jews and the Muslims in more detail in a later chapter. But for now, it is important to remember that when this final war (or, more accurately, final slaughter) occurs, according to Islamic tradition, Jesus is the primary instigator.

JESUS: A GOOD MUSLIM FAMILY MAN

One final aspect of the Muslim Jesus' return must be pointed out. After converting the world to Islam and killing unbelievers, the Dajjal, and his followers, Jesus is said to marry, have children, and eventually die:

> The Prophet said: There is no prophet between me and him, that is, Jesus.... He will destroy the Antichrist and will live on the earth for forty years and then he will die. The Muslims will pray over him.[21]

> After his descention [sic] on earth, Jesus will marry. He will have children, and he will remain on the earth nineteen years after marriage. He will pass away and Muslims will perform his funeral prayer and bury him next to the Prophet Muhammad.[22]

SUMMARY

Now let's review the various defining characteristics and actions of the Muslim Jesus upon his return to the earth:

1. Jesus is said to return to the earth in the last days near a mosque in Damascus.

2. He will arrive at a time when the Mahdi and his army will be preparing to pray.

3. He will be offered to lead the prayer by the Mahdi, but will decline in direct deference to the Mahdi whom Jesus declares to be the leader of the Muslims.

4. He will then pray behind the Mahdi as a subordinate.

5. He will be a faithful Muslim.

6. He will make a pilgrimage to Mecca.

7. He will visit Muhammad's grave and salute Muhammad, whereby Muhammad will return the salute from the grave.

8. He will destroy Christianity.

9. He will repeal the *jizyah* tax, thus leaving Jews and Christians only the options of conversion to Islam or death.

10. He will establish Islamic *shariah* law throughout the entire earth.

11. He will kill the Antichrist and his followers made up largely of Jews and women.

12. He will remain on the earth for roughly forty years, during which time He will marry, have children, and then die.

As we have clearly seen, the Muslim Jesus, in both His nature and actions is *far* different from the biblical Jesus. Rather than coming to reign as king and messiah over all the earth from Jerusalem, Jesus instead comes to convert the world to Islam or kill those who refuse to do so. Instead of coming to save and deliver faithful Christians and Jews, He comes instead to slaughter them. We will discuss what the Bible has to say about the return of Jesus more in a later chapter.

COMPARING THE FALSE PROPHET
AND THE MUSLIM JESUS

A*mazingly, the similarities* between the biblical narratives of the end times and the Islamic narratives do not end with the Antichrist and the Mahdi. If it were so, then it might be easier to dismiss the many similarities as mere coincidence. The parallels, however, do not stop with the Antichrist and the Mahdi, but extend again quite clearly into the person of the man biblically known as the False Prophet and the man known in Islam as Isa al-Masih—Jesus the Messiah.

The Bible clearly articulates the specific plan of Satan down through the ages. The Bible teaches that Satan will raise up not one, but two, men as his agents on the earth to lure men away from the worship of the One True God. The first man that Satan will use is the Antichrist. We have already examined his role in chapter five. The second man is known biblically as the False Prophet. We will examine his role next.

THE UNHOLY PARTNERSHIP OF THE ANTICHRIST AND THE FALSE PROPHET

The nature of the relationship of the biblical False Prophet to the Antichrist is one of a partner in crime, so to speak. Only in the final book of the Bible do we learn about the False Prophet. The Apostle John was the first and only author of Scripture who received revelation about this assistant to the Antichrist.

In Revelation chapter thirteen, John introduces us to the man described as "another beast" but spoken of later in Revelation as the False Prophet:

> Then I saw another beast, coming out of the earth. He had two horns like a lamb, but he spoke like a dragon. He exercised all the authority of the first beast on his behalf, and made the earth and its inhabitants worship the first beast.... And he performed great and miraculous signs, even causing fire to come down from heaven to earth in full view of men. Because of the signs he was given power to do on behalf of the first beast, he deceived the inhabitants of the earth... (Revelation 13:11-14).

From this passage, we can determine a few things about the False Prophet. First he is called a beast—he is, like the Antichrist, a man possessed by Satan. He is another human pawn of the dragon, exercising the will of the dragon on the earth. But instead of ten horns, he only has two. The horns speak of authority. The power and authority of the False Prophet is clear, but not nearly equal to that of the Antichrist, said to have ten horns. We also see that the False Prophet can perform miracles. Among the many miracles he is said to work, one is mentioned specifically: He is said to make fire come down from the sky. The False Prophet's primary reason for performing miraculous signs is to cause the inhabitants of the earth to follow and worship the Antichrist. The two are pictured as a team, a partnership with one common goal—deception, seduction, and a luring away of anyone who worships Yahweh, the God of the Bible.

THE UNHOLY PARTNERSHIP OF THE MAHDI AND THE MUSLIM JESUS

Likewise, in the Islamic narrative of the last days, we do not find a lone character coming to rescue the world, but instead we find a team. We find both the Mahdi and the Muslim Jesus. And as in the case of the Antichrist and the False Prophet, we find that one clearly fills a supporting role while the other leads.

While the Mahdi is clearly described as "the vice regent (*caliph*) of Allah,"[1] Jesus is described as one who will "espouse the cause of the Mahdi"[2] and "follow him."[3] The partnership between the Mahdi and Jesus is one of a leader and his subordinate. And as we have already seen, and will continue to see, the partnership of the Mahdi and Jesus is indeed an unholy partnership—particularly if you are not a Muslim and have no intention of becoming one. If this is the case, then you are marked for death—plain and simple. The Muslim Jesus is a twisted version of the biblical Jesus who said:

> For I have come down from heaven not to do my will but to do the will of him who sent me. And this is the will of him who sent me; that I shall lose none of all that he has given me, but raise them up at the last day. For my Father's will is that everyone who looks to the Son and believes in him shall have eternal life, and I will raise him up at the last day" (John 6:38-40).

Instead of espousing the "cause" of the Father, the Muslim Jesus espouses the cause of the Mahdi. Instead of saving those followers of His whom the Father has placed under His oversight, the Muslim Jesus instead slaughters those who remain faithful to the words of Jesus as found in the Bible. The Muslim Jesus is not the tender yet strong shepherd of the Gospels, but rather *the Wolf* himself in the shepherd's clothing.

THE FALSE PROPHET AS THE ANTICHRIST'S CHIEF ENFORCER

> The coming of the lawless one [the Antichrist] will be in accordance with the work of Satan displayed in all kinds of counterfeit miracles, signs, and wonders, and in every sort of evil that deceives those who are perishing. They perish because they refused to love the truth and so be saved. For this reason God sends them a powerful delusion so that they will believe the lie and so that all will be condemned who have not believed the truth but have delighted in wickedness (2 Thessalonians 2:9-12).

> Then I saw another beast, coming out of the earth.... He performed great and miraculous signs, even causing fire to come down from heaven to earth in full view of men (Revelation 13:11, 12).

We see in the Bible that the False Prophet will come with "all kinds of counterfeit miracles, signs, and wonders and in every sort of evil that deceives those who are perishing." He will perform "great and miraculous signs, even causing fire to come down out of heaven... [to deceive] the inhabitants of the earth." But after his miracle-working power fails to convert every last person on the earth, his primary drive becomes to set up a system whereby the inhabitants of the earth will have only two options: worship the Antichrist or die. The False Prophet is said to create some form of "image," possibly some form of idol or statue that has the ability to "speak." Exactly what this "image" will be remains to be seen:

> He [the False Prophet] was given power to give breath to the image of the first beast, so that it could speak and *cause all who refused to worship the image to be killed* (Revelation 13:15, emphasis mine).

There is something highly unusual about this image that "could speak and cause all who refused to worship the image to be killed." Somehow the image itself will have the ability to enforce the law of the False Prophet; it will have the ability to cause people to be killed. This seems to work in tangent with the infamous "mark of the beast" that is part of the False Prophet's system. All the inhabitants of the earth will be "forced, everyone, small and great, rich and poor, free and slave, to receive a mark on his right hand or on his forehead, so that no one could buy or sell *unless he had the mark*, which is the name of the beast or the number of his name" (Revelation 13:17, emphasis mine).

So biblically speaking, the False Prophet enforces the Antichrist's global worship movement. Imagine for a moment a miracle-working evangelist completely possessed by Satan and who refuses to take no for an answer at the threat of death. This is exactly what the False Prophet will be.

THE MUSLIM JESUS AS THE MAHDI'S CHIEF ENFORCER

The False Muslim Jesus according to Islam will likewise be the greatest evangelist that the world has ever seen. He fulfills the description of the False Prophet in this regard to a T! We see that the false Muslim Jesus, like the False Prophet, comes to convert the Christian world to a new religion. In the case of the Muslim Jesus, the religion is, of course, Islam:

> When Jesus returns he will personally correct the misrepresentations and misinterpretations about himself. He will affirm the true message that he brought in his time as a prophet, and that he never claimed to be the Son of God. Furthermore, he will reaffirm in his second coming what he prophesied in his first coming bearing witness to the seal of the Messengers, Prophet Muhammad. In his second coming many non-Muslims will accept Jesus as a servant of Allah Almighty, as a Muslim and a member of the community of Muhammad.[4]

From this description, Jesus' power to convert seems based more on the simple fact of the persuasiveness of His words, presence, and actions than any specific mention of miracles. Just like the False Prophet, however, the Muslim Jesus refuses to take no for an answer. Along with the Mahdi, He institutes Islamic law all over the earth. In so doing, He abolishes the *jizyah* tax, which non-Muslims historically have had the option of paying as "protection" money, much like the "protection" money that *Mafia* bosses enforce onto businesses in their areas. After the *jizyah* tax is abolished, "all people will be required to embrace Islam and there will be no other alternative."[5] But what if some still refuse to convert? Then, as we have already seen, the leaders of the so-called "religion of peace," the Mahdi and the Muslim Jesus, will execute them.

THE FALSE PROPHET AS EXECUTIONER

From the Bible's description of the False Prophet we learn that one of the primary motives behind his plan in creating this "image in honor of the beast" is to kill those who refuse to worship it:

> He ordered them to set up an image in honor of the beast who was wounded by the sword and yet lived. He was given power to give breath to the image of the first beast, so that it could speak and cause all who refused to worship the image to be killed (Revelation 13:14, 15).

Later there is a specific reference to the exact form in which these people will die:

> And I saw the souls of those who had been *beheaded* because of their testimony for Jesus and because of the word of God. They had not worshiped the beast or his image and had not received his mark on their foreheads or their hands (Revelation 20:4, emphasis mine).

The Bible tells us that those who refuse to participate in the system established by the False Prophet, who refuse to worship the Antichrist or his image, will die. The specific death that the Bible indicates is beheading. We will discuss this fact in more detail in a later chapter. The False Prophet will be the most infamous executioner that the world has ever known.

THE MUSLIM JESUS AS EXECUTIONER

And how different is the Muslim Jesus? We have already examined the Islamic traditions that establish that Jesus will abolish the *jizyah* tax, thus leaving only two options for Christians and Jews worldwide: convert to Islam or die:

> Jesus, the son of Mary will soon descend among the Muslims as a just judge.... Jesus will, therefore, judge according to the law of Islam...all people will be required to embrace Islam and there will be no other alternative.[6]

> The time and the place for [the poll tax] is before the final
> descent of Jesus. *After his final coming, nothing but Islam will
> be accepted from them,* for taking the poll tax is only
> effective until Jesus' descent (emphasis mine).[7]

We have also seen the Islamic traditions that picture Jesus as the
leader of an army that slaughters tens of thousands of Jews said
to follow the Dajjal (Antichrist).

> The Yahudis [Jews]...will be his main followers.[8]
>
> Isa [Jesus] kills the Dajjal at the Gate of Hudd, near an
> Israeli airport, in the valley of "Ifiq." The final war between
> the Yahudis will ensue, and the Muslims will be victorious.[9]
>
> In the Last Hour Muslims will fight with Jews. Since the
> Jews are an integral part of the army of the Dajjal, and
> Muslims are the soldiers of the Prophet Jesus, they will
> fight each other and the Muslims will become triumphant
> until even a stone or a tree would say: Come here,
> Muslim, there is a Jew hiding behind me; kill him.[10]

The biblical False Prophet and the Muslim Jesus are both
described as establishing a system of law that will enforce the
mass execution of everyone who refuses to convert to the new
global religion.

A DRAGON IN SHEEP'S CLOTHING

We have all heard the expression "a wolf in sheep's clothing."
Most people don't know that Jesus coined this saying.
Interestingly, when Jesus coined this expression, He was
referring specifically to false prophets. The exact phrase was,
"Watch out for false prophets. They come to you in sheep's
clothing, but inwardly they are ferocious wolves" (Matthew
7:15). Likewise, the Apostle John describes *the* False Prophet,
whom all other false prophets merely foreshadow, as one who,
"had two horns like a lamb, but he spoke like a dragon"
(Revelation 13:11). This is to say that the False Prophet will
appear to be mild and gentle—a "lamb-like" person—but

inwardly he will be possessed by Satan himself. He will be filled with deception, murder, rage, and hatred. His purpose will be to deceive as many people as he can into worshipping the dragon.

The appearance of the False Prophet as "a lamb" may also quite possibly refer to the notion that the False Prophet will claim to be *the Lamb*, Jesus Christ (John 1:36; Revelation 5:6,13). This would make sense if we look a bit more closely at Jesus' warnings to His disciples in Matthew chapter twenty-four. Repeatedly, Jesus warns His disciples of the many false prophets who will come in the last days, but in the very first warning that Jesus gives His disciples when they ask Him about the nature of the final hour before His return, Jesus says, "Watch out that no one deceives you. For many will come in my name, claiming, 'I am the Christ,' and will deceive many" (Matthew 24:4-5). While I do not believe that every false prophet that will emerge in the last days will claim to be Christ Himself, it is clear from this passage that some will. And if *the* False Prophet of Revelation chapter thirteen is the archetype and model for all other false prophets, then it also stands to reason that the False Prophet may very well claim to be Jesus Christ Himself. This of course is a perfectly brilliant (though infinitely evil) plan. Who else better could you imagine to have as your backup man and your primary minister of propaganda than someone whom much of the world believes to be Jesus Christ Himself? It appears that this is what Satan has planned for the Antichrist/Mahdi.

CONCLUSION

Muslims are very fond of using Jesus as an evangelistic tool among Christians. Numerous Muslim books extol the greatness of Jesus and express a deep love for Him. One Muslim Web site even proclaims that "Jesus led me to Islam." Muslims use Jesus as a lure to draw Christians in, in order to convince them of the truth of Islam. But the advertised Jesus of Islam differs greatly from the Muslim Jesus Who comes to reveal His true identity as the most radical of fundamentalist Muslims. The Jesus that returns in Muslim tradition makes Osama Bin Laden look like a novice. He is pictured as coming to establish Islamic law across the face of the planet that would legalize the execution of anyone who refuses to convert to Islam. He is pictured as leading the army that will slaughter tens of thousands of Jews said to follow the Dajjal. If ever such a person existed that could rightly be described as a "beast," then surely, the Muslim Jesus is such a man.

Muslims await a man who will claim to be Jesus Christ. He would be presented as a lamb. If such a man ever exists, he will claim, according to Islamic tradition, that he has been alive in heaven for the past two thousand years, waiting to return to complete his life and accomplish his mission on the earth. Such a man would be a liar—a true student of his master, the father of lies. He would come to fulfill what the Bible expresses to be the chief boiling desires of Satan: to either deceive Christians and Jews—indeed the entire earth—into worshipping him, or to slaughter them. In the Bible, we see that it is for these very purposes that Satan will empower his False Prophet. The biblical description of the False Prophet and the Islamic description of the Muslim Jesus, on all the essential points, are identical.

CHAPTER EIGHT

THE DAJJAL: ISLAM'S ANTICHRIST

The third primary character that dominates Islamic eschatology is a man whose full title is Al-Maseeh (the Messiah) Ad-Dajjal, (the Liar/Deceiver). Usually just referred to as the Dajjal, he is a bizarre character whose description and story seem far more fantastic than that of either the Mahdi or the Muslim Jesus. Numerous *hadiths* contain descriptions of the Dajjal. Here we will just touch on the most common of these traditions to give an overview of just who this mysterious and strange person is.

THE GREAT DECEIVER

The Dajjal is described as a deceiver who will have miraculous powers and who will temporarily hold power over the whole earth:

> The Prophet was warning us that in the last days there would be someone who would deceive all of humanity. The Dajjal will possess power over this world. Thus, Muslims must be careful not to have the love of the world in their hearts so they won't leave their religion and follow him. He will be able to heal the sick by wiping his hand on them, like Jesus did, but with this deceit the Dajjal will lead people down the path to hell. Thus the Dajjal is the false Messiah, or Anti-Christ [Massih ad-Dajjal]. He will pretend to be the Messiah, and deceive people by showing them amazing powers.[1]

BLIND IN ONE EYE

Possibly the most frequently quoted reference to the Dajjal is that he is blind in one eye. The *hadiths*, however, are contradictory regarding which eye is blind:

> Allah's Messenger made a mention of Dajjal in the presence of the people and said: Allah is not one-eyed and behold that Dajjal is *blind of the right eye* and his eye would be like a floating grape.[2]

> Allah's Messenger said: Dajjal is *blind of left eye* with thick hair and there would be a garden and fire with him and his fire would be a garden and his garden would be fire.[3]

INFIDEL

The Dajjal is sometimes said to have the word "infidel" (*kaafir*) written between his eyes, possibly on his forehead, but this word will be perceptible only to true Muslims and no one else:

> Allah's Messenger said: Dajjal is blind of one eye and there is written between his eyes the word "*kaafir*" (unbeliever/infidel). He then spelled the word as k. f. r., which every Muslim would be able to read.[4]

> Very important is that this word "*kaafir*" will be readable only by the believer, literate or illiterate. Non-believer: let him be educated from "Oxford" or "Harvard" will not be able to read it.[5]

A FALSE MIRACLE WORKER

Sheikh Kabbani describes some of the Dajjal's miraculous powers:

> The Dajjal will have powers of the devil. He will terrorize the Muslims into following him, converting them into unbelief. He will conceal the truth and bring forth falsehood. The prophet said that the Dajjal will have the power to show the image of one's dead ancestors on his hand, like a television screen. The relative will say, "Oh my son! This man is correct. I am in Paradise because I

was good and I believed in him." In reality that relative is in hell. If the relative says, "Believe in this man, I am in hell because I didn't believe," one must say to the Dajjal, "No, he is in Paradise. This is false."[6]

The Prophet said: the Dajjal will say to a Bedouin Arab, "What will you think if I bring your father and mother back to life for you? Will you bear witness that I am your lord? The Bedouin will say, "Yes." So two devils will assume the appearance of his father and mother, and say, "O my son, follow him for he is your lord..."[7]

THE DAJJAL WILL CLAIM TO BE JESUS CHRIST AND WILL CLAIM TO BE DIVINE

The above tradition shows that the Dajjal's deceptive signs will lead people into believing that the Dajjal is actually their "lord." Muslim scholars universally have concluded that the Dajjal will claim to be divine. According to the very well known Muslim scholar Abu Ameenah Bilal Phillips, the Dajjal "will claim to be God."[8]

While there are no specific traditions that state such directly, as a result of the fact that the Dajjal is, according to Islamic tradition, the false Jewish Messiah who claims to be God, most Muslims have deduced that the Dajjal will thus claim to be Jesus Christ by name.

THE DAJJAL AND HIS MAGIC MULE

Muslim Scholar Muhammad Ali ibn Zubair Ali says of the Dajjal, "He will travel at great speeds and his means of conveyance will be a giant mule.... He will travel the entire world."[9] As strange as this seems, it also bears a faint resemblance to Jesus the Messiah Who also rode a donkey as He entered Jerusalem during the final week of His ministry.

CITIES OF REFUGE

It is said that there are three cities that the Dajjal may not enter; Mecca, Medina, and Damascus. Muslims are encouraged to seek refuge from the Dajjal in one of these three cities:

> The Prophet said, "Ad-Dajjal will come to Medina and find the angels guarding it. So Allah willing, neither Ad-Dajjal nor plague will be able to come near it."[10]

> The coming of the Antichrist [Dajjal] must occur in the Last Days. This dreadful event is approaching, and in that time only three cities will be safe: Makka, Madina, and Sham [Damascus]. If anyone wants safety in that time he will have to run to one of these three cities.[11]

Apart from these three cities, it is said that the Dajjal will enter every single city, town, and village in the world to test and possibly deceive every human alive.[12]

A SURAH OF PROTECTION

Muslims believe that if they memorize a particular portion of the Qur'an that they will be protected from the Dajjal. It is somewhat like a verbal amulet that protects one from the powers of evil:

> If the Dajjal comes upon someone who has memorized the first ten verses of *Surat al Kahf* [Chapter of the Cow] he cannot harm him. And whoever memorizes the last verses of *Surat al-Kahf* will have light on the day of Judgement.[13]

HE WILL BE JEWISH AND WILL BE FOLLOWED BY JEWS AND WOMEN

Based on various Islamic traditions, Muslims believe that the Dajjal will be Jewish. The title of a book by Muslim author Matloob Ahmed Qasmi, *Emergence of the Dajjal, the Jewish King*, couldn't make this point more clearly. Imam Sheikh Ibrahim Madhi of the Palestinian Authority articulated the Islamic perspective regarding the expectation of the Jewish people quite well in one of his sermons:

> The Jews await the false Jewish messiah, while we await with Allah's help...the Mahdi and Jesus, peace be upon him. Jesus' pure hands will murder the false Jewish messiah. Where? In the city of Lod, in Palestine. Palestine will be, as it was in the past, a graveyard for the invaders.[14]

Christian Arab scholar Samuel Shahid, in his scholarly study of Islamic eschatology, says of the Dajjal that he will be "the embodiment of the Jewish hope and longing. The bulk of his army is recruited from the Jews."[15]

As mentioned in the last chapter, the followers of the Dajjal will primarily consist of Jews and women. It is mentioned that women are very ignorant and easily misled. Veliankode states, "Meanwhile, women will also fall to the deviant line of the Antichrist because of their unawareness and ignorance of Islam."[16]

SLAIN BY THE MUSLIM JESUS

As mentioned in the last chapter, the Muslim Jesus will kill the Dajjal and his followers:

> Allah's Messenger said: ...the time of prayer shall come and then Jesus son of Mary would descend and would lead them in prayer. When the enemy of Allah (Dajjal) would see him...Allah would kill them by his (Jesus') hand and he would show them their blood on his lance (the lance of Jesus Christ).[17]

CHAPTER NINE

COMPARING THE BIBLICAL JESUS AND THE DAJJAL

The third amazing parallel between biblical eschatology and Islamic eschatology is the person of the Dajjal, the Islamic Antichrist figure. Despite all of the wild and fantastic descriptions of the Dajjal, if we boil down the Muslim belief regarding the Dajjal to its simplest and most important terms, we basically have a man who will claim to be divine and will claim to be Jesus Christ, the Jewish Messiah. He will defend Israel against the Mahdi and the Muslim Jesus and he will deceive many people into leaving Islam.

While I certainly do not believe that there will ever come a figure into the world as described in the Islamic traditions—a great deceiver, blind in one eye, flying around the earth on some form of giant mule—there will come Jesus (the real one), Who will in many very crucial ways fulfill the Muslim expectations of the Dajjal.

THE RETURN OF JESUS CHRIST

The real Jesus, however, will indeed come as a divine defender of Israel and her people as well as Israel's spiritual children, the Christians. If the Islamic prophecies are indeed intertwined with the unfolding of biblical prophecy, then we can see that part of Satan's strategy is that, when the real Jesus returns, there will already be a worldwide religious leader claiming to be Jesus, namely the False Prophet. If this were the case, then Muslims worldwide would accuse the real Jesus of being the

Dajjal, the Muslim Antichrist/Great Deceiver. Muslims would be particularly convinced of this because the surviving Jews of the earth will acknowledge Jesus as their Messiah. At least six hundred years before Islam ever existed, the Jewish prophets and apostles described the event of Jesus returning to Israel, defeating her enemies, and finally gaining full acceptance among the Jewish people:

> On that day I [the Lord] will set out to destroy all the nations that attack Jerusalem. And I will pour out on the house of David and the inhabitants of Jerusalem a spirit of grace and supplication. They will look on me, the one they have pierced, and they will mourn for him as one mourns for an only child, and grieve bitterly for him as one grieves for a firstborn son (Zechariah 12:10).
>
> A day of the Lord is coming...the Lord will go out and fight against those nations, as he fights in the day of battle. *On that day His feet will stand on the Mount of Olives* (Zechariah 14:1, 3, 4, emphasis mine).
>
> And so all Israel will be saved, as it is written: "The deliverer will come from Zion; he will turn godlessness away from Jacob" (Romans 11:26).
>
> Put a seal on the foreheads of the servants of our God...Then I heard the number of those who were sealed: 144,000 *from all the tribes of Israel*...Then I looked, and there before me was the Lamb [Jesus the Messiah], standing on Mount Zion, and with him 144,000 who had his name and his Father's name written on their foreheads...*And they sang a new song...* (Revelation 7:3-4; 14:1, 3, emphasis mine).

We see that when Jesus returns to "to destroy all the nations that attack Jerusalem," "his feet will [literally] stand on the Mount of Olives." Jesus will be physically present in Israel. At this time, it is said, those Jews living in Israel will see Him and realize that He is "the one they have pierced, and they will mourn for him." Thus the acknowledgement of Jesus as the genuine Jewish Messiah and divine Savior will fill their hearts and "so all Israel will be saved."

THE ISLAMIC TRADITIONS

Of course, based on the Islamic traditions, Muslims expect Jews to acknowledge the Dajjal as the divine Jewish Messiah; thus, in the Islamic mind, the Jesus of biblical tradition will fulfill the three most primary Islamic expectations of the Dajjal. Clearly, these traditions will be used by Satan, not only to preempt the Muslims of the earth from receiving the real Jesus when He comes, but to inspire them to attack Him. The plot never seems to stop thickening. Consider the following statement by well-known Muslim apologist Osamah Abdallah. The question posited to him was, "What do Muslims believe about the end of the world and Jesus' part in it?" His answer is astonishing as it relates to this discussion:

> Briefly, Christians believe that Jesus will come down to earth and fight for the state of Israel.... What seems to be quite ironic to me is that those Jews that Jesus is supposedly going to fight for don't even believe in Jesus as GOD himself nor as a Messenger of GOD.... *Jesus never liked the Jews....* Now without being biased, we Muslims have a story that makes a lot more sense and is empty of contradictions! We believe that Jesus will come down to earth toward the end of the world time to fight the army of Satan which will be mostly from the "bad" Jews or "Zionist Jews" as we call them today, and the deceived from the Polytheist Christians or the Trinitarian Christians and the Pagan Polytheists such as Hindus, Buddhists, etc.... Some Jews and many Christians will be among the good and blessed who will fight with Jesus' side. *The army of Satan will be led by a person who will claim to be Jesus Christ himself. The Muslims will call him the Dajjal or the Deceiver. The real Jesus' army will fight the Dajjal's army and defeat him. The empire of Israel will fall, and the religion of Islam will prevail* (emphasis mine).[1]

This is quite amazing. We see that as a direct result of the Islamic apocalyptic traditions, Muslims expect two Jesuses to come: the real one and the false one. By Mr. Abdallah's admission, the real Jesus will be identifiable by the fact that He does not like Jews; indeed He is expected to attack and slaughter them. Likewise the false Jesus (according to Islam) will be clearly identifiable by the fact that He will defend the Jews. Thus, as we have seen, Mr. Abdallah and Muslims everywhere expect the Muslim Jesus, along with His leader, the Mahdi, to attack Israel and do battle against Him Who Christians understand to be the real Jesus. The battle of Armageddon as prophesied in the Bible may indeed be coming into very clear focus.

CHAPTER TEN

THE REVIVED ISLAMIC EMPIRE OF THE ANTICHRIST

W*hile the information* that we have covered thus far is certainly quite interesting, ultimately, if Islam is indeed the primary vehicle that Satan will use to fulfill his final rebellion against God, it is the Bible that must be the primary litmus test. What does the Bible say about the nature and the makeup of the Antichrist's empire?

The Bible abounds with proofs that the Antichrist's empire will consist only of nations that are, today, Islamic. If one were to do a thorough study of all of the various examples from the Hebrew prophets, it would be extensive. But for the sake of brevity and our purposes here, we will present a limited argument based on some portions of Scripture from the Book of Ezekiel and the Book of Revelation. Despite the numerous prevailing arguments for the emergence of a revived European Roman empire as the Antichrist's power base, the specific nations that the Bible identifies as comprising his empire are today all Muslim.

Pretty simple. This fact leaves us with only a couple of options. The first option is to assume that before the coming of the Antichrist, most of these Islamic nations will experience significant transformation and leave their Islamic roots behind. There are problems with this option: While there are ample reports of individual Muslims coming to follow Jesus from throughout the Muslim world, there are really no concrete signs of any of these nations abandoning their Islamic roots on a larger scale. In fact, many of the nations that we will look at are presently seeing a resurgence of Islamic fundamentalism sweeping throughout their lands. Nevertheless, I have heard Bible teachers for years express that before the coming of the last days, Islam as a religion would basically fizzle out and become entirely irrelevant. The present reality and long-term statistical trends, however, simply do not bear this out.

The other option, a far more reasonable one, is to conclude that the Antichrist's empire indeed will be Islamic. This fact alone should make most Bible scholars and students of eschatology consider the role of Islam in the last days very seriously. In this chapter we will examine exactly which modern nations the Bible says will play primary roles in the last days empire of the Antichrist.

EZEKIEL'S IDENTIFICATION

The Prophet Ezekiel lists the nations of this final empire quite specifically as he prophesies the future attack of the Antichrist against Israel. In the thirty-eighth chapter of his book, Ezekiel begins by directly addressing the Antichrist whom the Lord refers to by the unusual name of "Gog." The name "Gog" is a specific title for a ruler from the land of Magog. It could be likened to the Pharaoh and Egypt. Pharaoh is an ancient title for rulers of Egypt, and "Gog" was a title for rulers of Magog:

> The word of the LORD came to me: "Son of man, set your face against Gog, of the land of Magog, the chief prince of Meshech and Tubal; prophesy against him and say: 'This is what the Sovereign LORD says: I am against you, O Gog, chief prince of Meshech and Tubal. I will turn you around, put hooks in your jaws, and bring you out with your whole army—your horses, your horsemen fully armed, and a great horde with large and small shields, all of them brandishing their swords. Persia, Cush, and Put will be with them, all with shields and helmets, also Gomer with all its troops, and Beth Togarmah from the far north with all its troops-the many nations with you.' Get ready; be prepared, you and all the hordes gathered about you, and take command of them" (Ezekiel 38:1-7).

I encourage you to open your Bible and read through all of Ezekiel chapter thirty-eight slowly. The specificity with which Ezekiel describes modern-day Israel is quite astonishing. Prophesying to the Antichrist, Ezekiel says, "In future years you will invade a land that has recovered from war, whose people were gathered from many nations to the mountains of Israel, which had long been desolate." Israel is described as "the resettled ruins and the people gathered from the nations, rich in livestock and goods." Clearly Ezekiel was describing the Israel of today.

So Ezekiel gives us the specific names of countries that will be involved in the invasion of Israel led by Gog. Listed in order, they are Magog, Meshech, Tubal, Persia, Cush, Put, Gomer, and Beth Togarmah, as well as "many nations with you."

IS GOG ANTICHRIST?

Prophecy teachers and Bible scholars have different opinions regarding the identification of Gog and his coalition of nations. The majority position for the past few decades, however, has been that the invading army of nations described in Ezekiel 38-39 is not the army of the Antichrist, but another army led by another world leader. I personally reject the idea that Gog is anyone other than the Antichrist. While a smaller book could be written examining all of the various reasons why this is so, for now, we will only very briefly examine two of the primary reasons why I think this is untenable.

THOU SHALT HAVE NO OTHER GOG

There are two specific mentions of Gog and Magog in the Bible. Gog is mentioned not only in Ezekiel but also in the Book of Revelation. Let's look at the passage from Revelation:

> When the thousand years are over, Satan will be released
> from his prison and will go out to deceive the nations in
> the four corners of the earth—Gog and Magog—to gather
> them for battle. In number they are like the sand on the

seashore. They marched across the breadth of the earth and surrounded the camp of God's people, the city he loves. But fire came down from heaven and devoured them. And the devil, who deceived them, was thrown into the lake of burning sulfur, where the beast and the false prophet had been thrown. They will be tormented day and night for ever and ever (Revelation 20:7-10).

Even after the earthly thousand year reign of Christ from Jerusalem, the Bible says that yet another army will form to attack the holy city of Jerusalem. Again, the leader of this army is called Gog and his army, Magog. Those who take the position that Gog is not the Antichrist must wrestle through the fact that this "Gog" and his armies are resurrected, so to speak, at least a thousand years after the first Gog. This is a difficulty. Obviously, the first "Gog and Magog" shares more than a mere name with the second "Gog and Magog." There is a correlation between the two that extends beyond this very unusual title. Those who see Gog and the Antichrist as two separate entities must be able to explain just what similarities the Gog of Ezekiel and the Gog of Revelation bear that merits them both carrying the same name.

Actually, in order to estimate who Gog is, all one must really do is take a look at who the Antichrist is. The Antichrist, quite simply, is the Devil incarnate—or at least the closet thing to it. Some passages of Scripture actually shift from speaking of Satan to speaking of the Antichrist seamlessly as if they are one and the same (see, for instance, Isaiah 14). And as we have seen, Satan will share his worship with the Antichrist. Simply stated, Antichrist is Satan's puppet that he will use to attack Jerusalem. And, at least in the Book of Revelation, Gog is also Satan's puppet that will serve the very same purpose. In terms of both role and function, the Antichrist and the Gog of Revelation are essentially the same. Even as Satan will raise up a man to carry out his work in the days to come, so will Satan also raise up a man to carry out his final rebellion against God one more time at the end of the Millennium. Both times, the leader of Satan's rebellion against Jerusalem is referred to as Gog and his army is called Magog. Why should we view the basic nature of the first Gog as being any different than the second? Those who view Ezekiel's Gog as a competitor to Antichrist find themselves taking a very inconsistent position.

But if you are not yet sure, consider this second point. Ezekiel says specifically of Gog that the prophets spoke of him in times past:

> This is what the Sovereign LORD says: Are you not the one I spoke of in former days by my servants the prophets of Israel? At that time they prophesied for years that I would bring you against them (Ezekiel 38:17).

The question must be asked then—if Gog and Magog are spoken of by Israel's former prophets prior to Ezekiel, then where are all of these references? We will be very hard pressed to find any unless we do some serious stretching of the Scriptures. But if we take the position that Gog is the Antichrist, then it is very easy to find numerous passages about the Antichrist and his invading army throughout the prophets.

While there are several more very good arguments to support this view, I will assume that this is enough and move on. Gog and the Antichrist are one and the same. Now let's take a look at which specific nations will make up Gog's coalition.

ROSH?

> Son of man, set your face against Gog, of the land of Magog, the chief prince of Meshech and Tubal; prophesy against him... (Ezekiel 38:2).

Some Bible translations differ on how to interpret the portion of this verse that says "the chief prince of." In Hebrew, the word translated as "chief prince" is *rosh*. The problem is that while *rosh* most probably means "prince" or "head," some argue that it should be treated as a proper noun, referring to the name of a place. Those who feel as though it is a place use the word "Rosh" to find Russia here as one of the nations. The basis for doing so of course is due primarily to the similar sound of the two words. This opinion is also supported by the fact that Ezekiel specifically says that Gog would come from the north. While Russia indeed sits perfectly north of Israel, the actual interpretation of the word *rosh*, however, is based on a bogus principle. One cannot simply take a word from an ancient Semitic language (in this case Hebrew) and find a correlation to a modern name from a drastically different language (in this case an early form of Scandinavian) simply because the two words "sound the same."

The Hebrew word *rosh* is used well over five hundred times in the Bible and each time is interpreted as meaning "head, chief, top, best" or something similar. It is the same *rosh* that we find in *Rosh Hashana*—"the chief day of the year"—the Jewish New Year. Also consider this: Of the eight nations mentioned, all except one represent grandsons of Noah. The other is Persia. Persia, however, was a very well known nation in Ezekiel's day, having formerly been the head of the Medo-Persian Empire that ruled the entire Middle East. Now juxtapose this to Russia, which did not even exist in Ezekiel's day. To simply attempt to toss "Rosh" into the mix, an alleged name neither a descendant of Noah nor a well-known nation of that day, certainly seems out of place. As Bible scholar Dr. Merrill F. Unger admits, "Linguistic evidence for the equation [of Rosh with Russia] is confessedly only presumptive."[1]

During the Cold War, of course, this opinion was a popular one. Many reasoned that, because Russia led the great communist (read: atheist) Soviet Union, surely such an anti-God empire fulfilled Bible prophecy. But we must not read our assumptions or modern events into Scripture. We must allow Scripture to speak for itself. Unfortunately, many Bible teachers still seem to cling to this interpretation. The notion that Ezekiel specifically mentioned Russia is a strong, if not irresponsible, stretch—mere speculation built on a very weak foundation.

SATAN'S COALITION OF THE WILLING

Now let's identify the nations. Of the eight nations mentioned— Magog, Meshech, Tubal, Persia, Cush, Put, Gomer, and Togarmah—seven are mentioned in the Book of Genesis as descendants of Noah and his three sons. Bible scholars and historians can trace the names of Noah's sons to certain people groups and regions and thus identify them with modern nations. While the identification of some of these people groups is somewhat debatable, there is a general measure of agreement among Bible scholars as to their identification.

MESHECH AND TUBAL

Regarding Meshech and Tubal, here again, we find some prophecy teachers assigning a Russian identification. Many very well known prophecy teachers base their opinions primarily on the fact that the *Scofield Study Bible* identifies these two "nations" as correlating to the modern Russian cities of Moscow and Tobolsk. The problem again is that the basis of this interpretation comes primarily from the similar sound of the words: Meshech— Moscow, and Tubal—Tobolsk. While this may convince some, we have already discussed the weakness of this reasoning. Again, unless one can legitimately trace the roots of a particular word back to its Hebrew origin, then the argument stands on very weak evidence. It is a forcing of the puzzle piece where it doesn't naturally fit.

Mark Hitchcock, a well known Bible teacher, accurately points out that Ezekiel 27:13 describes Meshech and Tubal as trading partners with ancient Tyre, in what is today Lebanon. "It is highly doubtful," says Hitchcock, "that ancient Tyre was trading with people as far north as Moscow and Tobolsk." In fact, it is questionable whether or not these areas were even very well populated in Ezekiel's day. Hitchcock concludes that:

> A closer study of these names reveals that Meschech and Tubal are the ancient Moschi/Mushki and Tubalu/Tibareni peoples who dwelled in the area around, primarily south of, the Black and Caspian Seas in Ezekiel's day. These nations today are in the modern country of Turkey, possibly parts of southern Russia and northern Iran.[2]

Meshech was located near what was known as Phrygia, in central and western Asia Minor, while Tubal was located in eastern Asia Minor. So Meshech and Tubal form portions of modern Turkey. Today this region is predominantly Islamic. While modern Turkey has undergone a drastic secularization in the last century, within the past few years Turkey has also seen some quiet, though very strong trends toward a return to a stronger Islamic identification.[3]

MAGOG

Regarding the identity of Magog, there is some difference of opinion among Bible teachers and historians. Referring to the Magogites, the *Matthew Henry Complete Commentary on the Whole Bible* speaks of this diversity of opinion:

> Some think they find them [Gog and Magog] afar off, in Scythia, Tartary, and [Southern] Russia. Others think they find them nearer the land of Israel, in Syria, and Asia the Less [Turkey].[4]

Those who argue for a Scythian connection find their best argument in a reference from the ancient Jewish historian Josephus who wrote, "Magog founded the Magogians, thus named after him, but who by the Greeks are called Sythians." Hitchcock says of the Sythians:

> The ancient Sythians were a great nomadic tribe who inhabited the ancient territory from central Asia all across

the southern part of ancient Russia. The descendants of Magog were the original inhabitants of the plateau of central Asia. Today the land of Magog is inhabited by the former Soviet Republics of Kazakhstan, Kyrgystan, Uzbekistan, Turkmenistan, Tajikistan, and possibly even northern parts of modern Afghanistan.[5]

Former Muslim Walid Shoebat agrees. Shoebat points out that:

> *The Schaff-Herzog Encyclopedia of Religious Knowledge*, citing ancient Assyrian writings, places the location of Magog in the land mass between ancient Armenia and Media—in short, the republics south of Russia and north of Israel, comprised of Azerbaijan, Afghanistan, Turkestan, Chechnya, Turkey, Iran, and Dagestan. Significantly, all of them are Muslim nations.[6]

Thus, while the specific nations that comprise Magog may be partially in question, the same general area is agreed upon. We are dealing with Asia Minor, and possibly parts of central Asia—some of the southern regions of the former Soviet Union. Today, Islam dominates this entire region.

What if we take the alternative interpretation made by some Bible scholars—that Magog is Syria? Even if this were the case, we still have an Islamic nation.

But here is the real key to identifying Magog: *identifying Meshech and Tubal*—which we have already done. The reason for this is the wording of Ezekiel: "Gog, of the land of Magog, the chief (or head) of Meshech and Tubal." Magog is the "head" of the land of Meshech and Tubal. We have already seen that Meschech and Tubal are located in modern day Turkey. Thus it would be foolish to assume that Magog as their "head" is in some other distant region or nation. While it seems more likely that Magog is either a portion of Turkey or a conglomerate of the former Soviet Turkic "istans," whether it be these or Syria, we have an Islamic entity.

This point is essential. Because we know that Gog—the Antichrist—will come from the land of Magog, definitely an

Islamic region, it seems very unlikely that he will be a non-Muslim. While I suppose that anything is possible, particularly in the distant future, it is very hard to imagine a non-Muslim ruling over any one of these nations, at least not anyone who doesn't outwardly pose as a Muslim. Now, let's move on to identify the remaining member states of the Antichrist's coalition.

PERSIA

Persia is very easy to identify. Essentially, Persia is modern day Iran. Many Iranians in America, if asked where they are from, will say they are from Persia. In fact, Iran was called Persia until 1935. Obviously Iran is a predominantly Muslim nation. While there are some wonderful signs of change in Iran due to a growing dissatisfaction with Islam among Iran's massive youth population, it does not seem likely that a majority of Iranians will leave behind its Islamic roots anytime soon.[7]

CUSH

Cush is also relatively easy to identify. Some Bible translations merely interpret Cush as Ethiopia, though this is not accurate. The Cush of Ezekiel's day sat far more northwest than the Ethiopia of today. Scripture often associated Cush with Egypt, which bordered her:

> Egypt will become a desolate wasteland. Then they will know that I am the LORD. Because you said, "The Nile is mine; I made it," therefore I am against you and against your streams, and I will make the land of Egypt a ruin and a desolate waste from Migdol [Northern Egypt] to Aswan [today in southern Egypt], *as far as the border of Cush* (Ezekiel 29:9-10, emphasis mine).

Another of Cush's defining characteristics was her rivers (Isaiah 18:1). Because Cush bordered Egypt, the rivers were most likely the five rivers that feed the Nile. Of course, the context of Ezekiel is the best context by which to interpret the area to which Isaiah referred. If we look at a map, the Nile River flows directly into the southern border of Egypt from the modern nation of Sudan. In the nation of Sudan, five rivers merge to feed the Nile to the north. The only legitimate identification of Cush, then, is modern Sudan, known officially since 1989 as the Islamic Republic of Sudan. The Sudanese government is Islamist to its core and an absolute cesspool of Islamic oppression toward Sudan's Christian minority. As Hitchcock accurately says, "One would be hard pressed to find a more rabid enemy of Israel and the West today than Sudan."

PUT

Biblically, Put (or Phut) is the region west of Egypt. Today this is the nation of Libya. The Septuagint translates the word *Put* here as *Libue*. Most modern scholars seem to agree with this interpretation. Shoebat, however, includes Algeria, Morocco, and Tunisia along with Libya. Either way, we have another entirely Islamic region or nation.

GOMER

Gomer, scholars seem to almost universally agree, "refers to the Celtic Cimmerians of Crim-Tartary."[8] Regarding the identification of Gomer, Baptist Pastor Fred Zasper accurately points out that:

> Gomer is well known to the ancient world as Gimarrai of north central Asia Minor (Cappadocia). These people are also known as the Cimmerians. This seems to be the simplest, most obvious interpretation.[9]

So Gomer is Gimarra is Cimmeria is Cappadocia. Cappadocia is simply central Turkey, another Islamic region.

TOGARMAH

Zaspel sums up the identity of Togarmah quite well:

> Togarmah was a descendant of Noah through Japheth
> then Gomer (Genesis 10:1-3). He is known to Assyrian
> records as Tilgarimmu.... Tilgarimmu was a city state in
> Eastern Anatolia [Asia Minor, modern Turkey] more
> specifically, as Ryrie states, "the southeastern part of
> Turkey near the Syrian border." This identification is
> generally acknowledged by all.[10]

Once more, we have a region in present-day Turkey.

ASSESSING THE EIGHT NATIONS

Thus, in the final assessment, five of the eight nations
mentioned by Ezekiel occupy modern Turkey and possibly
some of the southern Russian regions near the Caucasus
Mountains, as well as some of the Turkic nations of central
Asia. Obviously, the Lord directed Ezekiel to significantly
highlight Turkey. The other three nations mentioned—Libya,
Sudan, and Iran—together with Turkey form a perfect circle
around Israel. Turkey covers Israel's entire northern horizon,
while Iran lies to the east of Israel, Sudan to the south, and
Libya to the west. Israel finds herself surrounded on all four
sides by the Islamic nations of the Antichrist's empire.

While many Bible teachers have for years prophesied a
coming invasion of Israel headed by Russia, we see that the
Bible simply does not substantiate this position. In fact, it is fair
to say that the entire argument for a primary Russian
involvement is based on weak scholarship and actually requires
a violation of basic linguistic norms. Instead, we see an Islamic
invasion of Israel, most likely led by Turkey and involving
minimally three or more other Islamic nations. While there is
always the temptation to read one's enemies into Scripture, we
should instead simply take the Bible for what it says. While
presently there is not any pressing reason to see Turkey as the
leader of an imminent world empire, this is nevertheless what
Ezekiel prophesied. And as we are about to see, this is
confirmed through other portions of Scripture as well.

WHAT IS THE SEVENTH AND THE EIGHT EMPIRE?

Before we proceed, I wish here to acknowledge someone who has greatly contributed to my understanding of this issue, my friend Walid Shoebat. He is a former Palestinian terrorist and the author of *Why I Left Jihad*. I highly recommend this book, which readers can order through his Web site at www.shoebat.com.

Beyond the above identification of the nations of Ezekiel 38, the Book of Revelation also confirms the notion that, indeed, the region of Turkey will head the future Antichrist's empire. Let's examine these passages: "There I saw…a scarlet beast that was covered with blasphemous names and had seven heads and ten horns (Revelation 17:3)." Here we see the final "beast" empire of the Antichrist. The beast has seven heads and ten horns. We already know from the Book of Daniel that the ten horns represent the ten nations or kings that will comprise the Antichrist's empire. But the seven heads stand for seven empires that have existed throughout history. All have foreshadowed the final empire to come. As usual, whenever the Bible gives a prophecy that may be difficult in its symbolism, the Bible clarifies the symbolism and explains the passage for us:

> This calls for a mind with wisdom. The seven heads are seven mountains on which the woman sits. They are also seven kings. Five have fallen, one is, the other has not yet come; but when he does come, he must remain for a little while. The beast who once was, and now is not, is an eighth king. He belongs to the seven and is going to his destruction (Revelation 17:9-11).

Now the seven heads are called seven mountains. The Bible often uses mountains as a symbol representing a kingdom or an empire. But most importantly this passage gives us insight into the fact that, before Jesus returns, there will actually have been a total of eight "beast" empires. The eighth empire will be ruled by the Antichrist. How can this passage help us gain insight into the identification of the final empire of the

Antichrist? First, we see that at the time that John wrote this passage, five of the empires had already fallen. This is seen in the phrase "five have been." These empires are generally accepted by Bible teachers as the following:

- The Egyptian Empire
- The Assyrian Empire
- The Babylonian Empire
- The Persian Empire
- The Greek Empire

After these five, the angel tells John that one empire "is." At the time that John wrote the Book of Revelation, Rome "was." It ruled the Middle East, Northern Africa, and much of Europe. Thus the sixth empire was the Roman Empire. The next empire, of course, is the seventh, and then the eighth will be the empire of the Antichrist. So the seventh empire is the empire that we need to identify, because according to the verse above, the eighth empire will be a resurrection or a revived version of the seventh empire: "The beast who once was, and is not, is an eighth king." Let me just paraphrase this portion for clarity: "The seventh beast (empire) that existed, but then did not exist, will come back as an eighth empire."

So if we are now waiting for the final eighth empire, then what was the seventh? What empire followed Rome?

Because of the harsh anti-Semitic nature of the German Third Reich, some Bible teachers have speculated that Germany was the seventh empire and thus Germany will come back as the eighth.[11]

The most common belief, however, held almost universally by Bible teachers, is that the Antichrist's empire will be a revived Roman empire. There are, however, some glaring problems with this theory: First, Rome was the sixth empire. If Rome was the sixth, and will also be the last, then what happened to the seventh? This theory has a gaping hole. Is

Rome the sixth, seventh, and eighth empires? Neither Scripture nor history nor common sense supports this notion. Second, every one of the previous six empires ruled the Middle East, including Jerusalem. *This is very important!* We must always remember that the Bible is thoroughly Jerusalem-centric. It is not America-centric, nor is it Western-centric. In the biblical view of things, Jerusalem is the center of the earth. This point cannot be underscored enough. Any theory that revolves around a revived Roman empire based in Europe—for instance on the European Common Market—is a concept foreign to the Bible. Unless the empire rules over or directly affects Jerusalem, it is actually a bit irrelevant to the biblical mindset.

Third, if we look at the first six empires, each succeeding empire either destroyed or absorbed the empire that preceded it. There is a very natural succession. If we look at each empire, we see that they all fulfill these two characteristics: they ruled over Jerusalem and they defeated or absorbed their predecessor. The Egyptian Empire ruled all of Egypt and Israel as well. But the Assyrian Empire defeated the Egyptian Empire and likewise ruled over a vast portion of the Middle East, including Israel. After this, the Babylonian Empire defeated the Assyrian Empire and became even larger than its predecessor, again, ruling over Israel. Such is the pattern with each successive empire: The Medo-Persian Empire succeeded the Babylonian Empire only to be succeeded by the Greek Empire. The Greek Empire was in turn succeeded by the Roman Empire. Which leads us to the seventh empire. Who overcame the Roman Empire? In order to answer this question, we need to briefly review the fall of the Roman Empire. What exactly happened?

In AD 395, the Roman Empire was divided into two portions; the eastern and the western portions. The eastern portion became known as the Byzantine Empire. In AD 410 the western capital city of Rome fell to invading Germanic tribes known as the Visigoths or Barbarians. The western/European half of the empire including its capital had fallen, but the Roman Empire nevertheless continued. How so? It simply shifted its capital and its throne from Rome to Constantinople— a thousand miles east. The western European portion of the Roman Empire fell but the Eastern Byzantine portion of the Roman Empire lived on for nearly another thousand years with Constantinople as its capital. The Roman Empire didn't actually completely fall until the eastern portion of the Empire finally fell in AD 1453 to the Turks. The Turkish Ottoman Empire succeeded the Roman Empire and ruled over the entire Middle East, including Jerusalem, for nearly five hundred years.[12] The Turkish Empire existed right up until 1909.

Thus we see that the only empire that fulfills the patterns necessary to be considered the seventh empire is the Turkish/Ottoman Empire. This of course corresponds perfectly with Ezekiel's list of nations with such a heavy emphasis on Turkey.

THE COMING RESTORATION OF THE *CALIPHATE*

The Turkish Empire was the seat of the Islamic *caliphate*. It was not until 1923 that the Islamic *caliphate* was officially abolished. Today the Islamic world awaits the restoration of that *caliphate*. The Bible teaches that someday soon the Turkish Empire will be revived:

> The inhabitants of the earth whose names have not been written in the Book of Life from the creation of the world will be astonished when they see the beast, because he once was, then he was not, and yet came again (Revelation 17:8).

At that time, we may expect to see the Islamic *caliphate* restored. Eventually a man might rise to this position whom the Muslim world would refer to as the Mahdi, but whom people of understanding would identify as the man known biblically as the Antichrist.

CHAPTER ELEVEN

THE DARK NATURE OF MUHAMMAD'S REVELATIONS

W*e begin our further critical examination* of Islam with the person of Muhammad and his revelations, for this is where it all started. If we expect to accurately discern the spirit of Islam then we must begin at the foundation; we must examine the seed. Muhammad is the founder of Islam and Muslims believe he is the sole human instrument that "received" the words of the Qur'an directly from Allah. This chapter will review the nature of Muhammad's spiritual encounters that led to his career as a "prophet" and birthed the religion that now has the attention of the world.

THE BIRTH OF THE QUR'AN

Muslims believe that when Muhammad received the revelations that make up the Qur'an, he received them word for word, directly from Allah. Consequently, in the Muslim mind, Allah actually authored the Qur'an. The Qur'an is thus intended to be read as if it were Allah speaking directly in the first person. Muhammad is viewed as merely the human messenger, or the apostle of Allah (*rasul-allah*). As one Muslim theologian has said, "The prophet was purely passive—indeed unconscious: the Book was in no sense his, neither its thought, nor language, nor style: *all* was of God, and the Prophet was merely a recording pen."[1] This stands in distinction to the Christian view of the nature of inspiration of the Bible. Christians understand that while God indeed *inspired* the authors of Scripture to convey His thoughts and words, each individual author brought to the Scriptures his own style and personality. God used the human agents as His vessels, but He did not override them. As we will see, this was not the manner of Muhammad's revelations.

Karen Armstrong, a popular and highly sympathetic writer about Islam and Muhammad, gives this account of the manner of Muhammad's initial encounter with what Muslims believe was Gabriel (*Jibril*) the angel in the Cave of Hira:

> Muhammad was torn from his sleep in his mountain cave and felt himself overwhelmed by a devastating divine presence. Later he explained this ineffable experience by saying that an angel had enveloped him in a terrifying embrace so that it felt as though the breath was being forced from his body. The angel gave him the curt command: "*Iqra!*" "Recite!" Muhammad protested that he could not recite; he was not a *kahin*, one of the ecstatic prophets of Arabia. But, he said, the angel simply embraced him again until, just as he thought he had reached the end of his endurance, he found the divinely inspired words of a new scripture pouring forth from his mouth.[2]

Armstrong mistakenly, however, does not mention that it was not actually until the third time that the "angel" had strangled Muhammad, demanding that he recite, that he finally did so.[3] This encounter stands in stark contrast to the gentle nature of angelic and divine encounters found throughout the Bible, where the angels (or the Lord Himself) almost always begin their conversation with the comforting phrase, "Do not be afraid" (Genesis 15:1, 26:24, 46:3, Daniel 8:15-19, 10:12, 19, Matthew 28:5, 10, Luke 1:13, Luke 1:26-31, 2:10, Revelation 1:17).

We should not be surprised to find out then, that after Muhammad's terrifying and violent encounter with the spirit in the cave, he believed that demons possessed him. Muhammad became so distraught that he grew suicidal. From Guillaume's translation of Ibn Ishaq's famous early biography of Muhammad, *Sirat-Rasul*, we read:

> So I (Muhammad) read it, and he (Gabriel) departed from me. And I awoke from my sleep, and it was as though these words were written on my heart…. Now none of God's creatures was more hateful to me than an (ecstatic) poet or a man possessed: I could not even look at them. I thought, "Woe is me poet or possessed—never shall Quraysh (a tribe of Muhammad's day) say this of me! I will go to the top of the mountain and throw myself down that I may kill myself and gain rest." So I went forth to do so and then) when I was midway on the mountain, I heard a voice from heaven saying "O Muhammad! Thou are the apostle of God and I am Gabriel."[3]

The reference to "poet or possessed" comes from the notion that Arabs contemporary with Muhammad believed that poets created their poetry under the inspiration of demons. At-Tabari, one of Islam's most highly respected early historians says, "The pre-Islamic Arabs believed in the demon of poetry, and they thought that a great poet was directly inspired by demons…"[4]

After the terrible experience, Muhammad returned home to his wife Khadija, still terribly disturbed by the encounter:

> Then Allah's Apostle returned with the Inspiration, his neck muscles twitching with terror till he entered upon Khadija and said, "Cover me! Cover me!" They covered him till his fear was over and then he said, "O Khadija, what is wrong with me?" Then he told her everything that had happened and said, "I fear that something may happen to me."[5]

But it was not only Muhammad who suspected a demonic source to his revelations; clearly many of Muhammad's contemporaries also believed that his revelatory experiences were demonic and that he was demon possessed:

> "Yet they turn away from him and say: "Tutored [by others], a man possessed!" -Surah 44:14 (Yusuf Ali)

> And say: "What! shall we give up our gods for the sake of a Poet possessed?" -Surah 37:36 (Yusuf Ali)

Apparently it grew necessary that Allah come to Muhammad's defense and respond to his critics within the Qur'an itself:

> No, your compatriot [Muhammad] is not mad. He saw him [Gabriel] on the clear horizon. He does not grudge the secrets of the unseen, nor is this the utterance of an accursed devil. -Surah 81:22-25

> It [the *Qur'an*] is no poet's speech: Scant is your faith! It is no soothsayer's divination: How little you reflect! It is revelation from the Lord of the Universe. -Surah 69:41, 42

Many scholars have become convinced that Muhammad was either epileptic or demon possessed or both.[6] After studying the nature of his revelatory experiences and reading the comments of his contemporaries, this is not surprising. In fact, after discussing some of the specific physical manifestations of Muhammad's experiences, John Gilcrest, a South African Christian author and well known authority on Islam, finalized his analysis of the various physical phenomena that accompanied Muhammad's revelatory experiences:

> It should be pointed out that men can be subjected to a different type of seizure which very closely resembles epilepsy. During the life of Jesus a young boy was brought to him who was "an epileptic" (Matthew 17:15) and who suffered extreme forms of epilepsy (he would suddenly fall down, be convulsed, and be unable to speak). There is no doubt, however, that this epilepsy was not naturally but demonically induced as all three records of the incident (in Matthew 17, Mark 9, and Luke 9) state that Jesus exorcised the unclean spirit in the child and healed the boy. Without passing judgment on Muhammad, let it nevertheless be said that anyone subject to occultic influences could well find that seizures similar to epileptic fits would occur at appropriate times and, instead of causing a loss of memory, would have just the opposite effect and leave firmly induced impressions on the recipient's mind. Throughout the world missionaries have related cases of precisely this nature. To this day such

phenomena are not uncommon among Oriental ecstatics
and mystics and they are widely reported.[7]

So while the Apostle Peter describes the experience of the authors of
biblical Scripture by referring to men who "spoke from God" as
they were "moved by the Holy Spirit" (2 Peter 1:21), Muhammad's
experience was much more direct, ecstatic, and dark. It is important
to note that none of the biblical prophets ever questioned the source
of their revelations. Muhammad's experience was far more similar
to the experience of a spiritist or someone who channels spirits than
the experience of a biblical prophet.

OTHER STRANGE PHENOMENA

Muhammad's frightening spiritual encounters did not end
with these examples. On another occasion, Muhammad was
"bewitched," whereby he believed himself to be having sexual
relations with his wives when he was actually doing no such
thing. Guillaume notes that one Muslim scholar says that the
spell lasted for an entire year. This episode of Muhammad's
life is well documented in Islam's sacred traditions:

> Narrated Aisha (one of Muhammad's wives): Magic was
> worked on Allah's Apostle so that he used to think that he had
> sexual relations with his wives while he actually had not.[8]

This absolutely bizarre portion of Muhammad's life should give
pause to anyone who might consider Muhammad a genuine
prophet of God—never mind the greatest of all prophets, as
Muslims claim. One can only conclude that in order to have
fallen into such a delusional state, Muhammad was indeed
either demon possessed or significantly ill or both. In light of
the occultic occurrences that defined Muhammad's initial
"revelatory" experiences, the conclusion is not hard to arrive at
for anyone with any genuine spiritual discernment. Of course
the contrast here is stark when we look at the life of Jesus, Who,

rather than being given over to any form of demonic influence, instead freed numerous people from such oppression.

CONCLUSION

In the final assessment, we see that Muhammad's revelations—the seeds out of which Islam sprouted—began amidst a violent and dark encounter with some form of spiritual being in the Cave of Hira. We have also seen that Muhammad's life contained periods of either significant delusion or blatant spiritual oppression. Note this dimension of Muhammad's life as we develop the greater theme of this book. Also, when attempting to discern the primary spiritual source of Islam, it is essential to see not only the dark nature of the initial seed but even more so its ultimate vision of the future—its fully mature fruit—as the demonic and anti-biblical revelations that began in the Cave of Hira find their culmination with the killing of every Jew, Christian, and other non-Muslim in the world.

CHAPTER TWELVE

THE ANTICHRIST SPIRIT OF ISLAM

W*hile we have already discussed* the actual person of the Antichrist, the Bible also talks of *an antichrist spirit.* Apart from the one direct reference in the Bible to *the* Antichrist, there are four other times that the Apostle John uses the word in a more general sense. Each time it is in reference to a particular spirit. This spirit is defined by its denial of some very specific aspects of Jesus' nature and His relationship to God the Father. Following are the verses that describe this "antichrist" spirit:

> But every spirit that does not acknowledge Jesus is not from God. This is the spirit of the antichrist, which you have heard is coming and even now is already in the world (1 John 4:3).

> Who is the liar? It is the man who denies that Jesus is the Christ. Such a man is the antichrist—he denies the Father and the Son. No one who denies the Son has the Father; whoever acknowledges the Son has the Father also (1 John 2:22, 23).

> Many deceivers, who do not acknowledge Jesus Christ as coming in the flesh, have gone out into the world. Any such person is the deceiver and the antichrist (2 John 1:7).

From these verses, we learn that the antichrist is a spirit that is identified as a "liar" and a "deceiver" which specifically denies the following:

1. That Jesus is the Christ/Messiah (the savior/deliverer of Israel and the world).

2. The Father and the Son (the Trinity or that Jesus is the Son of God).

3. That Jesus has come in the flesh (the incarnation—that God became man).

THE ANTICHRIST SPIRIT OF ISLAM

The religion of Islam, more than any other religion, philosophy, or belief system, fulfills the description of the antichrist spirit. The religion of Islam makes one of its highest priorities the denial of all of the above points regarding Jesus and His relationship to the Father. In fact, we can very fairly claim that Islam is a direct polemical response against the above essential Christian doctrines. Regarding the above points, however, Muslims will be quick to argue that Islam teaches that Jesus is indeed the Messiah. But this is really just trickery. While it is true that Islam does retain the title of Messiah for Jesus, when one asks a Muslim to define what the title "Messiah" actually *means* in Islam, the definitions given are always hollow and fall entirely short of containing any truly messianic substance. In Islam, Jesus is merely another prophet in a very long line of prophets. Biblically speaking, however, the role of the Messiah among other things entails being a divine priestly savior, a deliverer, and the king of the Jews. As we saw in earlier chapters, rather than delivering His followers, the Muslim Jesus leads Israel's enemies against her and seeks to kill or convert all the Jews and Christians. This would the equivalent of calling Adolph Hitler, rather than Moses, Israel's deliverer. But the Apostle John informs us that in the last hour, a man is coming who will fully personify the antichrist spirit and deny many of the essential biblical doctrines regarding Who Jesus is and what He came to do. That man will be *the* Antichrist.

TAWHID AND SHIRK

In order to properly understand the antichrist spirit of Islam, there are two doctrines that must first be understood. *Tawhid* refers to the belief in the absolute oneness of God. Islam adheres to the strictest form of unitarian monotheism possible. *In Islam, God is utterly alone.* But in order to understand *tawhid*, one must understand that it is more than just a doctrine; in Islam, belief in *tahwid* is an absolute commandment. And if adherence to *tawhid* is the highest and most important commandment in Islam, then the greatest sin is *shirk*. *Shirk* is, in essence, idolatry. From the "Invitation to Islam" newsletter published by a Muslim group from Toronto, we read a very telling statement that helps us to understand exactly how *shirk* is viewed by Muslims:

> Murder, rape, child molesting, and genocide. These are all some of the appalling crimes which occur in our world today. Many would think that these are the worst possible offences which could be committed. But there is something which outweighs all of these crimes put together: It is the crime of *shirk*.[1]

Thus many Muslims feel as though believing in the Trinity or ascribing divinity to Jesus are among the greatest sins conceivable. In fact, believing in these essential Christian doctrines is more than just a sin; *it is the most heinous of all crimes!* In the Muslim mind, *shirk* refers not only to the beliefs of polytheists or pagans, but also to the essential historical doctrines of the Christian faith. Below we will examine these three essential doctrines and how Islam specifically denies them.

ISLAM DENIES THE SONSHIP OF CHRIST

The religion of Islam has as one of its foundational beliefs a direct denial of Jesus as God's Son. This denial is found several times throughout the Qur'an:

> In blasphemy indeed are those that say that God is Christ
> the son of Mary. -Surah 5:17 (Yusuf Ali)

> They say: "God hath begotten a son!"—Glory be to Him!
> He is self-sufficient! His are all things in the heavens and
> on earth! No warrant have ye for this! Say ye about Allah
> what ye know not? -Surah 10:68 (Yusuf Ali)

> They said, "The Most Gracious has begotten a son"! You
> have uttered a gross blasphemy. The heavens are about to
> shatter, the earth is about to tear asunder, and the
> mountains are about to crumble. Because they claim that
> the Most Gracious has begotten a son. It is not befitting the
> Most Gracious that He should beget a son. -Surah 19:88-92
> (Rashad Khalifa)

> [T]he Christians call Christ the son of Allah. That is a saying
> from their mouth; [in this] they but imitate what the
> unbelievers of old used to say. *Allah's curse be on them: how
> they are deluded away from the Truth!* -Surah 9:30 (Yusuf Ali,
> emphasis mine)

The Qur'an pronounces a curse on those who believe that Jesus is
God's Son. People who say such things utter "gross blasphemies"
and are likened to "unbelievers" or infidels. Without question
then, in this regard, Islam is an antichrist religious system.
Remember Jim Hasting's comments from chapter one? He was the
priest in training who converted to Islam. "The thing I've always
latched to is that there's one God, he doesn't have equals, *he doesn't
need a son to come do his work.*" Islam attempts to create an
acceptable form of monotheistic worship yet it not only leaves out
the most essential aspects of a saving relationship with God, but it
also directly confronts these things and calls them the highest
forms of blasphemy. "Far be it from God that he should have a
son!" These words encircle the inside of the Dome of the Rock
Mosque in Jerusalem—the very location where for centuries God's
people, the Jews, worshipped in their Temple awaiting their
Messiah. This is also where Jesus, the *Son of God* and the Jewish
Messiah will someday rule over the earth. Islam has built a
monument of utter defiance to this future reality.

ISLAM DENIES THE TRINITY

Islam applies the same claim of blasphemy to those who believe in the Trinity:

> They do blaspheme who say: Allah is one of three in a Trinity: for there is no god except One Allah. If they desist not from their word [of blasphemy], verily a grievous penalty will befall the blasphemers among them. –Surah 5:73 (Yusuf Ali)

Thus belief in the Trinity is also defined as blasphemy. But what is the "grievous penalty" that shall befall those who believe such things? Well, as we saw in previous chapters, many Muslims ironically expect their version of Jesus to return and kill these "polytheist Trinitarian Christians."

And the Qur'an does not stop at denying that Jesus is the Son of God or that God exists as a Trinity.

ISLAM DENIES THE CROSS

With tears in his eyes, Paul the Apostle warned the Thessalonians that, "many live as enemies of the cross of Christ" (Thessalonians 3:18). It should not come as a surprise then that Islam also denies the most central event of all of redemptive history: the crucifixion of Jesus. Speaking to the Jews of Jesus' day, the Qur'an says:

> That they said [in boast], "We killed Christ Jesus the son of Mary, the Messenger of Allah"; but they killed him not, nor crucified him, but so it was made to appear to them, and those who differ therein are full of doubts, with no [certain] knowledge, but only conjecture to follow, for of a surety they killed him not: Nay, Allah raised him up unto himself; and Allah is exalted in power, wise. -Surah 4:157-8 (Yusuf Ali)

Islamic scholars put forth conflicting theories regarding exactly what happened to Jesus. (For ironically, regarding this issue, it is actually they who are the ones who have "only conjecture to follow.") But despite the inability of Muslims to arrive at any form of consensus regarding what happened to Jesus, they are very much in agreement on at least one issue: *He was not crucified!* This passage of the Qur'an makes at least this much clear.

HOW DOES THE ANTICHRIST SPIRIT OF ISLAM AFFECT MUSLIMS?

So we see that Islam very specifically and very deliberately denies all three of the doctrines that the Apostle John says the antichrist spirit will deny. The Qur'an does not merely deny these doctrines, but expresses utter disdain for them, actually cursing those who believe these things, accusing them of gross blasphemy. But how do these Qur'anic attitudes then affect Muslims? This statement may sound strong, but in all of my years of outreach, interfaith dialogue, and casual conversations with those who are not Christians, the two groups that I have personally witnessed express the strongest degree of contempt and mockery toward the Gospel have been Satanists and Muslims. (Yes, believe it or not, I've actually had quite involved conversations with more than a few Satanists.) Now, let me be clear that I am in no way trying to liken all Muslims to Satanists. I have met many wonderful and decent Muslims who would never express any form of blatant disrespect for Christian doctrine, even if they secretly felt that way. But I am speaking very truthfully when I say that in terms of my personal experiences of witnessing assaults toward the Gospel message, only Satanists and Muslims have expressed such a high degree of venomous disgust. While many religions and systems of belief exist that do not agree with the doctrines of Christianity—many which do not even believe in God—only Islam fills the role of a religion that exists to deny core Christian beliefs. And of course, following the lead of the Qur'an, the three doctrines most severely and most often attacked and mocked by Muslims are the doctrines of the Trinity, the divine incarnation, and the atoning sacrifice/crucifixion of Jesus. I recently saw a suggestion by a Muslim on an Internet discussion group for a bumper sticker. It read: "Divine Insanity: God died on the cross to save his own creation from his own wrath." One Muslim friend insists on referring to Jesus as a "god-man sandwich." I have weathered innumerable accusations that by believing in the historic Christian God I am no different than a pagan polytheistic idol worshipper. Many times, I have been told that the doctrine of the atoning sacrifice of Jesus is as archaic and pagan as a human sacrifice to some kind of "volcano god." I have been accused of believing in a God who is a "sadistic child abuser." I have seen attempts to liken Jesus' death on the Cross to a suicide bombing. I have even weathered the mocking of the Christian God as a "blood-thirsty vampire."

If you are a Christian and you love God, I'm sure these statements grieve you as they grieve me, and I apologize for repeating them. I don't relate these attacks in any way to provoke negative feelings against Muslims. Please do not come away with any such feelings! My reason for relating these examples is to acquaint you with the blatant antichrist spirit that resides within the religion of Islam and that many Muslims therefore manifest. We should not be surprised then to find that one of the descriptions of the Antichrist is that he will be very fond of uttering great blasphemies against the God of the Bible:

> The king will do as he pleases. He will...say unheard-of things against the God of gods (Daniel 11:36).

> He will speak against the Most High and oppress his saints (Daniel 7:25).

The Qur'an itself expresses such blasphemies. As someone who is in continual dialogue with numerous Muslims from all over the world, I can testify that the blatant antichrist spirit that we saw expressed in the Qur'anic passages above quite often blooms into an overt disdain and utter contempt, not only for Christian beliefs, but also for Christians themselves. While this is not always the case, should we really be surprised when Muslims act out against those whom the Qur'an curses as idolatrous infidel blasphemers? And if we are being realistic, should we expect the future of Islam to rest with those Muslims who identify with the Qur'anic scorn for Christians, or with those who show an amiable attitude despite the curses of their own holy book?

In regard to whether or not Islam is specifically *the* antichrist system that the Bible foretells, there can be no question that this, the second largest, fastest growing religion in the world, is and has been from its inception, the quintessence of the very antichrist spirit about which John the Apostle warned us.

CHAPTER THIRTEEN

ISLAM'S ANCIENT HATRED FOR THE JEWS

W*hile Islam envisions the day* when Christians and Jews will convert to Islam *en masse*, Islam's end-time narrative makes a distinction between the final destiny of Christians and that of Jews. In Islam's version of the last days, we see that all Christians will either accept Islam or be killed. Certainly, when we look at this final picture, it is impossible to say that Islam has any real affinity for Christians or Christianity. But when analyzing Islamic teaching and traditions about the Jews, one gets a very cold feeling that the only destiny that Islam has marked out for Jews is that of an absolute and total slaughter. We see in the Islamic traditions a dark and very persistent hatred for Jews nearly identical to the ideology expressed through Naziism. The Qur'an and the Islamic traditions fully support and nurture this ideology of hatred. For instance, speaking of Jews, the Qur'an says:

> Amongst them we [Allah] have placed enmity and hatred till the Day of Judgment. Every time they kindle the fire of war, Allah doth extinguish it; but they [ever] strive to do mischief on earth. And Allah loveth not those who do mischief. -Surah 5:64 (Yusuf Ali)

This verse makes it clear that there will be "enmity and hatred" against the Jews until the very end of the present age. So much for those who claim that the Qur'an's scorn for Jews is limited only to specific historical incidences in Muhammad's career. Not only does the Qur'an portray Jews as those who start wars and cause general mischief on the earth, but it also claims that Allah was so disgusted by the Jews that he cursed them and transformed many of them into "apes and swine," assigning them the lowest "rank" among humankind:

> When in their insolence they transgressed [all] prohibitions, we said to them: "Be ye apes, despised and rejected." -Surah 7:166 (Yusuf Ali)

> Those who incurred the curse of Allah and his wrath, those of whom some he transformed into apes and swine, those who worshipped evil—these are [many times] worse in rank, and far more astray from the even path! -Surah 5:60 (Yusuf Ali)

> And well ye knew those amongst you who transgressed in the matter of the Sabbath: We said to them: *"Be ye apes, despised and rejected."* -Surah 2:65 (Yusuf Ali, emphasis mine)

Among the more anti-Semitic and vocal Muslims, these verses have become absolute favorites. Walid Shoebat, a former Muslim, grew up in the Palestinian territories. Recalling a school trip to the Jerusalem zoo as a child, Walid relates, "The Islamic teacher would tell us, 'this gorilla was originally a Jew.' I look at this now and I think, this is what Naziism teaches—in its worst form. This is being taught throughout the entire Middle East."[1] Whereas the Nazis called Jews subhuman "vermin" in order to justify their inhumane treatment of the Jews, the Muslim world follows the lead of the Qur'an in dehumanizing the Jewish race.

Now, at this point, the enterprising Muslim apologist will be quick to argue that while many verses in the Qur'an speak of the Jews in such a negative manner, other verses speak of the Jews in a more positive manner. While true, this is also highly misleading. In his highly informative book, *Islam and the Jews*, Mark A. Gabriel, a former Muslim *imam* and professor of Islamic history at the prestigious Al-Azhar University in Cairo, addresses this misunderstanding of Islam's disposition toward the Jews. Gabriel explains that, according to Islamic theology, those verses in the Qur'an that appear to be "nice" towards the Jews are understood to be cancelled out (*mansookh*) by the verses revealed to

Muhammad later in his "prophetic" career. This is based on the idea of progressive revelation in Islam whereby if you have any verses that seem to contradict one another, the newer revelations given to Muhammad negate or cancel out the older revelations. This is an established and well-understood doctrine in Islam called *nasik*.[2] Many Qur'ans even include a chart in the back that lists which verses are older and which are newer so Muslims can know which verses are cancelled out and which verses remain. Because the verses which are inflammatory and aggressive toward the Jews are newer verses, they cancel out any that might have a more conciliatory tone. This understanding is well known throughout the Islamic world.

As we trace the growth and development of anti-Semitism in Islam, we see that, unfortunately, it is not limited to the Qur'an, but rather seems to find an even fuller expression in the infamous *hadith* about the final slaughter of the Jews. We have already quoted this tradition more than once, but shall quote it again here one last time:

> [Muhammad said] The last hour would not come unless the Muslims will fight against the Jews and the Muslims would kill them until the Jews would hide themselves behind a stone or a tree and a stone or a tree would say: *Muslim, or the servant of Allah, there is a Jew behind me; come and kill him*; but the tree Gharqad would not say, for it is the tree of the Jews (emphasis mine).[3]

This apocalyptic belief of a future battle against Israel and the murder of all Jews is a deeply held belief among many Muslims. And we must remember that these anti-Semitic traditions and verses from the Qur'an are over a thousand years old. These sacred Islamic traditions of a final slaughter of all Jews cannot be attributed to the present day conflict with the state of Israel. Although many today try to blame Muslim enmity toward Jews solely on Zionism and its alleged "Nazi-like" abuse of the victimized and oppressed Palestinians, it simply cannot be done in an honest and informed manner. The enmity of Islam toward the

Jews has existed since Islam's inception. It is not a new phenomenon. And today Islam and the Muslim world is undeniably the single most anti-Semitic force on the earth. Palestinians in particular use the anti-Semitic apocalyptic template as a basis for many of their actions toward Israel and the Jews. Although this template is in fact one of the primary factors fueling the ongoing present conflict in Israel, it is also the most often overlooked factor by secular observers who attempt to judge the present conflict on the basis of a moral equivalency. The following quotes are all translated portions of sermons from recent years delivered by Sheikh Ibrahim Madhi, the officially appointed *imam* of the Palestinian Authority. Notice the overwhelming reliance upon the previously discussed verses and traditions that are used to justify and support the hatred against the Jews:

> We the Palestinian nation, *our fate from Allah is to be the vanguard in the war against the Jews* until the resurrection of the dead, as the prophet Muhammad said: "The resurrection of the dead will not arrive until you will fight the Jews and kill them...." We the Palestinians are the vanguard in this undertaking and in this campaign, whether or not we want this... (emphasis mine).

> Oh, our Arab brethren.... Oh, our Muslim brethren.... Don't leave the Palestinians alone in the war against the Jews...even if it has been decreed upon us to be the vanguard.... Jerusalem, Palestine, and Al Aksa (The Temple Mount), the land that Allah blessed and its surrounding areas will remain at the center of the struggle between Truth and Falsehood, between the Jews and the non-Jews on this sacred land, regardless of how many agreements are signed, regardless of how many treaties and covenants are ratified. For the Truth is in the Qur'an, as verified by the words of the prophet Muhammad, that the decisive battle will be in Jerusalem and its environs: "The resurrection of the dead will not occur until you make war on the Jews..."

> The battle with the Jews will surely come...the decisive Muslim victory is coming without a doubt, and the prophet spoke about in more than one *hadith* and the Day

of Resurrection will not come without the victory of the believers [the Muslims] over the descendants of the monkeys and pigs [the Jews] and with their annihilation.[4]

Oh Allah, accept our martyrs in the highest heavens.... Oh Allah, show the Jews a black day.... Oh Allah, annihilate the Jews and their supporters.... Oh Allah, raise the flag of *jihad* across the land...[5]

Thus, as the world eagerly awaits and believes for the peaceful co-existence of the Jewish and the Palestinian people, the *imams*, the religious authorities of the Palestinian people, with the full support and approval of the political leadership, ceaselessly beat the drums of "the final war," the final slaughter of the Jews.

SATAN'S ANCIENT HATRED FOR THE JEWS

When we compare the spirit that we see in Islam with the spirit that we see manifest under the rule of the Antichrist and the False Prophet, we find the same ancient hatred against the Jewish people in both. This ancient hatred originates with Satan himself. From the day that God showed His favor to the Jewish people, Satan has raged against them. Satan's primary vehicles that he has used to do this have been several great world empires. These are the "beast" empires that we discussed in chapter ten. Throughout the Bible, we read of Satan's attempts to exterminate or persecute the Jewish people:

1. Through Pharaoh, the ruler of Egypt, when he ordered the slaughter of every male Hebrew child (Exodus 1:5-22).

2. Through Shalmaneser, the ruler of Assyria, when he conquered the northern kingdom of Israel and carried away and dispersed ten of the twelve tribes into exile (2 Kings 17:5, 6).

3. Through Nebuchadnezzar, the ruler of Babylon, when he attacked Jerusalem, the capital of the southern

kingdom of Judea, and carried the rest of the Jews off into exile (2 Kings 24:10-16).

4. Through Haman, the man appointed as second in command over the Medo-Persian Empire, when he attempted to have every Jew in the empire killed (Esther 3:9).

5. Through Antiochus Epiphanes, the Greek ruler of Syria, when he laid siege to Jerusalem in what the Jewish historian Josephus describes as one of the bloodiest sieges in Israel's history (Daniel 8:23-25; 1 Maccabees 1-6).[6]

6. Through Titus, the Roman emperor, who attacked and captured Jerusalem, killing over 1.1 million Jews and enslaving over ninety-seven thousand. (*Wars of the Jews*, VI, ix, 3).

7. Through various Islamic and Christian empires, which we cannot fail to mention. Even Christianity (albeit in a perverted form) has been *far* from innocent in the bloody history of the Jewish people.

8. Through Hitler, *führer* of Germany, who killed over six million Jews during World War II.

9. And eventually through the Antichrist and the False Prophet and their future empire, which is prophesied very clearly by the Prophets Zechariah and Ezekiel to attack Jerusalem and kill two-thirds of the inhabitants of the nation of Israel (Zechariah 13:8, 9; Ezekiel 38).

Any thinking person at this point must stop and ask: What else can explain such a consistently bloody and painful history of one people other than an inhuman, demonic hatred? Who could instigate such a black and persistent attack against one people who represent such a very small fraction of one percent of the earth's population—no matter where they dwell? Who else if not the Devil himself? The history of the Jewish people alone is proof to the open mind that Satan exists and that he hates those whom God loves and declares to be the very "apple of his eye" (Zechariah 2:8).

CONCLUSION

Throughout natural history we see willing vessels manifest Satan's hatred for the Jewish people. And, even more frightening, in the sacred texts of all three monotheistic religions, we see yet another future attack against the Jews, this one worse than all those that preceded it. In the Bible, it is specifically Satan's pawns—the Antichrist, his False Prophet, and all who follow them—who carry out the final onslaught. In Islam it is the Mahdi, the Muslim Jesus, and as the tradition says, "faithful Muslims," who carry out such atrocities. Indeed, in this regard, Islam again fulfills one of the primary characteristics of the Antichrist spirit; that of an unquenchable anti-Semitic spirit.

CHAPTER FOURTEEN

END TIME MARTYRDOM

W*hile the last chapter* dealt with the concentrated hatred and murderous spirit of Islam toward the Jewish people, this chapter deals in a more general sense with the worldwide persecution and martyrdom that the Antichrist's empire will wage against anyone who follows Jesus or who refuses to become a Muslim during the last days.

BEHEADINGS IN THE LAST DAYS

In the Book of Revelation, chapter twenty, the Apostle John sees a particular company of people. John gives us a very brief synopsis of what he sees. He specifically describes future end-time martyrs:

> I saw thrones on which were seated those who had been given authority to judge. And I saw the souls of those who had been beheaded because of their testimony for Jesus and because of the word of God. They had not worshiped the beast or his image and had not received his mark on their foreheads or their hands. They came to life and reigned with Christ a thousand years (Revelation 20:4).

I've dwelled on this verse many times. The Bible says that in the last days, beheading will be the primary method by which people will be for their "testimony of Jesus and because of the word of God." It is a strange picture to try to imagine. Is the Bible implying a worldwide resurrection of *guillotines* in every town square? What exactly will occur that will result in a worldwide standard of beheading as a means of executing Christians? As I have tried to envision the nature of the end times and what they will look like, I have often wondered about this verse. Other passages very similar to this one also speak of a future persecution and a global trend of executing Christians for their faith in Jesus: "Then you will be handed over to be persecuted and put to death, and you will be hated by all nations because of me (Matthew 24:9)."

Here Jesus warns His disciples that they will be hated and ultimately put to death as a result of their identification with Him. But then there is a prophetic expansion on this prediction. Jesus says that "you will be hated *by all nations* because of me." Jesus specifically predicted a global element to this future persecution against Christians. This next verse gives us even further insight:

> All this I have told you so that you will not go astray. They will put you out of the synagogue; in fact, a time is coming when anyone who kills you will think he is offering a service to God. They will do such things because they have not known the Father or me. I have told you this, so that when the time comes you will remember that I warned you (John 16:1-4).

In this passage from the Gospel of John, Jesus is initially speaking to the disciples outside of a strictly end-time context. He first warns the disciples that in the days ahead they would see His followers put out of the synagogues. This prophecy came to its fullest expression after what became known as the Bar Kochba Rebellion in AD 132-135. During the Bar Kochba Rebellion the final separation of church and synagogue took place. Bar Kochba was a false Jewish messiah supported and endorsed by the highest level of the rabbinic authority at the time, the renowned Rabbi Akiva. Akiva's support authenticated Bar Kochba as the Messiah in the eyes of the Jewish people. When Bar Kochba led the Jews in a rebellion against Rome, any Jew who did not participate was viewed as a traitor to the Jewish nation. The Jews who followed Jesus, however, who before this time still regularly participated in the synagogue services, could not support a rebellion led by someone whom they knew to be a false messiah. As a result the Jewish followers of Jesus were expelled from the synagogues *en masse* and Jesus' prophecy was fulfilled in the second century.

But in the second part of this verse, Jesus is speaking of the end times. "In fact," He goes on to say, "the days will come when your persecutors will do far more than merely expel you from a synagogue; they will kill you." But the most bewildering and intriguing aspect of this verse is the next portion of Jesus' statement. He says that those who kill you will think that in doing so, they are offering a service to God. This portion of the verse is key. How could someone in today's world think that God demands the killing of other human beings simply because they believe differently? It's such a completely foreign concept to most modern Western minds. It is not, however, a foreign concept to history. Both Islam and Christianity—Catholic and Protestant—have been guilty of this very thing, murdering those perceived as heretics from the only true religion. *Jihad*, the Crusades, the Inquisitions—all fit the bill of murder for and in the name of God. One thing is for sure, an absolutely necessary ingredient in any such bloody exchange would have to be a firm conviction that God is on one's side and that He commands such executions. It is impossible to imagine any belief system or philosophy on the earth that could carry out such a thing other than a well-established world religion. While totalitarian regimes are certainly capable of such a thing, this verse specifically says that the ones who carry out these executions will believe themselves to be serving God in doing so. No, the system that carries this out will be a religious system that views itself as the earthly steward of some form of global divine government. It must view itself as God's only organization or community on the earth. Only such a scenario can account for the actions that we read about in these verses.

In summary then, when we compare these three verses we get a very specific picture of what end-time persecution and martyrdom will look like. First, it will be global. Second, it will necessitate a belief system that views itself as having a divinely appointed governmental role on the earth. Third, it will involve the specific method of beheading as its primary method of execution. So we have a global religion that will view itself as a divinely appointed system on the earth, authorized by God to behead those who refuse to join. As we are about to see, in terms of religious systems that exist on the earth today, only the religion of Islam fulfills these requirements.

BEHEADINGS IN THE NEWS

When the first draft of this work was completed, in late 2004, there in Iraq, Saudi Arabia, and a few other countries a new story just about weekly of Islamic radicals beheading foreigners and Christians. Now, five years later, beheadings continue to be a normal part of life in the Islamic world, but the Western media seems to have grown tired of reporting them with the same shock that they once expressed. A debate rages about whether or not this practice is indeed "Islamic" or merely the barbaric practice of a few radicals violating the true principals of Islam. Among the public statements picked up by the Western media are the usual denouncements of such incidents as having anything to do with "true Islam." In most cases, the Western media gobbles these disavowals up and reprints them without much question. But if we examine not only Islamic tradition and history, but also the "word on the street" feelings of those Muslims who make their opinion known every day on Internet message and chat groups, we find a much different reality. Islamic message boards all over the Internet have debated the legitimacy or illegitimacy of such actions since they became front page news stories. CBS News also picked up on some of this Internet "chatter":

> And on Islamic Internet forums, mostly used by radicals,
> beheading has been a popular topic in recent weeks, with
> many participants describing it as the "easiest" way to kill
> an American or a Saudi from the ruling family.[1]

The only mistake that CBS made is to assume that most of the participants who use such forums are indeed "radicals." I have participated in several such Islamic "communities" and have befriended many Muslims through such groups. Many who participate in these forums presently live in the USA and Canada and many are converts from Christianity. While the writer of the CBS article assumes because of the barbaric nature of such discussions that these individuals are all "radicals," I have found that many of them simply take their Muslim faith seriously, even as I take my Christian faith seriously. While some of the members of these discussion groups seem disgusted and ashamed by the rise of beheadings, the overwhelming majority seem far more focused on doctrinal issues, such as whether the beheadings were done properly or if the victims were enemies or innocent parties. Sam Hamod, the former director of the Islamic Center in Washington, DC, when given the opportunity to chime in on this issue in an article featured in the *Washington Times*, used the moment not to condemn the beheadings, but to make the point that the men committing the beheadings in Iraq and elsewhere do it all wrong: "You can't do it like the idiots on TV. The right thing to do is slit the person's throat, not cut off the entire head."[2]

BEHEADING IN ISLAM: MUHAMMAD'S EXAMPLE

Beheading in Islam is not a new phenomenon by any means. Due to the utter disgust of many throughout the West with this practice, many moderate Muslims and Muslim apologists have repeatedly made the claim that beheading is not an officially sanctioned Islamic practice. They claim it defies the basic tenets of Islam. These claims are made to create a better image of Islam in the Western eye. Unfortunately, these claims are made either out of ignorance of Islam's history or with an active intent to deceive. Indeed, as we are about to see, *beheading is the very heritage of Islam*. Beheading is not only commanded as a specific method of killing one's enemies in the Qur'an, but was a favored method of killing by Muhammad and many of his followers.

When Muhammad began his career of violence and aggression, his band of Muslim warriors was still very small. Caravans traveling back and forth from Mecca and Damascus became Muhammad's favorite soft targets. Because the inhabitants of Mecca depended on these caravans for their lives, they were more than a bit disturbed after several attacks by Muhammad and his gang of marauders. Finally, men from the tribe of Quraysh came from Mecca to attack Muhammad and his men. This famous battle, the Battle of Badr, saw Muhammad and his fledgling army gain a surprise victory over the Quraysh. Among the people slain was Abba Hakam:

> Abba Hakam was severely wounded but still alive when Abdullah, the servant of Muhammad, ran up, put his foot on Abba Hakam's neck, got a hold of his beard and started insulting the fatally wounded man whom his own people had named "the father of wisdom." Abdullah cut off Abba Hakam's head and carried it to his master. "The head of the enemy of Allah!" exclaimed Muhammad joyously; — "Allah! There is no other god but he!" — "Yea, there is no other!" responded Abdullah, as he cast the severed head at the Prophet's feet. *"It is more acceptable to me;"* cried *Muhammad, hardly able to contain his joy, "than the choicest camel in all Arabia"* (emphasis mine).[3]

Sadly the blood lust of Muhammad and his followers only increased. In AD 627 Muhammad himself oversaw what can only be called a mass slaughter. Muhammad and his army laid a siege around the Jewish village of Qurayzah. After twenty-five days, the village surrendered, hoping that Muhammad would be merciful to them. Instead Muhammad had his soldiers dig several trenches and forced between six hundred to nine hundred men to march into them. At the hands of Muhammad's soldiers, they were all beheaded. The trenches became mass graves. From Ibn Ishaq's *Sirat Rasul*, Islam's earliest and most well received biography of Muhammad, we read the gruesome account:

> Then they (Qurayza) surrendered and the apostle confined them in Medina.... Then the apostle went out to the market of Medina (which is still its market today) and dug trenches in it. Then he sent for them and struck off their heads in those trenches as they were brought out to him in batches.... They were six hundred or seven hundred in all, though some put the figures as high as eight hundred or nine hundred.... This went on until the apostle made an end to them.[4]

Apparently this great slaughter awakened something in Muhammad. Beheading those six hundred to nine hundred men from Qurayza was not enough. Soon after this incident, Muhammad beheaded four hundred more Jews. Muhammad was allied with two groups of men, the Khazraj and the Aus. The Khazraj were in charge of beheading the four hundred Jews but the Aus stood by on the sidelines. When Muhammad looked and saw that the faces of the Khazraj showed their pleasure in the beheading and the Aus stood on the sidelines, he ordered that the Aus carry out the last twelve beheadings:

> Abu 'Ubayda told me on the authority of Abu 'Amir the Medinain, when the apostle (Muhammad) got the better of the sons of Qurayza he seized about four hundred men from the Jews who had been allies of Aus against Khazraj, and ordered that they should be beheaded. Accordingly Khazraj began to cut off their heads with great satisfaction. The apostle saw that the faces of the Khazraj showed their pleasure, but there was no such indication on the part of Aus, and...when he saw that there were only twelve of them left he gave them over to Aus, assigning one Jew to every two of Aus, saying, "Let so-and-so strike him and so-and-so finish him off."[5]

Later, another campaign of beheading took place under Muhammad. As he re-entered the city of Mecca with his army of ten thousand, he called to the warriors in his army from Medina and asked them, "Do you see the soldiers from Quraysh (from Mecca)? Go and slaughter them." Mark A. Gabriel explains the meaning of the word that Muhammad used for slaughter in Arabic:

> The Arabic word for slaughter presents the picture of a farmer harvesting his crop with a scythe. In other words, Muhammad was telling them, "Cut their heads from their bodies as you would cut fruit from the branch of a tree."[6]

So this is where it all began, with Muhammad. But it's certainly not where it ended. Remember that whatever Muhammad says or does is considered just as authoritative and as inspired as the very Qur'an itself. The actions of Muhammad dictate the model for living that Allah has ordained as his will for all Muslims:

> If you love Allah, then follow me (Muhammad). -Sura 3:31 (Shakir)

> Ye have indeed in the Apostle of Allah a beautiful pattern of (conduct) for anyone whose hope is in Allah and the Final Day. -Sura 33:21

By slaying the men of these Jewish villages this way, Muhammad set the example of what Allah has ordained and commanded for all faithful Muslims to follow.

BEHEADING AMONG MUHAMMAD'S FOLLOWERS

Abu Bakr, Muhammad's best friend and successor, became the first "rightly guided" *caliph* of Islam after Muhammad's death. Abu Bakr's general was Khalid bin al-Walid al-Makhzumi who also fought under the leadership of Muhammad. Under Muhammad, Khalid fought so effectively that he earned the title "the Sword of Allah."

Upon Abu Bakr's orders, in AD 633-634, Khalid extended an invitation to the people of Arabia to accept Islam. This "invitation," however, was actually nothing more than an overt threat of war and death to those who refused to convert and submit to the rule of Islam. The actual invitation read as follows:

> In the name of Allah, the Compassionate, the Merciful. From Khalid bin al-Walid to the governors of Persia. Embrace Islam so that you may be safe. If not, make a covenant with me and pay the *jizyah* tax. Otherwise, I have brought you a people who love death just as you love drinking wine.[7]

After this "invitation" to Islam, many refused to convert to Islam. Among those who refused were a group of Persians and Christians from Ullays on the Euphrates River. Khalid attacked them in AD 633. The battle was fierce and so Khalid made a vow to Allah during the battle that if he could defeat them that he would make the canal that surrounded their village literally *run* with their blood. He commanded that all who were defeated be taken alive. There were so many captives that it took a day and a half to behead all of the men. The blood however, coagulated and Khalid's troops were forced to release water into the canal in order that it would run red with the blood of the slain lest Khalid's vow remain unfulfilled. Abu Jafar Muhammad ibn Jarir At-Tabari, an early Islamic historian and theologian, recorded this event:

> Khalid said, "O Allah, if you deliver their shoulders to us, I will obligate myself to you not to leave any one of them whom we can overcome until I make their canal run with their blood." Then Allah defeated them for the Muslims and gave their shoulders to them. Khalid then commanded to his herald to proclaim to his men, "Capture! Capture! Do not kill any except he who continues to resist." As a result the cavalry brought prisoners in droves, driving them along. Khalid had detailed certain men to cut off their heads in the canal. He did that to them for a day and a night. They pursued them the next day and the day after, until they reached the Nahrayn and the like of that distance in every direction from Ullays. And Khalid cut off their heads.[8]

Some of Khalid's men proclaimed to him:

> "[E]ven if you were to kill all the population of the earth, their blood would still not run.... Therefore send water over it, so that you may fulfill your oath." Khalid had blocked the water from the canal. Now Khalid brought the water back, so that it flowed with spilled blood. Owing to this it has been called Blood Canal to this day.[9]

Amir Taheri, an Iranian-born journalist, outlines several other incidents throughout Islam's history of the practice of beheading:

> In 680, the Prophet's favorite grandson, Hussein bin Ali, had his head chopped off in Karbala, central Iraq, by the soldiers of the Caliph Yazid. The severed head was put on a silver platter and sent to Damascus, Yazid's capital, before being sent further to Cairo for inspection by the governor of Egypt. The *caliph's* soldiers also cut off the heads of all of Hussein's seventy-one male companions, including the one-year-old baby boy Ali-Asghar.[10]

Thus the pattern had been established and now the principle that Muhammad had modeled now came back and touched his own family. Eventually stories of beheading came to fill Islam's history. Andrew Bostom, editor of *The Legacy of Jihad*, points out that in the late fifteen century:

> Babur, the founder of the Mughal Empire, who is revered as a paragon of Muslim tolerance by modern revisionist historians, recorded the following in his autobiographical *Baburnama*, about infidel prisoners of a *jihad* campaign: "Those who were brought in alive [having surrendered] were ordered beheaded, after which a tower of skulls was erected in the camp."[11]

Skipping forward to a slightly more modern era, Taheri again picks up the gruesome tale:

> In 1842 the Afghani Muslims overtook the British garrison in Kabul and beheaded over two thousand men, women,

and children. The heads were placed on sticks around the city as decorations.[12]

The practice continued during the 1980s in Afghanistan, where Afghani warriors beheaded an estimated three thousand Soviet troops. The practice of beheading was also common during the Iranian Revolution:

> In 1992, the *mullahs* sent a "specialist" to cut off the head of Shapour Bakhtiar, the *shah's* last prime minister, in a suburb of Paris. When the news broke, Hashemi Rafsanjani, then president of the Islamic Republic, publicly thanked Allah for having allowed "the severing of the head of the snake."[13]

Taheri even makes reference to one Algerian "specialist" named Momo le nain, who was recruited by an Islamic group known as the GIA specifically for the purpose of chopping off heads:

> In 1996 in Ben-Talha, a suburb of the capital Algiers, Momo cut off a record eighty-six heads in one night, including the heads of more than a dozen children. In recognition of his exemplary act of piety, the GIA sent him to Mecca for pilgrimage. Last time we checked, Momo was still at large somewhere in Algeria.[14]

Taheri likewise relates the situation in Pakistan where:

> Rival Sunni and Shiite groups have made a habit of sending chopped off heads of each other's activists by special delivery. By one estimate, over four hundred heads have been chopped off and mailed since 1990.[15]

And today, we see the power of beheading on the Indonesian island of Borneo, where Muslims have been using beheading as a means to drive out the Christian majority. Nearly half of the Christians have fled the island.

And beyond all of these very incriminating examples there are the government-sanctioned beheadings that take place weekly in Saudi Arabia after Friday prayers just outside the mosques:

> The Saudi government beheaded fifty-two men and one
> woman last year for crimes including murder, homosexuality,
> armed robbery, and drug trafficking.... A condemned convict
> is brought into the courtyard, hands tied, and forced to bow
> before an executioner, who swings a huge sword amid cries
> from onlookers of "*Allahu Akbar*!" Arabic for "God is great."[16]

Allahu Akbar was also the phrase screamed by the murderers of
Nicholas Berg, the Jewish-American contractor, and Kim-Sun-il,
the Korean translator and evangelical Christian whose dream of
one day preaching the Gospel to Muslims was both fulfilled and
brought to an end in the very same moment.

So while it is clear what the *history* of Islam teaches, we
also need to look at what the scriptures and scholars of Islam
have to say about this subject.

THE VALUE OF A NON-MUSLIM LIFE

Whenever a Muslim "extremist" carries out a horrifying act in
the name of Islam, most Muslims that I know are very quick to
state that, "That is not Islam! Islam is not to be judged by the
behavior of a few, but needs to be studied to see what it really
teaches." Fair enough. So the question then is: What does Islam
really teach about the killing of non-Muslims?

The first thing that should be pointed out is that according
to Islamic law, Muslims are, for all practical purposes, allowed
to kill non-Muslims. This is based on the law of *qisas*. *Qisas* is
essentially the law of reciprocity. It is the Islamic version of
"an eye for an eye." *Qisas*, for instance, states that if a Muslim
murders another Muslim, then that Muslim will likewise be
executed. Amazingly though, this law does not apply to a
Muslim who murders a non-Muslim. This teaching is found in
a *hadith* from Sahih Bukhari:

> Narrated Ash-Sha'bi: Abu Juhaifa said, "I asked Ali, 'What
> is [written] in this sheet of paper?' Ali replied, it deals with
> the *diyya* [compensatory blood money paid by the killer to
> the relatives of the victim], the ransom for the releasing of

the captives from the hands of the enemies, and *the law that no Muslim should be killed in* qisas [*equality in punishment*] *for the killing of [a disbeliever]* (emphasis mine).[17]

In some cases of course, the murderer might receive other penalties such as prison or a fine. But sadly, reality bears out that in a culture that does not value the life of non-Muslims as much as that of Muslims, a blind eye is most often turned to the murder of non-Muslims. If you go to the Web site of the Voice of the Martyrs at www.persecution.org, or of the Barnabas Fund at www.barnabasfund.org, you can read hundreds of stories, updated daily, of Christians mistreated or murdered without any legal repercussions for the Muslim murderer. The statement below is a perfect example of the mentality that I have often encountered when talking to many Muslims from the Middle East. This statement was made on an Internet interfaith discussion group. Notice the attitude toward the killing of non-Muslims (*kaffirs*):

> The *kaffirs* [unbelievers] have been attacking Muslim countries killing Muslim people from the beginning of time...when we have done nothing. Like the people of Israel attack the Muslims from Palestine because they do it for the land and because they hate Arabs/Muslims...we defend them for Allah. We try and spread Islam, the one and only true word of Allah. They rejected it, therefore we are allowed to kill them. *It is not* haram [*forbidden/illegal*] *to kill a* kaffir. Of course we want to *inshallah* [by the will of Allah] peacefully live with them and *inshallah* teach them about the beautiful religion (emphasis mine).[18]

Do you see the altogether twisted mentality expressed in the above comment? The "beautiful religion" that allows the killing of those who do not belong to it?

THE QUR'AN ON KILLING INFIDELS

Perhaps the Qur'anic verse most often quoted by Westerners to demonstrate the violent nature of the Islamic religion is the verse known within and without Islam as "the verse of the sword":

> So when the sacred months have passed away, then slay the idolaters wherever you find them, and take them captives and besiege them and lie in wait for them in every ambush, then if they repent and keep up prayer and pay the obligatory charity, leave their way free to them; surely Allah is forgiving, merciful -Surah 9:5 (Shakir)

Each time this verse is quoted, a Muslim states that this verse is not applicable today. While I would certainly love to believe that, the real question that needs to be asked is: How do the teachers and scholars of Islam interpret this verse? Do they say that it still applies today? The overriding majority of modern and classical Muslim scholars agree that it does. Remember the concept that the behavior of all Muslims is dictated by both the Qur'an and the Sunna (sayings, actions, and behavior of Muhammad). From Ibn Kathir, the renowned eighth-century scholar, we learn the true Islamic interpretation of this verse. Kathir begins by citing for support of his interpretation several eminent early Muslim *hadith* narrators/scholars; Mujahid, 'Amr bin Shu'ayb, Muhammad bin Ishaq, Qatadah, As-Suddi and 'Abdur-Rahman. Kathir then explains the meaning of the verse:

> The four months mentioned in this verse refer to the four-month grace period mentioned in an earlier verse: "So travel freely for four months throughout the land." Allah said next, "So when the Sacred Months have passed," meaning upon the end of the four months during which [Allah] prohibited you from fighting the idolaters, Muslims are to "fight and kill the idolaters wherever you may find them." "Wherever you find them" means on the earth in general.... Allah said here to execute some and keep some as prisoners. "Besiege them and lie in wait for them in each and every ambush" means do not wait until you find them; rather seek and besiege them in their areas and forts, gather

132

intelligence about them in the various roads and fairways so that what is made wide looks ever smaller to them. This way, they will have no choice but to die or embrace Islam.... Abu Bakr [Muhammad's closest friend and successor upon Muhammad's death] used this and other honorable verses as proof for fighting against those who refrained from paying the obligatory charity tax. This verse allowed fighting people unless and until they embrace Islam and implement its rulings and obligations.[19]

This doesn't leave any room for debate. Ibn Kathir lays it out as clearly as anyone could. We see that Muslims are allowed and even commanded to fight against the unbelievers (*mushrikun*) and even seek them out where they are in order to force them to convert to Islam or accept death. Again it must be noted that Kathir is not an "extremist" Muslim but is perhaps one of Islam's most universally received classical scholars.

Another pertinent verse from the Qur'an that applies to our discussion is the infamous "beheading" verse:

If you encounter [in war] those who disbelieve, you may strike the necks. -Surah 47:4 (Khalifa)

When ye encounter the infidels, strike off their heads. -Surah 47:4 (Rodwell)

Ibn Kathir explains that the purpose of this verse is to:

[Guide] the believers to what they should employ in their fight against the idolators. Allah says, "So when you meet those who disbelieve [in battle], smite their necks," which means when you fight against them, cut them down totally with your swords. "Until you have fully defeated them" meaning you have killed and utterly destroyed them. This is referring to the prisoners of war whom you have captured.[20]

So when we look at these verses we see that Muslims are commanded to behead (or at a bare minimum "smite the necks") of those non-Muslims they fight. Sheik Omar Bakri Muhammad, judge of the *shari'ah* (Islamic law) court in Great Britain, as well as the secretary general of the Islamic World League and the spokesman for the International Islamic Front, however, has a slightly different opinion:

> What's the verdict? "The punishment of those who wage war against Allah and His apostle and strive to make mischief in the land is only this, that they should be murdered or crucified or their hands and their feet should be cut off on opposite sides or they should be imprisoned; this shall be as a disgrace for them in this world, and in the hereafter they shall have a grievous chastisement."[21]

After examining just a sampling of Islamic texts as well as the opinions of Islamic scholars, spokesmen, and ordinary Muslims, we see that Islam not only commands the killing of non-Muslims but also supports a culture where killing non-Muslims has become an acceptable practice. But before we finish this discussion, there is one more very specific tradition that will surely come into play if indeed the person of the Mahdi ever becomes a reality.

DEATH TO THOSE WHO DISPUTE THE AUTHORITY OF THE *CALIPH*

The leadership role of a *caliph* in Islam is a very powerful concept. The *caliph* is viewed as the successor of Muhammad and the leader of all Muslims. He is, in a sense, the Pope of the Muslim world. The last *caliph* that both Sunnis and Shi'a accept as justifiably elected was Ali, Muhammad's cousin and son-in-law. Ali died in AD 661. Since then, many other *caliphs* have held office, but none that held the universal sway that the first four *caliphs* held. Muslims have awaited the restoration of the *caliphate* to restore unity and leadership to Islam worldwide. As we have already seen, the Mahdi is expected to fulfill this role. From a *hadith* in *Sahih Muslim* we read of the punishment for those who dispute the authority of the *caliph*:

> Whoever wishes to be delivered from the fire and enter the garden should die with faith in Allah and the Last Day.... He who swears allegiance to a *caliph* should give him the pledge of his hand and the sincerity of his heart [i. e. submit to him both outwardly as well as inwardly]. He

should obey him to the best of his capacity. *If a man comes forward, disputing his* [the caliph's] *authority, they* [the Muslims] *should behead the latter* (emphasis mine).[22]

The Saudi Arabian government holds this opinion as well. On the official Saudi Arabian Islamic Affairs Department (IAD) Web site, we find a similar declaration:

The Noble Prophet said: "It is obligatory upon a Muslim to listen and obey [to the authority of the *caliph*] whether he likes it or not...one who has already taken an oath of allegiance to one leader [*imam*] and has committed his hand and heart to him, should obey him as much as may be possible for him. *If somebody else opposes and contests the authority of that leader* [imam], *the said opponent should be beheaded*" (emphasis mine).[23]

According to Islamic law, anyone who disagrees with the authority of a seated *caliph* should be beheaded.

SUMMARY AND CONCLUSION

Now let us review the points that have been made. First, we have seen that the end times as described in the Bible will be a time when Christians will face persecution and martyrdom for their faith. The specific manner of death that the Bible mentions for Christians is martyrdom by beheading. As we have most clearly demonstrated, it is quite undeniable that beheading is a tradition that stretches throughout Islamic history. Islam itself has thoroughly documented the fact that Muhammad and his immediate successors practiced beheading as the specific means to kill "the enemies of Islam." This practice has continued in certain quarters of Islam to this very day. The Qur'an itself actually encourages beheading, or at a bare minimum, "smiting the necks" of "idolaters" and any "prisoners of war." We noted some examples of the beheadings of such "prisoners of war" recently in Iraq and elsewhere. The death sentence is also prescribed for those who do not submit to or agree with the authority of the *caliph*. As

135

such it is actually very fair to assume that in the Islamic vision of the last days, if a *caliph*, specifically the Mahdi, comes forward and accepts the notion that all Christians, Jews, Israelis, and any who support them are considered "enemies of Islam," then it would be universally lawful and indeed obligatory for all Muslims to "make war" and "smite the necks" of all Christians, Jews, or Westerners, etc., as well as any who dispute the authority of the *caliph*.

Once again then, Islam, its practices, and its teachings, fulfill exactly the description of the forces that will gain power and dominate the world in the biblical end-time scenario. Having seen the murderous nature of the Islamic texts, as well as the proper Islamic interpretation of them, let us see the reality of how this mentality plays out in the mind of an ordinary Muslim from the Middle East. Following is a post from an Islamic/interfaith Internet message board. It is the kind of post that is only too common on such forums. We end this chapter with one Muslim's thoughts regarding the murder of Daniel Pearl, the slain American journalist:

> First Pearl is a Jew, a *munafiq* [hypocrite], a spy, and a *kaffir* [unbeliever]. Do not be fooled by these people. Their hatred for Islam can be seen from their mouths and what their heart conceals is much worse. I do not see where the sick part is in slaughtering.... In Islam we...can't even torture the *kaffir*—we just slit their throat, and it's proven when you pass a special area in the neck, they no longer feel pain. And remember when we Muslims capture a Muslim *munafiq*, we do the same to him, we slaughter him. What do you think of a dirty Jew, stupid *munafiq*, two-timing spy, and a *kaffir*? We do the same to him. *Walhumdulilah*. [Thanks be to Allah] And remember the *Rasoul* [Muhammad] slaughtered a great number of Jews in one battle; the best of creation did this, because the Jews backstabbed Prophet Muhammad. And if you think this is still sick, *inshaallaahi* [I hope by the will of Allah] you're alive when Mahdi is around cause your going to see many Jew/*munafiqqin* [Jews/hypocrites] heads on the floor.

CHAPTER FIFTEEN

ISLAM AND THE GOAL OF WORLD DOMINATION

*S*atan's goal has always been* to cause the inhabitants of the earth to worship him rather than God. As such Satan has long had a very specific plan to raise up his own worship movement that will cover the face of the earth. Those who believe the Bible know this to be true. Through the Antichrist and his False Prophet the Bible says that Satan will come very close to achieving his goal just prior to the return of Jesus:

> The dragon [Satan] gave the beast [the Antichrist] his power and his throne and great authority.... And he was given authority over every tribe, people, language, and nation. All inhabitants of the earth will worship the beast—all whose names have not been written in the Book of Life belonging to the Lamb that was slain from the creation of the world (Revelation 13:2, 4-8).

This future worship movement will touch "every tribe, people, language, and nation." The Bible teaches that at this time, whoever is not a worshipper of the One True God and His Son Jesus Christ will eventually be deceived into worshiping Satan, the invisible spirit behind the deceptive worship movement. As we have already seen, the vehicle that Satan uses to bring about his own movement is the Antichrist and his "beast kingdom," a powerful empire with an equally powerful military machine. Daniel the Prophet describes this empire and its military as a force "terrifying and frightening and very powerful" which "will devour the whole earth."

> After that, in my vision at night I looked, and there before me was a fourth beast—terrifying and frightening and very powerful. It had large iron teeth; *it crushed and devoured its victims and trampled underfoot whatever was left....* The fourth beast is a fourth kingdom that will appear on earth. It will be different from all the other kingdoms and *will devour the whole earth, trampling it down and crushing it* (Daniel 7:7, 23, emphasis mine).

Thus the Bible gives us a clear picture of the nature of Satan's final swan song before Jesus casts him into the Lake of Fire for eternity. The Bible has clearly forewarned us of Satan's coming empire, the goal of which will be nothing less than total world domination. The demands of this empire will be much more than mere allegiance to its governmental role: total submission to and worship of its leader, the Antichrist, and, ultimately, the Devil. Again, whoever does not submit to this brutal religious system will become its target.

ISLAM AND THE GOAL OF WORLD DOMINATION

In order to understand Islam properly, one must understand the way that Islam understands itself. Islam views itself as the only true religion—indeed the only religion worthy to be practiced. As such Islam has as one of its goals total world domination. Islam's driving goal is to literally eradicate what it sees as the false and misplaced worship of all other religions. Until the day that everyone says, "none has the right to be worshipped other than Allah," Islam will continue its fight against unbelievers and unbelieving nations. The texts and scholars of Islam teach that all Muslims must strive for global domination at all times, not just wait idly by for the Mahdi and the Islamic Jesus to accomplish it for them. This striving for Islam's furtherance and eventual world domination is called *jihad*. Indeed *jihad* is a basic requirement of all Muslims everywhere. It is an absolutely obligatory component of Islam.

Now Muslim apologists and propagandists will be quick to argue that *jihad* is not about fighting for world domination. Some will make such misleading remarks as "*jihad* is merely about overcoming adversity." Or they will point out that the "greater *jihad*" is a struggle against one's self. While this inner struggle is a legitimate aspect of *jihad*, do not be deceived: The *jihad* that is obligatory for all Muslims to fight against one's inner weaknesses in no way lessens the centrality of the demand of Islam upon all Muslims to wage *jihad* against the unbelieving world until Islam reigns supreme. This may include warfare in the intellectual or the political or other arenas, but wherever a Muslim engages in this fight, it is viewed as just that—a fight for the eventual global domination and universal supremacy of Islam.

JIHAD

The word *jihad* stems from the Arabic root word J-H-D, which means "strive." There are five types of *jihad*:

- *Jihad al-nafs* (striving against one's inner self)

- *Jihad al-Shaitan* (striving against Satan)

- *Jihad al-kuffaar* (striving against the disbelievers)

- *Jihad al-munafiqeen* (striving against the hypocrites)

- *Jihad al-faasiqeen* (striving against corrupt Muslims)

As already stated, all five forms of *jihad* are obligatory for all Muslims. If you pay attention to the discussion of *jihad* in the media, you will find endless articles and claims by Muslims that misrepresent *jihad*. But as stated earlier, those who deny the central aspect of an outward *jihad* in Islam are either ignorant or lying. In fact, lying to hide or misrepresent the true nature of Islam to the unbelieving world is actually part and parcel of Islam's method of carrying out *jihad* against non-

Muslims. We will take a look Islam's doctrine of lying in the next chapter.

Despite what the advertisers of a nicer, more peaceful Islam say, Muhammad clearly made the claim that his commission was to fight against the unbelievers until they all submit to Islam and worship Allah. Since the time of Muhammad, global domination has been the goal of Islam.

> Allah's Apostle (Muhammad) said, "I have been ordered to fight the people till they say: 'None has the right to be worshipped but Allah.'"[1]

> Fight those from among the People of the Book, who believe not in Allah, nor in the Last Day, nor hold as unlawful what Allah and His Messenger have declared to be unlawful, nor follow the true religion, until they pay the tax considering it a favor and acknowledge their subjection. -Surah 9:29 (Sher Ali)

> O ye who believe! Fight those of the disbelievers who are near to you, and let them find harshness in you, and know that Allah is with those who keep their duty (unto Him). -Surah 9:123 (Pickthall)

Unquestionably, we see that Muhammad encouraged the spread of his religion by force. Now, one might argue that Christianity also has a goal of spreading its message throughout the earth. While this is true, Christianity does not have a goal of fighting against non-Christians, but rather presenting the Gospel message, or "good news" to everyone in order that they have the option to freely accept or reject God's offer of forgiveness. As someone once said, "evangelism" (preaching the Christian message to non-Christians) is merely one beggar telling the other beggars where the food is.

In calling new believers to follow Him and serve God, Jesus makes this beautiful statement:

> Come to me, all you who are weary and burdened, and I will give you rest. Take my yoke upon you and learn from me, for I am gentle and humble in heart, and you will find

rest for your souls. For my yoke is easy and my burden is light (Matthew 11:28-30).

Muhammad calls his followers to something far more burdensome:

> Warfare is ordained for you, though it is hateful unto you; but it may happen that ye hate a thing which is good for you, and it may happen that ye love a thing which is bad for you. Allah knoweth, ye know not. -Surah 2:216 (Pickthall)

It would be quite easy to list several pages of verses from the Qur'an and *hadiths* that reflect this mindset of *jihad* and fighting against unbelievers for the express purpose of the furtherance of Islam. It is awfully difficult to take these verses out of context. Nevertheless, as I have said, many Western Muslims continue to claim that the Qur'anic verses that speak of *jihad* refer only to overcoming adversity or waging defensive war. As one Muslim commentator has said: "Don't believe those moderate Muslims in the Western media who tell you that *jihad* means 'overcoming adversity.'"[2]

Or as the popular Muslim author and teacher Muhammad Saeed al-Qahtani states:

> *Jihad* is an act of worship; it is one of the supreme forms of devotion to Allah.... They say that *jihad* is only for defense. This lie must be exposed...[3]

Rather than getting caught up in an in-house Islamic argument, we will simply examine the opinions of several prominent Muslim scholars throughout Islam's history as well as the leaders and representatives of Islam in Western countries today to see what Islam really teaches.

THE SCHOLARS ON *JIHAD*

Ibn Kathir lays out the prominent role of offensive *jihad* in Islam's early days as he comments on Surah 9:123 above:

Allah commands the believers to fight the disbelievers, the closest in area to the Islamic state, then the farthest. This is why the Messenger of Allah started fighting the idolaters in the Arabian Peninsula. When he finished with them...he then started fighting the People of the Scriptures (Jews and Christians). After Muhammad's death, his executor, friend, and *caliph*, Abu Bakr, became the leader.... On behalf of the Prophet, Abu Bakr...started preparing the Islamic armies to fight the Roman cross worshippers, and the Persian fire worshippers. By the blessing of his mission, Allah opened the lands for him and brought down Caesar and Kisra and those who obeyed them among the servants. Abu Bakr spent their treasures in the cause of Allah, just as the Messenger of Allah had foretold would happen. This mission (of world domination) continued after Abu Bakr at the hands of he whom Abu Bakr chose to be his successor...Umar bin Al-Khattab. With Umar, Allah humiliated the disbelievers, suppressed the tyrants and hypocrites, and opened the eastern and western parts of the world. The treasures of various countries were brought to Umar from near and far provinces, and he divided them according to the legitimate and accepted method. Umar then died.... Then, the Companions among the Muslims...agreed to choose after Umar, Uthman bin Affan.... During Uthman's reign, Islam wore its widest garment and Allah's unequivocal proof was established in various parts of the world over the necks of the servants. Islam appeared in the eastern and western parts of the world and Allah's Word was elevated and His religion apparent. The pure religion reached its deepest aims against Allah's enemies, and whenever Muslims overcame a community, they moved to the next one, and then the next one, crushing the tyrannical evil doers. They did this in reverence to Allah's statement, O you who believe! Fight those of the disbelievers who are close to you.[4]

It is clear that Muhammad, and then his successors, Caliph Abu Bakr, Caliph Umar, and Caliph Uthman, all attacked the surrounding nations offensively for the purpose of spreading Islam. These were not, as is claimed by the historical revisionists, defensive wars. They were offensive wars whose goal was to force the victims to submit to Islam or be "crushed."

Ibn Khaldun, a famous fourteenth-century Islamic historian and philosopher, in his classic and most notable work, the *Muqaddimah*, says of *jihad*:

> In the Muslim community, the holy war is a religious duty, because of the universalism of the (Muslim) mission and (the obligation to) convert everybody to Islam either *by persuasion or by force*. Therefore, the *caliphate* (spiritual), the royal (government and military) authority are united in Islam, so that the person in charge can devote the available strength to both of them at the same time (emphasis mine).[5]

In his book *Jurisprudence in Muhammad's Biography*, the renowned Egyptian scholar from Al-Azhar University, Dr. Muhammad Sa'id Ramadan al-Buti, writes that offensive and not defensive war is the "noblest Holy War" within Islam:

> The Holy War [Islamic *Jihad*], as it is known in Islamic jurisprudence, *is basically an offensive war*. This is the duty of Muslims in every age when the needed military power becomes available to them. This is the phase in which the meaning of holy war has taken its final form. Thus the apostle of Allah said: "I was commanded to fight the people until they believe in Allah and his messages..." *The concept of Holy War* [Jihad] *in Islam does not take into consideration whether defensive or an offensive war*. Its goal is the exaltation of the Word of Allah and the construction of Islamic society and the establishment of Allah's Kingdom on Earth *regardless of the means*. The means would be offensive warfare. In this case, it is the apex, *the noblest Holy War* (emphasis mine).[6]

According to the *Encyclopedia of Islam*, "the fight is obligatory even when the unbelievers have not started it."[7] The concept of *jihad* in Islam is to literally attack unbelievers for the purpose of converting them to Islam "by persuasion or by force," "even when they have not started it."

GLOBAL DOMINATION

Born in 1905, Mawlana Sayid Abul Ala Mawdudi was an Islamic scholar from the Indian subcontinent. His sermons (*khutbat*) and writings are world-renowned. He is viewed throughout the Islamic world as one of Islam's greatest scholars. Here is what he had to say about Islam and global domination:

> Islam is not a normal religion like the other religions in the world, and Muslim nations are not like normal nations. Muslim nations are very special because they have a command from Allah to *rule the entire world and to be over every nation in the world* (emphasis mine).[8]

Mawdudi explains Islam's goals and purpose:

> Islam is a revolutionary faith that comes to destroy any government made by man. Islam doesn't look for a nation to be in a better condition than another nation. Islam doesn't care about the land or who owns the land. The goal of Islam is to rule the entire world and submit all of mankind to the faith of Islam. Any nation or power that gets in the way of that goal, Islam will fight and destroy. In order to fulfill that goal, Islam can use every power available every way it can be used to bring worldwide revolution. This is *Jihad*.[9]

We have seen what some of Islam's most respected scholars have said about *jihad* and Islam's goal of global domination. Their viewpoint is undeniably clear. But what do the more modern, Western Muslim leaders have to say about this subject?

MODERN WESTERN MUSLIMS ON THE ISLAMIC GOAL OF WORLD DOMINATION

Aduallah al-Araby in his book *The Islamization of America* cites a very frightening letter from one Catholic archbishop to the Pope. In this open letter to the Pope, the Archbishop of Izmir (Smyrna), Turkey, the Reverend Guiseppe Germano Barnardini, spoke of a recent gathering of Christians and Muslims for the purpose of interfaith dialogue. An excerpt from his letter recounts that during the meeting, an authoritative Muslim stood up and spoke very calmly and assuredly: "Thanks to your democratic laws, we will invade you. Thanks to our religious laws, we will dominate you."[10]

If you go to the Web site of almost any mosque in the United States, you will invariably see a link to the Council on American-Islamic Relations. CAIR, as it is called, is a Washington-based Islamic group that likes to present itself as a moderate Islamic civil rights group. "We are similar to a Muslim NAACP," says spokesman Ibrahim Hooper. "Since its founding in 1994, CAIR has been garnering sizeable donations, invitations to the White House, respectful media citations, and a serious hearing by corporations."[11] Yet, according to Omar Ahmed, chairman of the board of CAIR:

> Islam isn't in America to be equal to any other faith, but to become dominant. The Qur'an should be the highest authority in America, and Islam the only accepted religion on Earth.[12]

This is the same Omar Ahmed who tore into the Reverend Franklin Graham for calling Islam "an evil religion." Mr. Ahmed addressed Graham in an open statement:

> Learn more about Islam and Muslims before you repeat your erroneous and divisive statements about one of the three great Abrahamic religions, Judaism, Christianity, and Islam. Such statements only sow animosity and mistrust among Americans. As a religious leader you should instead work to rebuild our national foundation instead of trying to tear it down.[13]

Perhaps Reverend Graham was more in touch with the true totalitarian doctrines of Islam than Mr. Ahmed realized. Perhaps Mr. Graham had read Mr. Ahmed's statement regarding Islam's goal of domination in America and abroad when he made his statement. In any case, through these two statements, it is easy to see the double-speak displayed by Mr. Ahmed and many like him. When speaking privately to Muslims, Mr. Ahmed speaks of Islam as the only valid religion with a goal to take over America, but when addressing the media, he speaks of "the three great Abrahamic religions" and then he accuses Mr. Graham of being "divisive."

Daniel Pipes, a scholar of militant Islam and director of the Middle East Forum, points out the case of one prominent American Muslim's open aspirations to take over America. Pipes introduces one Isamil Al-Faruqi:

> Ismail Al-Faruqi a Palestinian immigrant who founded the International Institute of Islamic Thought and taught for many years at Temple University in Philadelphia. "Nothing could be greater," Al-Faruqi wrote in the early 1980s, "than this youthful, vigorous, and rich continent [of North America] turning away from its past evil and marching forward under the banner of *Allahu Akbar* [Allah is great]."[14]

In England, and throughout Europe, Islam has progressed in strength far beyond that of Islam in America. Therefore, in such a context, we see aggressive statements made far more openly. As early as 1989, Europeans were shocked to see thousands of Muslims openly protest in the streets of Britain, France, Germany, Belgium, and the Netherlands, carrying signs with the provocative slogan: "Islam—our religion today, your religion tomorrow."[15]

Dated June 15, 1990, *The Muslim Manifesto*, published by the late Dr. Kalim Siddiqui, then the head of the Muslim Institute (now the Muslim Parliament of Great Britain), states:

> Jihad *is a basic requirement of Islam* and living in Britain or having British nationality by birth or naturalisation does not absolve the Muslim from his or her duty to participate in *Jihad* (emphasis mine).[16]

Dr. Siddiqui does not exclude Britain from the places where "armed struggle" is necessary. *Jihad* is obligatory everywhere. And as time has passed, the call to *jihad* in Europe has progressed to the point where radical Muslim leaders proclaim it openly in the streets. From the *New York Times*, April 26, 2004, we read:

> The call to *jihad* is rising in the streets of Europe.... In this former industrial town north of London, a small group of young Britons...say they would like to see Prime Minister Tony Blair dead or deposed and an Islamic flag hanging outside No. 10 Downing Street. They swear allegiance to Osama bin Laden and his goal of toppling Western democracies to establish an Islamic superstate under *shariah* law, like Afghanistan under the Taliban. They call the Sept. 11 hijackers the "Magnificent 19" and regard the Madrid train bombings as a clever way to drive a wedge into Europe. Their leader, Sheik Omar Bakri Mohammad, spoke of his adherence to Osama bin Laden. If Europe fails to heed Mr. bin Laden's offer of a truce—provided that all foreign troops are withdrawn from Iraq in three months—Muslims will no longer be restrained from attacking the Western countries that play host to them, the *sheik* said. "All Muslims of the West will be obliged," he said, to "become his sword" in a new battle. Europeans take heed, he added, saying, "It is foolish to fight people who want death—that is what they are looking for".... And he warned Western leaders, "You may kill bin Laden, but the phenomenon, you cannot kill it—you cannot destroy it. Our Muslim brothers from abroad will come one day and conquer here and then we will live under Islam in dignity," he said.[17]

Dr. Siddiqui and Sheik Omar Bakri Mohammad are far from alone in their calls for radical Islamic *jihad* against their homes in Europe:

> Abu Hamza, the cleric accused of tutoring Richard Reid before he tried to blow up a Paris-to-Miami jetliner with explosives hidden in his shoe, urged a crowd of two hundred outside his former Finsbury Park mosque to embrace death and the "culture of martyrdom."[18]

It is not surprising then, that in the war with Afghanistan, American forces captured at least three British citizens. Or that in

April of 2003, two British citizens conducted a suicide bombing that killed three others at a café in Tel Aviv. And when Muslim fanatics beheaded *Wall Street Journal* reporter Daniel Pearl in Pakistan, the world learned that Omar Sheik Saeed, a well-educated native of Britain once described as "a perfect Englishman," had transformed into a radical Muslim, eventually masterminding the kidnapping and videotaped beheading of Pearl. Should we really be surprised? Should we be surprised that Islam has this effect on people? If prominent Muslim leaders in Europe openly praise Osama bin Laden and call for *jihad* and "martyrdom," then why should we be surprised when impressionable young Muslims answer this call all over the world? While fifteen of the nineteen 9/11 hijackers were Saudi Arabians, will the world be shocked when British Muslims carry out such an act? How would the West have reacted if the "black boxes" salvaged from the wreckage of the World Trade Center had contained recordings of young men yelling "*Allahu Akhbar!*" in distinctly British or American accents?

CONCLUSION

Muslims in the West regularly refer to Islam as the "religion of peace," yet this so-called "religion of peace" is responsible for over 90 percent of all fighting presently occurring in the world. Think about that fact. Islam motivates the vast majority of world terrorism, violence, and war. There are about four hundred recognized terrorist groups in the world. Over 90 percent of these are radical Islamic terrorist groups. Over 90 percent of the current world fighting involves Islamist terror movements.[19]

The endless goal of moderate Muslim apologists is to make the claim that the radical terrorist groups are not behaving in an Islamic way. While I have no doubt that many moderate Muslims have a strong disdain for the murderous behavior of many of the most violent groups, the terrorists are actually carrying out a very legitimate aspect of Islam as defined by Islam's texts, scholars, and representatives. They indeed behave in an Islamic way. They are behaving like Muhammad and his successors. While it is often said that the terrorists have "hijacked" Islam, judged by what Islam really teaches, it is in reality the so-called moderate Muslims who are trying to change the true teachings of Islam.

When we look at the growth rates of Islam combined with the concept of *jihad* in Islam, and the growing popularity of its most radical interpretation, even in the West, the concept of a future Islamofascist world dictator becomes a genuine possibility. Based on trends and statistics alone, it really doesn't take a stretch to see the possibility of this reality within this century. The Bible teaches that in the future, a man will arise whose sole driving goal will be to achieve complete world domination through his political-military-religious empire. Islam has this very same goal inherent in its most core doctrines. And today, as we hear the call to *jihad* trumpeted ever louder by radical Muslim leaders all over the world, Islam slowly moves ever so much closer to achieving that goal.

CHAPTER SIXTEEN

UNDERSTANDING DISHONESTY AND DECEIT IN ISLAM

The following discussion is so very important for two reasons. First, because of the prominence of deception in the last days, and second, because of the grave implications that deception for the cause of Islam has for the spread of Islam in the West.

When people first become curious and wish to begin learning about Islam, it is imperative that they first understand the degree to which lying is not only permitted, but actually fostered and even, at times, commanded in Islam. When a Christian wishes to teach others about Christianity, it is simply understood that honesty will be an essential aspect of that sharing. Westerners, however, have a hard time relating to the fact that purposeful exaggerations, covering of the truth, and occasionally outright lying form a core part of the religion of Islam. Specific doctrines and traditions foster a culture of dishonesty within Islam. Now, of course, some verses and traditions in Islam do discourage lying: "And cover not truth with falsehood, nor conceal the truth when ye know (what it is) -Surah 2:42 (Yusuf Ali)." But unfortunately, as we are about to see, for many Muslims, it is the exceptions to the rule that have actually become the rule itself.

DECEPTION AND JIHAD

In order to understand how a religion can rationalize and justify lying, we must first briefly revisit the concept of *jihad* and the goals of Islam. We have already discussed this in the last chapter, but will point out again that Islam essentially views *jihad* as a struggle to bring all things into submission to Allah and Islam. The battlefields that *jihad* is fought on can be viewed on a spectrum. On one side of the spectrum is the personal inner struggle fought by every Muslim who wishes to overcome his or her own personal weaknesses or inner demons. As we move across the spectrum there is the need to wage *jihad* to cause other individuals to submit to Islam. This is, of course, what Christianity calls evangelism. In Islam it is called *dawah*. Flowing on down the spectrum, there is the imperative for Islam to take over local and eventually national governments. This is the point, unfortunately, where the true face—the violent face—of Islam is often revealed and where *jihad* usually begins to get bloody. This reality is seen throughout the world today. So while many people in the West think of *jihad* as simply fighting against non-Muslim governments and nations, the concept in Islam actually includes all aspects of life. So, in the Muslim mind, even the struggle to convert non-Muslims to Islam is part of *jihad*. Evangelism in Islam is more than just "sharing the good news;" *it is war*. With this in mind, it is vital that we note Muhammad's famous saying that "war is deception."[1] Thus, when dealing with non-Muslims, Islam encourages Muslims to use an aggressive *jihad*/wartime mentality defined by deception. Indeed, until non-Muslims come to realize the degree to which this mentality plays out when dealing with Muslims, it will be only too easy to lose touch with a healthy sense of objectivity. When dealing with someone who is purposefully deceptive, trusting individuals—as so many in the West are these days—are like sheep led to the slaughter.

This mentality of *evangelism as jihad* finds its support in Islam under the category of two specific doctrines called *kithman* and *taqiya*.

KITHMAN: HIDING THE TRUTH

Kithman is a command to deliberately conceal one's beliefs. Primarily practiced by the minority Shi'a Muslims, this doctrine is articulated by Imam Jafar Sadiq, the sixth *imam* of Shi'a Islam:

> One who exposes something from our religion is like one who intentionally kills us.[2]

> You belong to a religion that whosoever conceals it, Allah will honor him and whosoever reveals it, Allah will disgrace him.[3]

So Shi'a Muslims are commanded to hide what they truly believe in order to mislead outsiders as to the true nature of their religion. One cannot help but to immediately think of Jesus' words when He told His followers never to hide their religion:

> You are the light of the world. A city on a hill cannot be hidden. Neither do people light a lamp and put it under a bowl. Instead they put it on its stand, and it gives light to everyone in the house. In the same way, let your light shine before men, that they may see your good deeds and praise your Father in heaven (Matthew 5:14-16).

But instead, Shi'a Muslims "belong to a religion that whosoever conceals it, Allah will honor him and whosoever reveals it, Allah will disgrace him." That is the doctrine of *kithman*. To most Westerners, this concept is unimaginable and completely contrary to reason. If you have something good, then share it. If you have something to hide, then I probably don't want it anyway.

There is essentially no difference between the doctrine of *kithman* and the doctrine of *taqiya*. *Taqiya* is defined by one Shi'a Muslim commentator thusly:

> The word "*al-Taqiyya*" literally means: "Concealing or disguising one's beliefs, convictions, ideas, feelings, opinions, and/or strategies at a time of imminent danger, whether now

or later in time, to save oneself from physical and/or mental injury." A one-word translation would be "Dissimulation."[4]

This same commentator, however, in an article in *A Shiite Encyclopedia*, goes on to state that "the true spirit of '*al-Taqiyya*' is better embodied in the single word 'diplomacy.'" Indeed diplomacy is quite a "diplomatic" definition.

The doctrines of *kithman* and *taqiya* are often said to be strictly Shi'a doctrines, and Sunni Muslims deny that either doctrine is part of their tradition. Unfortunately, this is merely another deception. Next, we will run through some of the Sunni traditions that prove the universal application of *taqiya* within Islam.

TAQIYA: FOUNDATION FOR DECEPTION

The Qur'an teaches that Muslims may deny their faith in order to protect themselves. Muslims who deny their faith will receive forgiveness as long as their true faith was not really shaken (i.e., their denial was a lie in the purest sense) and only if their denial of faith was for the purpose of avoiding harm (primarily while living among non-Muslims):

> Anyone who, after accepting faith in Allah, utters unbelief, except under compulsion, his heart remaining firm in faith—but such as open their breast to unbelief, on them is wrath from Allah, and theirs will be a dreadful penalty." -Surah 16:106

Sunni scholar Ibn Kathir elaborates on the meaning of this verse in his classic commentary on the Qur'an:

> This refers to a group of people who were oppressed in Mecca and whose position with their own people was weak, so they went along with them when they were tried by them.... Allah tells them that after this, meaning after their giving in [to the non-Muslims by denying their faith] when put to the test, he will forgive them and show mercy to them when they are resurrected.[5]

As long as a Muslim lives in a country where Islam exists as a minority, in "a weakened state," then deceptiveness is allowed. When challenged by non-Muslims to blaspheme Allah, they "went along with them."

> The nonbelievers arrested 'Ammar Ibn Yasir and tortured him until he uttered foul words about the Prophet (Muhammad), and praised their gods and idols; and when they released him, he went straight to the Prophet. The Prophet said: "Is there something on your mind?" 'Ammar Ibn Yasir said: "Bad news! They would not release me until I defamed you and praised their gods!" The Prophet said: "How do you find your heart to be?" 'Ammar answered: "Comfortable with faith." So the Prophet said: "Then if they come back for you, then do the same thing all over again." Allah at that moment revealed the verse: "…except under compulsion, his heart remaining firm in faith…" -Surah 16:106[6]

So Muhammad actually encouraged Muslims to lie and blaspheme and deny their beliefs if that would protect them, as long as they remained "comfortable with faith." Ibn Abbas, the most renowned and trusted narrator of tradition in the sight of the Sunnis, confirms this notion. "*Taqiyya* is (merely) the uttering of the tongue, while the heart is comfortable with faith."[7]

This stands, of course, in direct contrast to the attitude of millions of Christians throughout history who have refused to renounce Christ and have accepted instead death and martyrdom.

The Qur'an also commands Muslims not to befriend non-Muslims—again, though, unless doing so can help protect the Muslim from harm:

> Let not the believers take for friends or helpers unbelievers rather than believers: if any do that, in nothing will there be help from Allah: except that you guard yourselves fully against them. -Surah 3: 28

Ibn Kathir again comments that:

> Allah prohibited his believing servants from becoming supporters of the disbelievers, or to take them as comrades

with whom they develop friendships.... Allah warned against such behavior when he said, "O you who believe! Take not my enemies and your enemies as friends, showing affection towards them. And whosoever of you does that, then indeed he has gone astray from the straight path." And, "O you who believe! Take not the Jews and the Christians as friends; they are but friends of each other. And whoever befriends them, then surely, he is one of them." Allah said next, "Unless you indeed fear a danger from them," meaning, except those [Muslims] who in some areas or times fear for their safety from the disbelievers. In this case, such believers are allowed to show friendship to the disbelievers outwardly, *but never inwardly.* For instance, Al-Bukhari recorded that Abu Ad-Darda' said, *"We smile in the face of some people although our hearts curse them"* (emphasis mine).[8]

Ibn Kathir, then goes on to utterly destroy the notion that *taqiya* is for Shi'a Muslims only when he says, *"Taqiya* is allowed until the Day of Resurrection."

We see that *taqiya* is indeed a doctrine for all Muslims that allows them to deny any aspect of their faith in order to protect themselves from harm. The problem, however, is that in practice, the definition of "harm" has come to include a mere harming of one's reputation as a representative of Islam. Thus Muslims may deny or misrepresent any aspect of their faith in order to help correct the negative image of Islam in non-Muslim countries. Ibn Taymiyah, the renowned Muslim philosopher, validates this point very strongly in his book titled *The Sword on the Neck of the Accuser of Muhammad*:

> Believers when in a weakened stage in a non-Muslim country should forgive and be patient with People of the Book (i.e., Jews and Christians) when they insult Allah and his prophet by any means. Believers should lie to People of the Book to protect their lives *and their religion* (emphasis mine).[9]

DECEPTION JUSTIFIED TO GAIN WEALTH

Despite Ibn Taymiyah, however, many will make the claim (possibly as a deception tactic itself) that Muslims should use *taqiya* only to protect life. Far from it. Muhammad even allowed lying for the sake of gaining wealth:

> After the conquest of the city of Khaybar by the Muslims, the Prophet was approached by Hajaj Ibn 'Aalat and told: "O Prophet of Allah: I have in Mecca some excess wealth and some relatives, and I would like to have them back; am I excused if I badmouth you to escape persecution?" The Prophet excused him and said: "Say whatever you have to say."[10]

The "any end justifies the means" approach to life and religion that Muhammad displays shines through clearly here. And there are numerous other examples of Muhammad encouraging his followers to lie as a means to achieve the end goal of the furtherance of Islam.

DECEPTION JUSTIFIED TO MURDER THE ENEMIES OF ISLAM

> Allah's Apostle said, "Who is willing to kill Ka'b bin Al-Ashraf who has hurt Allah and His Apostle?" Thereupon Muhammad bin Maslama got up saying, "O Allah's Apostle! Would you like that I kill him?" The Prophet said, "Yes." Muhammad bin Maslama said, "Then allow me to say a (false) thing (i.e. to deceive Kab)." The Prophet said, "You may say it."[11]

Abdullah Al-Araby, a Middle-Eastern-born authority on Islam, in an article entitled *Lying in Islam*, details another story of Muhammad's permissiveness toward lying to achieve the death of his enemies. This time the victim's name was Shaaban Ibn Khalid al-Hazly:

> It was rumored that Shaaban was gathering an army to wage war on Mohammed. Mohammed retaliated by ordering Abdullah Ibn Anis to kill Shaaban. The would-be

killer asked the prophet's permission to lie. Mohammed agreed and then ordered the killer to lie by stating that he was a member of the Khazaa clan. When Shaaban saw Abdullah coming, he asked him, "From what tribe are you?" Abdullah answered, "From Khazaa." He then added, "I have heard that you are gathering an army to fight Mohammed and I came to join you." Abdullah started walking with Shaaban telling him how Mohammed came to them with the heretical teachings of Islam, and complained how Mohammed badmouthed the Arab patriarchs and ruined the Arabs' hopes. They continued in conversation until they arrived at Shaaban's tent. Shaaban's companions departed and Shaaban invited Abdullah to come inside and rest. Abdullah sat there until the atmosphere was quiet and he sensed that everyone was asleep. Abdullah severed Shaaban's head and carried it to Mohammed as a trophy. When Mohammed sighted Abdullah, he jubilantly shouted, "Your face has been triumphant (*Aflaha al- wajho*)." Abdullah returned the greeting by saying, "It is your face, Apostle of Allah, who has been triumphant. (*Aflaha wajhoka, ye rasoul Allah*)."[12]

So we see that, again, lying is permissible for any number of reasons. As long as the end goal is to further the cause of Muhammad or Islam, it is permissible and overrides the initial prohibition against lying. In this case it was permissible in order to achieve the end goal of an assassination of someone whom Muhammad wanted dead. Unfortunately, because Islam holds up Muhammad as the supreme example of behavior for all Muslims, Muhammad's followers carry on this same attitude today.

DECEPTION TO ATTAIN GOALS AND PROSPERITY

Imam Al-Ghazali, one of the most famous Muslim theologians and philosophers of all time, takes the permissibility of lying even further. To Ghazali, lying is permissible so long as virtually any positive or beneficial goal may be achieved:

> Speaking is a means to achieve objectives. If a praiseworthy aim is attainable through both telling the truth and lying, it is unlawful to accomplish through lying because there is no need for it. *When it is possible to achieve such an aim by lying but not by telling the truth, it is permissible to lie if attaining the goal is permissible* (emphasis mine).[13]

> Know this that lying is not sin by itself, but if it brings harm to you it could be ugly. *However, you can lie if that will keep you from evil or if it will result in prosperity* (emphasis mine).[14]

It is impossible to deny that deceit has found a rich seedbed in Islam to deposit its roots and call home. We see that Islam as a religious system permits and even encourages lying and deceit as a specific aspect of its religious life. This unusual fusion of religion and deceit has profound implications, both in matters relating to the spread of Islam in the West and in matters relating to our discussion about the last days.

IMPLICATIONS FOR ISLAM IN THE WEST

In terms of the implications for today, Abdullah Al-Araby comments:

> The principle of sanctioning lying for the cause of Islam bears grave implications in matters relating to the spread of the religion of Islam in the West. Muslim activists employ deceptive tactics in their attempts to polish Islam's image and make it more attractive to prospective converts.[15]

I have personally witnessed this dynamic to the point of utter exhaustion. And equally frustrating is the fact that so many Christians, due to either a lack of knowledge or simply not wanting to appear contentious, allow the deception to flow unchecked. When Americans witnessed numerous so-called moderate Muslims make speeches to defend the benign nature of "the Religion of Peace," after 9/11, for instance, many of these speakers knowingly misrepresented the true nature of Islam. Many have been documented speaking in far more aggressive terms in private meetings with other Muslims. We pointed out the example of Omar Ahmed, chairman of the board of the Council of American Islamic Relations (CAIR) in the last chapter. These Muslims, posing as "moderates," justified their misrepresentations of Islam because in their minds, they were protecting Islam, and thus American Muslims, from "harm." It was "damage control" in its truest form. Christians, Americans, and unfortunately, even much of the political leadership, either desperately wanting to believe the best of people in order to comfort themselves in times of great uncertainty or through the inevitable dumbing down of the West through the constant hammering of moral relativity and political correctness, bought much of this deception—hook, line, and sinker. Those few bold enough to speak the truth regarding the true nature of Islam were viewed as intolerant or hateful or both. This is the pattern followed whenever Islam carrries out a great evil. Pay attention and you will see it again and again.

IMPLICATIONS FOR THE LAST DAYS

Of course the implications for Islam's doctrines of lying are obvious in relation to our discussion of the last days. The biblical picture of the last days is one where deception is the absolute rule of the day. In virtually every passage where the New Testament discusses the end times, the author stresses that believers must guard against deception. Following are some examples of such warnings.

Just before Jesus was taken away to be crucified, he had a discussion with his disciples about the last days. His very first exhortation was that they be careful not to be deceived:

> As Jesus was sitting on the Mount of Olives, the disciples came to him privately. "Tell us," they said, "when will this happen, and what will be the sign of your coming and of the end of the age?" Jesus answered: "Watch out that no one deceives you..." (Matthew 24:3, 4).

Jesus goes on to warn of the power of this deception:

> At that time many will turn away from the faith and will betray and hate each other, and many false prophets will appear *and deceive many people....* For false christs and false prophets will appear and perform great signs and miracles *to deceive even the elect—if that were possible.* See, I have told you ahead of time (Matthew 24:10-11, 24-25, emphasis mine).

Likewise the Apostle Paul in his letter to the Thessalonians warns the church of the need to be cautious against deception: "Concerning the coming of our Lord Jesus Christ and our being gathered to him.... Don't let anyone deceive you in any way..." (2 Thessalonians 2:1-3). Paul refers to the future deception as "a powerful delusion."

> The coming of the lawless one will be in accordance with the work of Satan displayed in all kinds of counterfeit miracles, signs, and wonders, and in every sort of evil that *deceives* those who are perishing. They perish because they refused to love the truth and so be saved. For this reason God sends them *a powerful delusion so that they will believe the lie* and so that all will be condemned who have not believed the truth but have delighted in wickedness (2 Thessalonians 2:9-12, emphasis mine).

CONCLUSION

I understand that to call anyone a liar is quite an insult. That is why I felt it important to demonstrate thoroughly the fact that Muhammad, the Qur'an, and *hadiths*, as well as Islam's most respected scholars, allow lying as a means to achieve any number of goals. I have documented this fact quite plainly. This is not an unfounded accusation made by the "people of falsehood" (a name that the Qur'an ironically applies to non-Muslims) but is indeed an established doctrine and practice within Islam. While I understand that this may feel like quite strong language, the simple truth is that Islam as a religious system is a son of its true father. The demonic being that assaulted Muhammad in the Cave of Hira is the same being that inspired the ungodly doctrines of deception that have so obviously affected the religion of Islam as we know it today. While I am quite sure that these comments may offend most Muslims, my response would be to ask that they do not get upset with me for reporting this information, but rather that they express their anger toward the traditions of Muhammad and the scholars of Islam who not only condone but encourage such behavior. It is behavior that simply should not be found among those who call themselves godly. The Bible calls on all people to strive to resemble their true heavenly Father, the Author of all light and truth.

While most people will agree that religion and deception are not intermixable, it is clear that in Islam, deception and religion mutually support one another. Likewise we can be sure that in the last days, deception and religion will be so intertwined that it will be difficult even for "the elect" to discern the truth. Once again, Islam finds itself fulfilling yet another of the primary descriptions of the last days system of the Antichrist.

THE GREAT APOSTASY, TERROR, AND ISLAM'S CONVERSION RATES

Perhaps the saddest and most devastating aspect of the last days is what the Bible calls the Great Apostasy. The Bible teaches that in the last days, many of those who name the name of Jesus, who call themselves Christians, will turn away from the faith and renounce Christ. Referring to this most horrific and chaotic period, Jesus said: "At that time many will turn away from the faith and will betray and hate each other (Matthew 24:10)."

Paul the Apostle warned the believers on more than one occasion not to be deceived into believing that Jesus had already returned. For until the Great Apostasy and the emergence of the Antichrist, the "Day of the Lord"—the return of Jesus, will not come:

> Let no one in any way deceive you, for it will not come unless the apostasy comes first, and the man of lawlessness is revealed, the son of destruction (2 Thessalonians 2:3, NASB).

> But the Spirit explicitly says that in later times some will fall away from the faith, paying attention to deceitful spirits and doctrines of demons (1 Timothy 1:4, NASB).

In this chapter we will examine how the dramatic growth of Islam may be tied into the coming Great Apostasy as well as the relationship between terror and the success of the Antichrist.

ISLAM'S RISE TO GLOBAL PROMINENCE

Because one of Islam's core doctrines is faith in Allah's absolute and complete sovereignty, many Muslims have had a hard time psychologically with the idea that Islam has had to play second fiddle to Christianity for such a long time. If Allah is all-powerful and Islam is his only religion, then why does Islam play such a secondary role to Christianity throughout the world? Why does Allah allow this? These are some of the things that many Muslims wrestle with. My speculation, however, is that in the next few decades, as Islam begins to draw closer to bypassing Christianity as the world's largest religion, the psychological boost to Islam will be tremendous. The psychological blow to Christianity, on the other hand, will be equally profound. Suddenly many Christians will ask themselves, "If God is all powerful, how can He allow Islam to in essence take over the world?" Muslims will triumphantly exclaim that it can no longer be said that Jesus Christ is the most influential man in human history, but rather Muhammad! There will be an atmosphere of excitement among Muslims that has not existed since the initial phases of Islam's conquests.

I don't intend to be negative here, but based on my simple observations of people, I expect that we will see a "tipping point" just before Islam actually bypasses Christianity when there will be a sudden burst forward of bandwagon conversions and growth. At this time, the power of testimony will be a powerful tool for Muslims. As more and more Westerners convert, the claims and challenges of Islam will become far more difficult for many Western Christians to brush aside. Existing prejudices that have insulated many Western Christians from actually having to face Islam as a relevant factor in the world will suddenly be stripped away as sincere and intelligent people that they know become Muslims. No longer will people be able to hide behind their prejudices and ignore Islam as a more primitive religion of a less cultured or less educated people. Many Westerners, consequently, will be forced to revisit the religion of Islam. Today in America, when the majority of people previously without religion come to accept monotheism and make a decision to follow God, most do not ever wrestle through which religion they should choose, but rather which denomination. As Islam grows in the West, such people will be forced to face this decision. Between the only two real choices, which will it be: Christianity or Islam?

We should expect at this time a frenzy among the Islamic community toward the goal of completing the task of Islamic world domination. The Muslim world will experience a tremendous psychological boost. This exhilaration will only be heightened if, during this time, anything happens to America which significantly weakens her as a world power. Admittedly, this is only speculation, but based on the apparent lack of any real significance of America in biblical prophecy, many prophecy teachers have argued that sometime prior to the last days America will suffer some form of significant decline in her place of prominence and power in the world. While I certainly do not hope for such a bleak scenario to unfold, the continual rise and fall of various world powers is a pattern as old and as predictable as the rising of the sun.

Again, we are just speculating, but if these two factors—the decline of America and the rise of Islam—did occur in a relatively close proximity of time, then surely the vindication that Muslims have longed for would invigorate the Islamic movement throughout the world in a way that has never before been seen. The final goal line would suddenly be in sight for Muslims throughout the world. Observers of apocalyptic movements have consistently made the point that one of the most dangerous combinations in any individual is the feeling that God is absolutely on his side and the belief in a divine mandate to do violence. Accordingly, when atrocities occur under the Mahdi, it will be far easier to excuse and overlook them. In the eyes of Muslims, the Mahdi will purge the last vestiges of infidel spiritual cancer from the earth in preparation for an age of peace. Consider the following statement made in Ayatollah Ibrahim Amini's *Al-Imam Al-Mahdi: The Just Leader of Humanity*. Referring to those who refuse to convert to Islam and submit to the Mahdi's leadership over the earth, we read:

> This group will indisputably be opposed to justice and will never give up their stubborn antagonism against any power. Such people will do anything against the promised Mahdi to protect their vested interests. Moreover, they will do anything within their power to demoralize and combat those who support the Imam (Mahdi). To crush the negative influence of this group there is no other solution except warfare and bloodshed.[1]

The end, the final victory, which will feel as if it is at arm's reach, will unquestionably justify the means. Anything, including blatant murder, will be excusable, so long as the goal of Islam's vindication is finally achieved. The psychology here cannot be underestimated.

A GLOBAL CASE OF THE STOCKHOLM SYNDROME

But beyond the emotional invigoration that we would expect to see among Muslims, we would also expect to see an equal measure of terror among those who do not wish to become Muslims. This brings us to another very important psychological factor that will likely come into play during the last days—terror. Specifically, it is what psychologists have labeled as "the Stockholm Syndrome." Allow me to explain. Perhaps the oddest quality to the Antichrist's empire is that it is a religious worship movement and a demonically inspired military machine hell-bent on crushing, devouring, and trampling "the whole earth." These two elements seem at first like a completely incompatible combination. We in the West with our religious freedom view worship as a voluntary act of reverence and love directed toward the one whom we deem worthy of such worship. We see, however, in the Book of Revelation, a hint of the mentality of the worshippers of Satan and the beast. It says that "men worshiped the dragon because he had given authority to the beast, and they also worshiped the beast and asked, *'Who is like the beast? Who can make war against him?'"* We see in the worshippers an "if you can't beat him may as well join him" mentality motivated by fear and terror. We see a clear example here of *the Stockholm Syndrome.* The Stockholm Syndrome essentially refers to the psychological dynamic that has been repeatedly observed in which those held prisoner or abused eventually identify with and support their captors or tormentors. A classic case in the United States was the kidnapping of newspaper heiress Patricia Hearst by the Symbionese Liberation Army, as a result of which she eventually joined their cause. In the case of the future worshippers of the beast, the trampled down and dominated will eventually give in and worship their dominator. In utter awe, they will ask, "Who is like him?"

Not surprisingly then, many psychologists equate the behavior of victims of terrorism or other abuses with the behavior of those captives. The comparisons are quite fascinating as they relate to our discussion. In an article entitled *The Stockholm Syndrome: Not Just For Hostages,* we read:

> The Stockholm Syndrome is an emotional attachment, a bond of interdependence between captive and captor that develops "when someone threatens your life, deliberates, and doesn't kill you...." *The relief resulting from the removal of the threat of death generates intense feelings of gratitude and fear* which combine to make the captive reluctant to display negative feelings toward the captor *or terrorist.* "The victim's need to survive is stronger than his impulse to hate the person who has created his dilemma...." The victim comes to see the captor as a "good guy," *even a savior*[2] (emphasis mine).

Should we be surprised then that the Stockholm Syndrome is at work in the terrorism-plagued nation of Israel? George E. Rubin, in *Commentary Magazine,* May 2000, sees symptoms of the Stockholm Syndrome among many in Israel:

> After fifty years of unending conflict, most Israeli Jews seem to have concluded that the burden of maintaining their nation is just too difficult to bear. The country's secular leftist elites—who control education, culture, the news media, and the government—blame the Jews for the Arabs' desire to destroy Israel, and the majority seems to be afflicted with the "Stockholm syndrome": though the victims of Arab hate, they identify with their oppressors.[3]

Rubin is not alone in this observation. Aharon Megged, an Israeli novelist, mirrors Rubin's comments:

> We have witnessed a phenomenon which probably has no parallel in history; an emotional and moral identification by the majority of Israel's *intelligentsia* with people openly committed to our annihilation.[4]

Even as psychologists and intellectuals have observed the Stockholm Syndrome present among victims of Islamic terrorism in Israel and elsewhere, the beast empire led by the Antichrist will likewise inspire a global case of this syndrome. People will be overcome with a terror that will eventually lead to literally worshipping the beast. The tormentor will become the savior.

HAS IT ALREADY BEGUN?

This dynamic may be one of the primary reasons responsible for the explosion of conversions to Islam among Westerners since 9/11. While common sense would tell us that 9/11 would have caused many to be repulsed by Islam, instead we see in many quarters just the opposite effect. We see this phenomenon in one young American woman's "testimony" of how she converted to Islam. In a story from the *New York Times* about the "thousands" of converts to Islam after 9/11:

> Shannon Staloch is not sure why, but upon hearing of the hijackings, she immediately grabbed a book from her backpack and recited the Arabic declaration of belief; she made the conversion official twelve days later.[5]

The aspect of this story and many others like it that amazes me is the complete absence of any intellectual or spiritual reasons that many converts can lay their fingers on when examining their decision to convert. "Not sure why," this woman simply felt the overwhelming need to convert to Islam upon hearing of the horrific murder of thousands of people in the name of the very religion she converted to. In Ms. Staloch's case, Islamic "terror" had its desired effect. Certainly the news would please Osama Bin Laden.

In the last days, terror will increase a thousand fold. And the Bible makes it clear that terror will have its desired effect upon the inhabitants of the earth. "Who is like the beast? Who can make war against him? Why resist him? He is simply too powerful," they will say. And the Bible says, "every tribe, people, language, and nation—all inhabitants of the earth will worship the beast."

The budding trends that we see today—the conversion of the terrorized to the religion of the terrorists—will come to full fruition in the days to come as the beast and his kingdom terrorize the whole earth in the name of his religion. So once again, we see that the methods of terror and fear utilized by the Antichrist and the methods of Islam are the same. The parallels and the psychology here cannot be ignored.

CHAPTER EIGHTEEN

A SUMMARY OF COMPARISONS BETWEEN THE ISLAMIC AND BIBLICAL NARRATIVE OF THE END TIMES:

So in summary we conclude this section with a final review of the many startling similarities that exist between the biblical narrative of the last days and the Islamic narrative of the same period.

- Bible: The Antichrist is an unparalleled political, military, and religious leader that will emerge in the last days.

- Islam: The Mahdi is an unparalleled political, military, and religious leader that will emerge in the last days.

- Bible: the False Prophet is a secondary prominent figure that will emerge in the last days who will support the Antichrist.

- Islam: the Muslim Jesus is a secondary prominent figure that will emerge in the last days to support the Mahdi.

- Bible: The Antichrist and the False Prophet together will have a powerful army that will do great damage to the earth in an effort to subdue every nation and dominate the world.

- Islam: The Mahdi and the Muslim Jesus will have a powerful army that will attempt to control every nation of the earth and dominate the world.

- Bible: The False Prophet is described essentially as a dragon in lamb's clothing.

- Islam: The Muslim Jesus comes bearing the name of the one that the world knows as "The Lamb of God, Jesus Christ." Yet the Muslim Jesus comes to murder all those who do not submit to Islam.

- Bible: The Antichrist and the False Prophet establish a new world order.

- Islam: The Mahdi and the Muslim Jesus establish a new world order.

- Bible: The Antichrist and the False Prophet institute new laws for the whole earth.

- Islam: The Mahdi and the Muslim Jesus institute Islamic law all over the earth.

- Bible: The Antichrist is said to "change the times."

- Islam: It is quite certain that if the Mahdi established Islam all over the earth, he would discontinue the use of Saturday and Sunday as the weekend or days of rest but rather Friday, the holy day of Islam. Also, he would most certainly eliminate the Gregorian calendar and replace it with the Islamic calendar used in every Islamic country.

- Bible: The Antichrist and the False Prophet will both be powerful religious leaders who will attempt to institute a universal world religion.

- Islam: The Mahdi and the Muslim Jesus will institute Islam as the only religion on the earth.

- Bible: The Antichrist and the False Prophet will execute anyone who does not submit to their world religion.

- Islam: Likewise, the Mahdi and the Muslim Jesus will execute anyone who does not submit to Islam.

- Bible: The Antichrist and the False Prophet will specifically use beheading as the primary means of execution for non-conformists.

- Islam: The Mahdi and the Muslim Jesus will use the Islamic practice of beheading for executions.

- Bible: The Antichrist and the False Prophet will have a specific agenda to kill as many Jews as possible.

- Islam: The Mahdi and the Muslim Jesus will kill as many Jews as possible until only a few are left hiding behind rocks and trees.

- Bible: The Antichrist and the False Prophet will attack to conquer and seize Jerusalem.

- Islam: The Mahdi and the Muslim Jesus will attack to reconquer and seize Jerusalem for Islam.

- Bible: The Antichrist will set himself up in the Jewish Temple as his seat of authority.

- Islam: The Mahdi will establish the Islamic *caliphate* from Jerusalem.

- Bible: The False Prophet is said to do many miracles to deceive as many as possible into supporting the Antichrist.

- Islam: The Mahdi himself is said to control the weather and the crops. His face is said to glow. We can also assume that since Jesus is viewed as having been empowered by Allah to work miracles when He was here on earth the first time, He will most likely be expected to continue to do so when He returns.

- Bible: The Antichrist is described as riding on a white horse in the Book of Revelation.

- Islam: The Mahdi is described as riding on a white horse (ironically in the same verse).

- Bible: The Antichrist is said to make a peace treaty with Israel for seven years.

- Islam: The Mahdi is said to make a peace treaty through a Jew (specifically a Levite) for exactly seven years.

- Bible: Jesus the Jewish Messiah will return to defend the Jews in Israel from a military attack from a vast coalition of nations led by the Antichrist and the False Prophet.

- Islam: The Dajjal, the Islamic Antichrist, will gain a great Jewish following and claim to be Jesus Christ and fight against the Mahdi and the Muslim Jesus.

- Bible: The antichrist spirit specifically denies the most unique and central doctrines of Christianity, namely the Trinity, the incarnation, and the substitutionary death of Jesus on the Cross.

- Islam: Islam doctrinally and spiritually specifically denies the most unique and central doctrines of Christianity, namely the Trinity, the incarnation, and the substitutionary death of Jesus on the Cross.

- Bible: The primary warning of Jesus and the Apostle Paul was to warn Christians of the abundance of deceit and deception in the last days.

- Islam: Islam is perhaps the only religion on earth that practices deceit as one of its tools to assist its own ascendancy. It actually has a specific doctrine which allows and even calls for deception to be used to achieve its desired end.

- Bible: The specific nations pictured in the Bible as part of the final empire of the Antichrist are all Islamic nations.

- Islam: All Muslims are commanded to give their allegiance to the Mahdi as the final *caliph* and *imam* (leader) of Islam.

- Bible: From the Bible and history we learn that the final Antichrist empire will be a revived version of the empire that succeeds the Roman Empire.

- Islam: The empire that succeeded the Roman/Byzantine Empire was the Islamic Ottoman Empire.

- Bible: When the Antichrist emerges, a system will already exist poised to receive him as a savior and to give allegiance to him.

- Islam is already the second largest religion and will at present growth rates become the largest religion within a few decades. Islam awaits the coming of the Mahdi with universal anticipation.

In the next section we will both analyze this information and discuss some proper responses.

CHAPTER NINETEEN

POTENTIAL PROBLEMS WITH THE THESIS

I *believe it only responsible* to address what I anticipate may be some of the arguments and objections raised against the thesis presented in this book. In this chapter I will address the potential difficulties that I have personally pondered myself and share why I feel as though they are easily resolved. In fact, some of the challenges may actually help shed even greater light on the details of how things just may unfold according to the biblical template.

JUMPING TO CONCLUSIONS

Throughout Christian history, many Christians have seen the Antichrist and his system in whoever happened to be their archenemy or bogeyman of the day. Many Protestants have singled out—and some still do—the Pope as the most likely candidate to be the Antichrist. More recent speculations have ranged from Mikhail Gorbachev to Saddam Hussein to Prince Charles. For quite some time communism with its atheist doctrines was the favorite Antichrist system for many. Before the European Union was formed, many speculated that when the number of participants in the EU reached ten, then the Antichrist would surely emerge as the ruler of the "revived Roman Empire." In the popular *Left Behind* series, it is Nicoloae Carpathia, a Romanian politician, who plays the role of the Antichrist. A whole book could be written about all of the various missed and zany speculations of Christians over the years. In fact, just such a book has been written.

Paul Boyer, professor of history at the University of Wisconsin, in his informative though quite jaded book entitled *When Time Shall Be No More*, thoroughly examines pre-millennial belief throughout the history of the church.[1] Boyer succeeds in demonstrating the repeated gullibility and hastiness of Christians all too quick to jump to conclusions regarding the identification of the Antichrist or his system. In our times, I would hazard to say that the occupation of some end-time teachers of speculating about the identity of the Antichrist and his system has become a bit of a sport and an industry.

So the challenge might arise which asks, "Aren't you doing the same thing? Aren't you just taking today's bogeyman (Islam) and making it into the Antichrist system?" I don't believe so. Here's why: I didn't go looking for a way to identify Islam as an Antichrist system, but rather I went looking to befriend Muslims and get to know Islam. And I still love Muslims. But through my journey of understanding and becoming intimately acquainted with Islam, the material covered in this book pretty much forced itself on me. It is not through any negative feelings or biased agenda that I have come to the conclusions I reached—the information speaks for itself. Also, the simple fact of the matter is that someday the Antichrist system *will* emerge. When it does, will we simply look the other way for fear of being the next gullible Christians to falsely identify the Antichrist? When the real thing arrives, will the church allow the fear of looking dumb to cloud her discernment?

At this point, my response to those who would challenge the idea that Islam is the primary driving force behind the Antichrist system would be to issue a challenge to show biblically why it is not. What aspect of the Antichrist spirit and system as described in the Bible *does not* line up with the spirit and doctrines of Islam? What weaknesses are there in the argument presented here? And if not Islam, then what other system fulfills the long list of biblical requirements necessary to fulfill such a role?

Ultimately, the purpose of this book is not so much to prove a point, but merely to present the information to the church. I believe that in doing so I have fulfilled my responsibility before God to warn the church regarding this undeniably startling information. This book is ultimately about turning the reader to the Scriptures and prayer in order to study and meditate to see if these things are so. If they are, then many others will follow with their own insights and add to what has been presented here. And of course, world developments will continue to substantiate this theory as well. But rather than viewing this information as some form of end-time trivia, or merely some interesting information to satisfy our intellectual curiosity, I appeal to every reader to take this information as a strong warning to remain both prayerful and watchful. The days that we live in have an intensity to them that requires a diligent attitude of prayerfulness and watchfulness. We all need to be aware of world developments both naturally and spiritually. If ever a day existed that demanded such a high level of sobriety, then surely this is that day.

We now turn to some potential "holes" in the argument.

THE ANTICHRIST HIMSELF DEMANDS WORSHIP

Perhaps the strongest argument that could be made against the idea that the system of Islam will fulfill the role of the Antichrist system is the fact that, despite all of the specific parallels and similarities between the two, the Antichrist demands personal worship and surely Islam does not allow for the worship of any man. Indeed this is the big problem that Islam has with Christianity. While I am plainly speculating, I believe that a thoughtful examination of this future scenario can clear up any doubts that might attempt to negate the notion that Islam is the Antichrist system.

The first point to remember is that while the Antichrist accomplishes much in the first half of the seven years of his rule, he does not actually demand worship until after the middle point of the seven years. Not until after the Antichrist has achieved several significant military victories and gained a great measure of allegiance will he invade Israel and establish his position of authority in the Jerusalem Temple. It is at this time that Paul the Apostle explains that Antichrist will "set himself up in God's temple, proclaiming himself to be God" (2 Thessalonians 2:4). This is also the time that Paul said that "the man of lawlessness is revealed" (2 Thessalonians 2:3). While many Christians with discernment will already have recognized the Antichrist by this point, he will not be fully revealed until the middle of the "week" of seven years.

We need to understand that the Antichrist will not demand worship until well after the Islamic world has universally acknowledged and accepted him as the Mahdi. The *imams, mullahs, sheikhs,* and *ayatollahs*—all of the world's Islamic leadership—will have already given their allegiance to the Mahdi. To deny him after this point would be the ultimate shame for Islam. It would come at a time when Islam will experience its greatest rush of vindication and fulfillment. In the midst of all of this incredible elation, to suddenly declare and acknowledge that an absolute evil charlatan has deceived the entire Islamic world would simply be unthinkable. Once the deception has taken place, it will be impossible to undo. The die will have been cast.

Other important factors will be at play here as well. Throughout this time period, the False Prophet, whom the Islamic world will believe to be Jesus, will work as the Antichrist's miracle-working "campaign manager," as it were. As Paul the Apostle says:

> The coming of the lawless one will be in accordance with the work of Satan displayed in all kinds of counterfeit miracles, signs, and wonders, and in every sort of evil that deceives those who are perishing. They perish because they refused to love the truth and so be saved. For this

reason God sends them a powerful delusion so that they
will believe the lie and so that all will be condemned who
have not believed the truth but have delighted in
wickedness (2 Thessalonians 2:9-12).

So the followers of the Mahdi/Antichrist are already in a deep
spiritual state of deception founded on a combination of factors,
including some very powerful psychological dynamics as well
as the spiritual dimensions that Paul describes above. Because
"they refused to love the truth and so be saved...God sends
them...*all kinds of counterfeit miracles, signs and wonders...in every
sort of evil that deceives...a powerful delusion* so that they will
believe the lie." This is strong language. And it is God Himself
who sends the delusion. God Himself causes them to become
cemented in their own poor decisions, just as God hardened
Pharaoh's heart in order that he could accomplish His purposes
for His people Israel. Indeed, Pharoah's Egypt foreshadowed
the coming followers of the Antichrist.

The Bible also gives us a hint into one of the specific powerful
delusions that will cause the world to awe over the Antichrist. He
is said to experience some sort of deadly head wound and yet
come back to life, forming a parallel to the death and resurrection
of Jesus. The Apostle John, in the Book of Revelation, describes
this fatal head wound for us:

> One of the heads of the beast seemed to have had a fatal
> wound, but the fatal wound had been healed. The whole
> world was astonished and followed the beast (Revelation 13:3).

Of course this great event will be "promoted" and exploited
for gain by The False Prophet/False Jesus:

> He exercised all the authority of the first beast on his behalf,
> and made the earth and its inhabitants worship the first beast,
> whose fatal wound had been healed. And he performed great
> and miraculous signs, even causing fire to come down from
> heaven to earth in full view of men. Because of the signs he
> was given power to do on behalf of the first beast, he
> deceived the inhabitants of the earth. He ordered them to set

up an image in honor of the beast who was wounded by the sword and yet lived (Revelation 13:12).

Exactly what this "fatal head wound" will be remains to be seen, but it is described in two ways; in the first reference it "seemed" to be fatal, and in the next reference it is simply called "fatal." The Antichrist is then specifically described as "the beast who was wounded by the sword and yet lived." Whatever this specifically means, it undoubtedly refers to some form of false sign that the Antichrist/Mahdi and the False Prophet/False Jesus will use to deceive and capture the wonder of the people. The very "sign" that Jesus pointed to as the greatest vindicating fact of his earthly ministry was His resurrection. The Antichrist, as the ape of Christ, may indeed fabricate his own counterfeit resurrection as a response to the central redemptive event of all time.

And of course, another important factor to consider here is that it will also be at this time that those who do not support the Antichrist/Mahdi or give him the worship that he demands will be killed under the new globally enforced Islamic law. "He was given power to give breath to the image of the first beast, so that it could speak and cause all who refused to worship the image to be killed" (Revelation 13:15). Speaking of this specific time, Jesus says:

So when you see standing in the holy place "the abomination that causes desolation," spoken of through the Prophet Daniel—let the reader understand—for then there will be great distress, unequaled from the beginning of the world until now—and never to be equaled again. If those days had not been cut short, no one would survive, but for the sake of the elect those days will be shortened (Matthew 24:16-22).

Clearly, multitudes will be killed. Multitudes will not accept or worship the Antichrist/Mahdi. I believe that it is quite likely that at this time multitudes of Muslims will see the evil person that the Antichrist really is and will turn to the true Jesus for salvation. Who knows?

So we need to try to envision this total scenario: the Antichrist/Mahdi has emerged. The entire Islamic world acknowledges him as such. Having been primed throughout their entire lives psychologically, doctrinally, and spiritually to receive him, much of the Islamic world rallies to his cause and joins his ranks. He gains several military victories and grows in power as an unparalleled world leader with an equally unparalleled military force under his control. All the people of the earth stand in awe and say, "Who is like him and who can make war with him?" On top of all this, the other man whom the Islamic world has been awaiting, the Muslim Jesus, is also on the scene, openly declaring the Mahdi Allah's man of the hour. Along with the False Jesus' stunningly powerful rhetorical skills, he will perform "all kinds of counterfeit miracles, signs, and wonders" to deceive and hook as many people as possible. Among these great signs is one that seems to utterly amaze the people of the earth. The Antichrist undergoes some form of false resurrection from the dead. He recovers from a "fatal head wound." And as if all of this is not enough, the Antichrist then proceeds to accomplish that which the Muslim world has longed and yearned for probably more than any other event: He utterly defeats Israel and establishes the Islamic *caliphate* from Jerusalem. Islam is now vindicated! It is now mere inches away from its absolute final victory over the entire earth. And it is now, in the midst of all this, that the Mahdi throws the ultimate curve ball. In the same way that Christians view Jesus to be the incarnation of God, so the Mahdi now declares himself an incarnation of Allah, and as such, he demands worship. A more suspenseful novel has never been written.

Satan often masks his true identity with something wonderful in order to allure and hook his victims. In most cases, Satan's true nature is eventually revealed. When this happens, it is because of the absolute mercy of God. In such cases, God gives the deceived person or people the opportunity to see the real face of evil behind all of the makeup. For some, the mask of deception will not be removed in this lifetime. For these, it will be too late. But for those who have the opportunity to see the truth behind what has been holding them sway, as I said, it is the mercy of God in their lives. When the Antichrist demands worship, he will reveal his true identity to many. The mask will fall and many eyes will open. For many, however, an utter determination to believe in the legitimacy of the Madhi and Islam will overwhelm them. These would rather be swept up into a great deception with an Islamic nature than to acknowledge having been wrong all along. Oddly enough, the choice that will suddenly be set before them will be to worship the Antichrist/Mahdi claiming to be Allah incarnate or to turn to Jesus, Yahweh—the God of the Bible—incarnate. All of the excuses that Islam used to cling to in order to reject Jesus, namely that Allah would simply never become a man and draw near to us as such, will be taken away. In allowing the Mahdi to be "revealed," God will be showing great mercy to the followers of Islam. When the Antichrist is revealed, Islam will finally be fully "unveiled." This will be a final demonstration of God's wonderful ability to turn even the most horrific time in history into an opportunity for multitudes to find repentance. He will be giving them one last great opportunity in this world to turn to Jesus. To do so at this time, however, will of course mean one thing: martyrdom. "Multitudes, multitudes in the valley of decision! For the day of the LORD is near in the valley of decision" (Joel 3:14).

While the Lord certainly speaks of allowing those who are deceived to continue in their deception, I believe that many Muslims will see the truth at this time and multitudes will find both salvation and possibly martyrdom at this time. Indeed, God's mercy is strong.

THE PROBLEM OF UNFULFILLED SIGNS

Another objection that might be raised is the problem of unfulfilled signs. Some might argue that unless Muslims see the fulfillment of *all* of the Minor and Major Signs of Islamic apocalyptic tradition, including the one-eyed Dajjal, or several other significant signs, they will not accept a false Mahdi. This argument makes some sense, but is easily resolved.

First of all, the primary factor at play here is the flexibility of the *hadith* traditions. In examining some of the *hadiths* about the Dajjal, for instance, we saw that while they were clear that indeed the Dajjal would be "one-eyed," the *hadiths* could not agree which eye was blind. One *hadith* said he was blind in the left eye, while the other said it was his right eye. Due to the obvious corruption and inconsistency throughout the *hadith* traditions, the *hadiths* are simply easy to ignore. I have personally found this reality too many times to count when discussing Islam with Muslims. A Muslim might quote a *hadith* as a proof text to validate his point for one argument, only to deny the "trustworthiness" of the very same *hadith* in another discussion. Many Muslims feel free to declare any *hadith* unreliable when it suits them and likewise to declare any *hadith* as fully reliable when it suits them on another occasion. There is no universal acceptance as to which *hadiths* are absolutely authoritative and which are not. For those who find themselves within the system of Islam, the *hadith* traditions create the perfect "loophole" to almost any argument that might be raised against the authority of Islam. The flexibility of the *hadith* traditions creates the perfect fuzzy atmosphere for a false religion to thrive. It is a deceiver's dream come true—allowing its adherents to remain in a haze of circular reasoning without ever realizing it.

While I concede that some Muslims will be looking for various signs to be fulfilled, so long as the Mahdi is on the scene and accomplishing all that we have discussed for the cause of Islam, I really don't think that any Muslims will actually reject the Mahdi simply because one or more of the particular "signs" of the last days has failed to materialize. Simply stated, when Jerusalem falls to the Antichrist, very few Muslims will protest.

The best way for most Christians to relate to this is to imagine how most Christians would respond if Jesus returned to the earth from heaven and established His rule over the earth from Jerusalem. Imagine that almost the entire world is becoming Christian as Jesus teaches from the Scriptures from His throne in Jerusalem. Imagine that the restoration of all things is gradually taking place—powerful supernatural healings are in abundance. The Jews are restored to their Messiah, and everything looks just perfect. Yet, in the midst of all of this, there never appeared an Antichrist or a "tribulation" or anything of the sort. Would most Christians thus reject Jesus? Or would they simply shrug their shoulders and say, "Oh well, I guess my eschatology was off a bit"? I think I know the answer.

And this is an excellent analogy because the Mahdi is in so many ways to the Muslim what Jesus is to the Christian. While I am quite sure that most Christians would not protest under such a scenario, but rather fully embrace Jesus, so will Muslims worldwide embrace the Antichrist/Mahdi despite the lack of several other confirming signs.

CONCLUSION

Although I'm sure that there will be other challenges to the thesis of this book, for now, I believe that we have sufficiently addressed the two primary potential objections that might be raised. In the next chapter I will share my own personal analysis and ponderings of the information that we have covered so far.

FURTHER THOUGHTS

Having *addressed and offered resolution* to some of the potential challenges to the thesis presented in this book, we now move on to some final thoughts.

MERE COINCIDENCE?

When I first grew acquainted with Islamic eschatology and the many similarities between the biblical Antichrist and the Islamic Mahdi, I was quite taken aback. But as I began to see that these similarities extended far beyond just the Mahdi and the Antichrist, I knew that this subject merited a comprehensive study. I had to "see just how deep this rabbit hole goes." As the similarities between the two eschatological systems fell in line, one subject after another, my personal conclusion was that these numerous similarities were not mere coincidence. There is clear evidence here of purpose and design. In chapter seventeen, I listed twenty-two striking parallels between the biblical and Islamic templates for the last days, and I'm sure that I could extend this list. Several of the parallels by themselves are quite impressive. Think about this fact for instance: Bible scholars and students of Bible prophecy have concluded that the Antichrist will make a "peace treaty" with Israel for exactly seven years. This treaty is believed by many to include a concession allowing Israel to rebuild the Jewish Temple. The exact same scenario is mirrored by the Islamic tradition that the Mahdi will mediate a "peace treaty" with the Christians through a Jew from the priestly tribe of Levi. A Levite would be the necessary agent to represent the Jewish people in rebuilding their Temple. Amazingly, the Islamic timeframe here is *for exactly seven years*. This is just too detailed and specific a parallel to write off as mere coincidence. And this is perhaps the most insignificant element of all of the many parallels which exist.

In thinking through the implications of the fact that the biggest bad guy in the Bible, the Antichrist, has transformed into the coming savior of Islam, while the biggest good guy in the Bible, namely Jesus, has transformed into the biggest bad guy in Islamic eschatology, one must be willing to ask the obvious question: *Has Satan been specifically involved in the inspiration of Islam's end-time doctrines?* Has Satan devised in the Islamic traditions a preemptive means to carry out his final plan? Now of course in natural history there were real men and numerous developments that contributed to the formation of these traditions as we have them today. But I am speaking of invisible spiritual factors and beings behind the formation of these traditions. The specificity, detail, and extent of the parallels demand the acknowledgement of design, while the twisted and cynical nature of these "anti-parallels" clearly point to the malevolent nature of the "person" doing so. I understand that that may initially sound like quite a paranoid statement to make. But think through the facts: When God revealed the Book of Revelation to the Apostle John, he was at the same time pulling the lid off of Satan's grandest plan to deceive the world. Satan's plans were exposed *a priori*. Finding himself in such a position, did Satan, being crafty as always, decide it was necessary to create a strong tradition that contained an "anti-parallel" of his plan? If so, Satan could still brazenly carry out what God has already said he would do and deceive a great portion of the world while doing it. If this is the case, then when the Antichrist comes forward as prophesied in the Bible, Satan has seen to it that at least 1.5 billion Muslims, rather than

recognizing the Antichrist for who ´
fourteen-hundred-year-old   traditi、
predict the advent of such a wonderfu
the establishment of such an antichrist
world religion, Satan has already preparea
to receive his coming Antichrist with arms wi、
as though the entire Muslim world, which is expa
has been set up in a way only accounted for by the
plans of God's greatest enemy. If this is the case, then
can it be said that "Satan is alive and well on Planet Eart、
even more specifically: Satan is alive and well in the fas
growing religion in the world.

THE GOOD SIDE OF ISLAM

Now, before we move on, I must point out that while this book
has in many ways focused on the negative aspects of Islam, it
must also be qualified here that Islam as a religion is filled with
many very good, godly, admirable, and noble traits. One could
point out Islam's strong emphasis on modesty or prayer or
Islam's stunningly beautiful architecture and art. In fact I
personally find many things about Islam and Islamic culture
incredibly attractive and appealing. To outright deny this side
of Islam would be to put our collective heads in the sand. But
as Oswald Chambers has said in his classic Christian
devotional, *My Utmost for His Highest*, "The good is always the
enemy of the best."[1] This is an essential concept for us to grasp.
The reason for this is that Satan figured this out long ago and
has effectively utilized this concept as one of his greatest tools
to lead many astray.

Islam has many inward and outward religious expressions
that are quite good; many bear a strong resemblance to the
expressions that I have experienced in Christianity. Of course, the
religion of Islam without the genuine gospel of Jesus will never
lead anyone into a true relationship with God. No matter how
many admirable traits and traditions Islam possesses, ultimately

short and fails to deliver where it truly matters the most. [He] s not merely another prophet; rather he is "the way and the [truth] and the life" (John 14:6). So in this sense, again, we see the [unde]r antichrist nature of Islam. How so? Because the word [ant]ichrist has a duel meaning. Not only does *antichrist* mean ["against Christ," it also means "instead of Christ" —a substitute.] In Islam, I see a masterfully crafted substitute form of Christianity. Islam bears as much resemblance to the real thing as possible without actually having the most essential aspect of all—a genuine living relationship with the One True God of the universe through Jesus Christ. This is the essential mode whereby God has chosen to deal with humans. Islam attempts to bypass this. It would be hard to create a better example of a Christ-less version of Christianity than Islam. And in this sense, Islam is the "good" that is the ultimate enemy of "the best." Thus, the danger of Islam is not only its obvious dark side but also its light side. For it is those aspects of Islam that resemble a genuine relationship with God that make it seem acceptable to many who base their decision on a less than complete examination of both religions. Satan is crafty and wise. Without a veneer of godliness, Islam would be unacceptable to everyone, but Satan has always candy-coated his poison. Satan was perfectly happy to suffer and allow many godly elements into the religion of Islam in exchange for the absence of the essential and foundational element of any true relationship with God, which is the real Jesus—the only Savior of the world.

IF NOT ISLAM, THEN WHAT?

After all of the information is examined, there is one last important question that needs to be asked: *If Islam is not the antichrist system, then what is?*

In America, we are infamously America-centric. As American Christians we read into the Bible our own American experience. Presently, in America and elsewhere, the greatest "enemy" today of Christianity is generally the "progressive"

secularists—the left wing and adherents to the various forms of New Age religions. David Limbaugh, social and political commentator, in his timely book *Persecution: How Liberals Are Waging War Against Christianity*, details the ever-growing trend of prejudice, discrimination, and hatred toward Christians in America. Many American Christians may envision a day when the hatred of progressive secularists toward Christians will boil over into a fomenting rage and some people will actually feel justified in the killing of Christians.

While I have seen some pretty strong hatred directed toward Christians, and while Limbaugh's analysis is entirely accurate, I personally find it rather hard to believe that mere liberalism or secular humanism accounts for the kind of worldwide murderous behavior that the Bible speaks of as taking place in the last days. Perhaps the vision of American Christians has been far too myopic when they have tried to visualize or speculate about who their real persecutors will be in the end times.

When Jesus says that the day is coming "when those who murder you will think that they are offering God a service," it necessitates not only a belief in God but also some form of religious system whereby the mentality that killing in the name of God is actually reasonable. I do not personally see mere liberalism, humanism, or even occultism as being enough to account for the specific description that Jesus gives us in this warning. Perhaps, if within the next several decades, humanism, occultism, and various forms of New Age religions somehow merge into some form of a popular cohesive world movement that experiences some form of significant revival, then maybe a case could be made for such a system being responsible for worldwide persecution. But right now, such a system does not exist. I simply do not see enough tangible evidence to accept the notion that any of the "isms" that we just mentioned could be legitimate candidates to fulfill the prophecies of Jesus regarding people killing Christians and thinking themselves to be serving God in doing so.

Islam, however, fits Jesus' prophecy perfectly. And, as we discussed in previous chapters, Islam also fulfills John's prophecy of a worldwide system that will use beheading as its primary method or mode of operation to enforce its rule. But how have we missed this? After all, Islam is the world's second largest and fastest growing religion. Are we really that blind?

To be fair, until 9/11, Islam stayed pretty much off the radar of most American Christians. And in many ways, Islam as a religion has been somewhat dormant as a world power for much of the last century. But Islam's slow and steady growth throughout the twentieth century began to churn and froth later in the century with the advent of radical Islam in Iran and Egypt that has already given rise to a world-wide network of *jihad* movements that has never before existed in the history of Islam or the world.

Many now declare that "the twenty-first century will be the century of Islam."[2] As many speculate that America is involved in the Third World War, Muslims are declaring all over the earth that they are at the onset of the third great *jihad*.[3] So now, possibly at an hour that is quite late, Islam has finally grabbed our attention. And as we assess Islam's nature in the light of biblical prophecies, we see that it not only fits the description of the biblical prophecies down to every last detail, but that it also has now had over fourteen hundred years to infiltrate every corner of the earth. I believe that the stage is now set.

CHAPTER TWENTY-ONE

HOW SHOULD WE RESPOND?

A *fter reading this book,* I'm sure that many may feel hopeless. "Well then," you might ask, "If this Satanic/Islamic empire is going to take over the world and kill millions of people, then what can we do? It seems so pre-determined, so hopeless." This chapter addresses God's primary provision and antidote to all seemingly hopeless situations: prayer.

Prayer is absolutely the most significant power available to mankind. Yet sadly, it is significantly neglected, even within the church.

So here's the question we must ask: If the Bible says that all of these things are going to happen, then why not simply resign ourselves to "God's will" and simply let Islam take over our nations and get it over with? Why prolong the inevitable? These are legitimate questions. But they are based on some very false assumptions. Let me explain.

IS OUR FATE ALREADY DETERMINED?

Some Bible teachers have speculated that every nation of the earth will be taken over by the antichrist system. We have already looked at some of the Bible verses that suggest this. My take on this subject is slightly different. Let me explain why. First let's look at the verses used to conclude that every last nation will fall to the Antichrist and join him in his attack against Jerusalem:

> I am going to make Jerusalem a cup that sends all the surrounding peoples reeling. Judah will be besieged as well as Jerusalem. On that day, when *all the nations of the earth* are gathered against her, I will make Jerusalem an immovable rock for all the nations. All who try to move it will injure themselves (Zechariah 12:2, 3, emphasis mine).

> I will gather *all the nations* to Jerusalem to fight against it (Zechariah 14:2, emphasis mine).

> I will gather *all nations* and bring them down to the Valley of Jehoshaphat. There I will enter into judgment against them concerning my inheritance, my people Israel (Joel 3:2, emphasis mine).

> The beast...was given power to make war against the saints and to conquer them. *And he was given authority over every tribe, people, language, and nation* (Revelation 13:7, emphasis mine).

Let's look at the first three verses first. Since these verses use the word "all" and specifically the phrase "all the nations of the earth" when speaking of the attack against Jerusalem at the battle of Armageddon, then surely it has already been determined that every last nation will fall to the Antichrist's empire and support him in this battle. I can fully understand how many would arrive at this conclusion.

There are at least two problems with this interpretation, however: First, other verses in the Bible use this very same type of language, yet clearly do not speak of every single last nation in the world. These verses, as well as the ones above, all employ a Hebrew grammatical construct—an exaggeration of sorts or an emphatic type of statement—in order to convey their point. Grammarians call this construct hyperbole. It is a statement like, "Everyone loves ice cream!" or "You never clean the kitchen," or the ancient, "Cretans are always liars, vicious brutes, lazy gluttons." Oftentimes, for the sake of brevity, elaborating on the exceptions would entirely blunt the impact of the statement. For instance, imagine a speed limit sign that had several various exceptions painted on it: "Speed limit fifty five, except ambulances, fire trucks, police giving chase, etc." It simply wouldn't work. Thus exceptions cannot be ruled out on the basis of exclusive language. This type of language is actually found quite frequently in the Bible. For instance, Daniel the Prophet, speaking to King Belshazzar, said this:

> O king, the Most High God gave your father Nebuchadnezzar sovereignty and greatness and glory and splendor. Because of the high position he gave him, *all the peoples and nations and men of every language* dreaded and feared him (Daniel 5:18, 19, emphasis mine).

So, I ask you this question: Did every single nation on earth fear Nebuchadnezzar? Or did only those nations that had heard of Nebuchadnezzar dread him? Was Daniel speaking of every single last nation of the earth? Or only those nations that were in close enough proximity to Babylon to be affected by her? Were the native peoples of Papua New Guinea living in dread of Nebuchadnezzar? Personally, I think that Daniel's use of the phrase, *"all the peoples and nations and men of every language"* was more of an emphatic expression used to convey his point. Or how about another similar example:

> Men of *all nations* came to listen to Solomon's wisdom, *sent by all the kings of the world,* who had heard of his wisdom (I Kings 4:34, emphasis mine).

Was Solomon's wisdom so impressive that not a single king in all the earth failed to hear of it? Or is this verse another expression used to convey the great amount of renown that Solomon had? How about this one: "And he took Agag the king of the Amalekites alive, *and utterly destroyed all the people with the edge of the sword"* (1 Samuel 15:8).

Should we find it odd that a people here recorded as being "utterly destroyed" come back making trouble just a few chapters later in 1 Samuel? Again, there are numerous such examples like this throughout the Bible. Do you see my point?

Now, if we look at the verses in Zechariah again, we see a more specific mention of just which nations will be primarily involved in the attack: "I am going to make Jerusalem a cup that sends *all the surrounding peoples* reeling" (Zechariah 12:2, emphasis mine).

Of course the surrounding nations are the Muslim nations that encircle Israel on every side. In fact, the Prophet Joel confirms this as well. Speaking of the final attack against Jerusalem, Joel prophesied:

> I will gather all nations and bring them down to the Valley of Jehoshaphat. There I will enter into judgment against them concerning my inheritance, my people Israel.... "Now what have you against me, O Tyre and Sidon and all you regions of Philistia?... Proclaim this among the nations: Prepare for war! Rouse the warriors! Let all the fighting men draw near and attack. Beat your plowshares into swords and your pruning hooks into spears. Let the weakling say, 'I am strong!' Come quickly, all you nations *from every side,* and assemble there. Bring down your warriors, O LORD! Let the nations be roused; let them advance into the Valley of Jehoshaphat, for there I will sit to judge *all the nations on every side*" (Joel 3:2, 4, 9-12, emphasis mine).

The *New American Standard Bible* words the italicized segments of the above passages as, "all you surrounding nations." Again, who are the "surrounding nations?" Does this include New Zealand? Canada? It could. But contextually, the Bible specifically refers to the Islamic nations that surround Jerusalem/Israel on every side.

The second reason that the position that every last nation will fall to the Antichrist is impossible is quite simply because the Scriptures state outright that not every nation will fall to him. In fact, some nations will resist the Antichrist after he attacks Jerusalem. Consider the following verses from Daniel:

> At the time of the end the king of the south will engage him in battle, and the king of the north will storm out

against him with chariots and cavalry and a great fleet of ships. He will invade many countries and sweep through them like a flood. He will also invade the Beautiful Land. Many countries will fall, *but Edom, Moab, and the leaders of Ammon will be delivered from his hand. He will extend his power over many countries*; Egypt will not escape. He will gain control of the treasures of gold and silver and all the riches of Egypt, with the Libyans and Nubians in submission. But reports from the east and the north will alarm him, and he will set out in a great rage to destroy and annihilate many. He will pitch his royal tents between the seas at the beautiful holy mountain. Yet he will come to his end, and no one will help him (Daniel 11:40-45, emphasis mine).

At a minimum it clearly says here that Edom, Moab, and the leaders of Ammon will be delivered from the Antichrist's hand. This is speaking of modern Jordan. So at least Jordan will not submit to the Antichrist nor fall to his control. The verse specifically goes on to define the nations that will fall to him. It says "*many* countries." Not *all*. Does the Bible contradict itself? I don't believe so. I do believe that every tribe, people, language, and nation will be utterly affected by the Antichrist's influence. I believe that the Antichrist will be given a measure of influence and authority over every last nation in that within every nation he will have many followers. Many nations will be completely dominated by him, but not every nation will completely fall to him. I believe that this is the only way that we can fully reconcile all of the verses relating to this issue.

Okay, so let's say that I have demonstrated that not every single last nation of the earth will attack Jerusalem with the Antichrist, but instead enough nations that Zechariah and Joel were justified in using such emphatic expressions. Why am I taking so much time making this point in a chapter on prayer? Simple. The reason is that I believe that, while the Bible indeed gives us a general prophetic framework of what will happen in the last days, *many of the specific details have yet to be determined.* God did not reveal every final detail for a reason.

He rarely does. If He did, then we would be justified in simply waiting for the Antichrist to come and get us. We would be entirely justified in digging holes in the ground as secret hideouts to store our survival food. But instead, God desires us to actually wrestle with Him in prayer, not only for our own souls and those of our families, but also for the very nations that we live in and call home. God did not, for instance, warn David Pawson, that Islam may indeed eventually take over England in order to give him fair time to flee, but rather to warn the church in England to join together and fight for the very soul of their country through prevailing prayer! Islam may have an attitude of almost fatalistic resignation to Allah's will: *"Inshallah"* (If it be Allah's will…it will be), they say. But we serve a God who asks us to participate with Him as He affects the nations. We serve a God who expects us to spread *His* beautiful kingdom throughout the earth through preaching (invitation) *and prayer*.

The point here is that if you find yourself feeling a tad hopeless after reading the scenario that has been opened up in this book, do not fear; you can always do something: You can pray, you can pray, and you can pray some more. And you can join with those doing likewise. Never underestimate the ability of prevailing prayer to affect reality and the final end of *any* matter. Remember, the story is not over until it has come to pass. I believe the lack of, or the presence of, an abundance of prevailing prayer will determine the final chapter in the story of *many* nations. The Lord has given us the ability to affect the measure of His mercy verses the measure of His judgment that will touch our homes, our cities, our regions, and our nations. Every nation will receive its own measure of God's judgment. Indeed, every person on earth will undergo a deep refining process during the last three and a half years of this terrible period. *Everything that can be shaken will be shaken.* So now is the time to cry out for God's mercy for the days to come.

I should also mention another very important aspect of prayer. I also believe that prayer can forestall the judgment of God and buy more time for positive changes. We must remember that the reason that the Lord has held off His return thus far is for the sake of more people coming to know Him and be saved. "The Lord is not slow in keeping his promise, as some understand slowness. He is patient with you, not wanting anyone to perish, but everyone to come to repentance" (2 Peter 3:9).

There are today dramatic revivals in many nations that would be cut short if the end came now, and there may very well be future revivals that would never take place if the end came now. While I personally believe that the day will indeed come when all of the terrifying prophecies in the Bible will come to pass, I believe that we can beseech God to give us more time and to pour out revival on our nations before these dark days come. Prayer can forestall His wrath in order that His mercy will have more time to work in the heart of a nation.

God came and spoke to Moses. He said that he was about to judge and destroy the children of Israel. For most of us, that would have been enough. God said it—it was a done deal. But Moses would not accept it. He interceded with God:

> "I have seen these people," the Lord said to Moses, "and they are a stiff-necked people. Now leave me alone so that my anger may burn against them and that I may destroy them. Then I will make you into a great nation." But Moses sought the favor of the Lord his God. "O Lord," he said, "why should your anger burn against your people, whom you brought out of Egypt with great power and a mighty hand? Why should the Egyptians say, 'It was with evil intent that he brought them out, to kill them in the mountains and to wipe them off the face of the earth'? Turn from your fierce anger; relent and do not bring disaster on your people. Remember your servants Abraham, Isaac, and Israel, to whom you swore by your own self: 'I will make your descendants as numerous as the stars in the sky and I will give your descendants all this land I promised them, and it will be their inheritance

forever.'" Then the Lord relented and did not bring on his people the disaster he had threatened (Exodus 32:9-14).

Now go back and rewind this scene. First God speaks to Moses and says, "Now leave me alone so that my anger may burn against them and that I may destroy them. Then I will make you into a great nation." Okay, press pause… Now let's insert a few theologians into the scene at this point to discuss whether or not God will destroy the Israelites. "Of course He will," they all agree, "God said it and that settles it." Many might argue the same thing today. Maybe you feel as though judgment is inevitable for our nation. Okay, fine. What are you doing about it? Are you complaining really loudly? Or are you interceding for mercy like Moses? Indeed, maybe God will pour out His judgment on your nation. Or perhaps He will desist:

> Seek the Lord, all you humble of the land, you who do what he commands. Seek righteousness, seek humility; perhaps you will be sheltered on the day of the Lord's anger (Zephaniah 2:3).

> "Even now," declares the Lord, "return to me with all your heart, with fasting and weeping and mourning." Rend your heart and not your garments. Return to the Lord your God, for he is gracious and compassionate, slow to anger and abounding in love, and he relents from sending calamity. *Who knows?* He may turn and have pity and leave behind a blessing (Joel 2:12-14, emphasis mine).

I personally believe that we now live in a crucial time when the future of many nations hangs in the balance. Now is not the time to fear. Nor is it the time to gripe. Now is the time to pray!

I want to end this chapter by quoting a portion of an article written by prominent Bible teacher and author Francis Frangipane. I felt particularly inspired by Francis's article as he addressed this very issue that we are discussing and I believe you will as well. The title of the article is "This Day We Fight!"

The conflict before our generation is no less threatening than Nazism and Soviet Imperialism. Radical Islam is a demonic power that seeks world domination. We cannot lose the war against terrorism or morality. We must not open to fear or unbelief, for we were born to fight and win the battles of our times. Again the argument arises, "I was taught that life is supposed to only grow more evil until Christ returns." *Yes, such a day will come, but we must not assume that it has arrived. In every age God requires we walk as overcomers.* The very fact that there are nations today that are experiencing great harvests and breakthroughs reminds us there is still time for our nations. One of our readers sent us the following excerpt from Aragon, king of Gondor, in *The Return of the King*. The book's author, J.R.R. Tolkien, an Englishman, denies his work had anything to do with the Great War. Yet, much of his manuscript was written during the height of WWII. The book is a metaphor of all the battles that each generation must face to conquer evil...

Hopelessly outnumbered, King Aragon sought to inspire his men against what seemed like sure defeat against the swarming hordes of their hellish enemies. Riding in front of his gathered, but rather lowly army, he shouted, "I see in your eyes the same fear that would break the heart of me. A day may come when the courage of men fails, when we forsake our friends, and break all bonds of fellowship. *But it is not this day. This day, we fight...by all you hold dear on this good Earth, I bid you stand with me, men of the West!*"[1]

To which I can only add a very heartfelt *Amen*!

CHAPTER TWENTY-TWO

RESPONDING WITH OUTREACH

While the power and necessity of prayer are indisputable, there is another dimension to our response that is absolutely necessary. We must also reach out to Muslims with the consummate Christian message of good news. It is a message of freedom to those held captive by the false Islamic gospel of fear. It is a message of love and acceptance to those who have never really known what it feels like to be accepted and fully loved by God. It is the message that says "God loves you this much. And here's how He proved it forever..." We must never take the Gospel message for granted. We must never underestimate its power. Indeed, *"It is the power of God for the salvation of everyone who believes"* (Romans 1:16).

REACHING OUT

> How can they believe in the one of whom they have not heard? And how can they hear without someone preaching to them? (Romans 10:14).

The purpose of this chapter is not to discuss methods of outreach to Muslims, but rather the spirit in which God desires us to reach out to Muslims in order that not only they, but also we, might be transformed. Nevertheless, I want to make just a few comments regarding outreach to Muslims. There are of course two primary ways that Christians can reach out to Muslims at home or abroad. While most Christians might assume that plenty of missionaries already labor away among Muslim peoples, consider this statistic: Only two percent of the Protestant missionary force is reaching out to the Muslims of the world who make up practically half of the non-Christian world population.[1] That's astounding, and much could be said about this. But while the majority of those who read this book may never actually move themselves and their families overseas to become missionaries to Muslims in foreign lands, that does not mean, however, that outreach to Muslims is not possible. Today, with approximately eight million Muslims living in America, America is part of the Islamic world. The same can be said of any number of Western countries. Most Muslims have moved to America from countries where you or I could face imprisonment or death for sharing the Gospel message with them. But here they are in America—the land of the free—and most Christians ignore their presence. Has there ever been a time when Jesus' words rang more true? "The harvest is plentiful, but the workers are few" (Luke 10:3).

If you are a follower of Jesus then I encourage you to meditate on Jesus' words when he told us all to "go and make disciples of all nations, baptizing them in the name of the Father and of the Son and of the Holy Spirit, and teaching them to obey everything I have commanded you." To what degree are you obeying this commandment?

Perhaps you think that outreach to Muslims is impossible. Perhaps after reading this book you are more afraid of Muslims than you previously were. Let's talk about those feelings.

A MUSLIM JUST LIKE ME

After reading this book, you may be surprised to find out that I actually love Muslims. And if you are someone who has been embraced by the love of God in Christ, then you should too. One of my biggest fears in writing this book was that it would foster a negative reaction in people toward Muslims. Of course the natural reaction after reading so much negative information is probably to shrink back from Muslims in fear. But when faced with such fear, the Lord does not want us to retreat, but rather to boldly shine forth his love to those in the darkness, *despite our fears*. Let me declare very loudly: "Our struggle is not against flesh and blood, but against the rulers, against the authorities, against the powers of this dark world and against the spiritual forces of evil in the heavenly realms" (Ephesians 6:12). In other words, *Muslims are not the enemy*! This book is not about Muslims—it is about Islam. It's about the spiritual forces and deceptive doctrines that hold people captive. Despite the fact that I've argued that Muslims follow an "antichrist" religion, I want to make it clear that as followers of Christ we need to see in every Muslim, never an enemy, but someone created in the image of God—*just like us*.

As a matter of fact, this is perhaps one of the issues that takes many Westerners by surprise when they begin to get to know Muslims. Instead of discovering small-minded, angry people, many are taken aback to discover that most Muslims are just like anybody else. I have met many very warm, very kind, and very intelligent Muslims. And the reason that they *seem* just like us is because they *are* just like us. The majority of Muslims that you meet sincerely desire to live a good life before God and do what pleases Him. So this is how we should view most Muslims: as genuine God seekers.

FINDING THE OCEAN IN EVERY DROP

Jalal al Din al Rumi was one of Islam's greatest mystics. He practiced a mystical form of Islam known as Sufiism. Rumi often spoke of God as "the Beloved" or "the Friend." Sufis such as Rumi also placed far more emphasis on Jesus as their model for life than other Muslims. One cannot read many of Rumi's writings without feeling as though he was very close to being a Christian. There is at least one quote of Rumi's that I have truly come to appreciate. Rumi said, "One day I was going along looking to see in people the shining of the Friend, so I would recognize the ocean in a drop." Rumi attempted to see God in all of His creation, and particularly in every one of His creatures. Maybe you say that we cannot find any goodness and light in the religion of the Antichrist. But, believe it or not, you can. And here's the reason: Islam is made of Muslims, and Muslims are people created in the image of God. Many of them are genuine God seekers and Christians can learn from them. And if this is so of a dead-end antichrist religious system, then how much more of its followers who are each one God's creatures! While the natural tendency of our hearts might be to shrink back from fear, instead the Lord desires us to approach Muslims with an attitude of confidence and humility that sees not an "other," but rather another of God's creatures. This attitude of humility, of boldness, and of confidence is what God desires for His people throughout time but particularly in the last days. *He desires us to be overcomers.*

OVERCOMERS

An overcomer is someone who does not allow fear to overcome him or her but rather overcomes fear with love. An overcomer does not allow hatred to overcome him or her but rather overcomes hatred with reconciliation. There was one man who reached out in just such a spirit to Muslims. He did so in the midst of one of the darkest periods of Christian history. The relationship between Islam and Christianity was at this time perhaps comparable to the atmosphere today. It was during the third Great Crusade that Francis of Assisi decided to go and preach the Gospel to the Muslims. The spirit that Francis showed is a powerful model for Christ-likeness in Christian outreach to Muslims today.

FRANCIS'S STORY

In AD 1219 Francis of Assisi and twelve of his brothers traveled with the Crusader army to the front lines in the war between the

Crusaders and the Muslim Saracens of Sultan al-Kaamil in Egypt.[2] Francis and his friends set up camp within the Crusader camp as the army prepared to lay siege to the port city of Damietta. Francis preached the Gospel among the Crusaders and many of those who impacted by Francis's message laid down their arms and joined the Franciscan order. Francis's approach was never to discriminate when preaching the Gospel. He preached to the "Christian" Crusaders and the Muslim Saracens alike. Francis followed Jesus directly into the camp of the *sultan*, the leader of the Muslim armies. Among the Christians, Sultan al-Kaamil was viewed as a brute beast. But Francis found a man who was kind, sincere, very open, and a genuine God-seeker.

Francis and his close friend Illuminato walked directly into the camp of the "enemy." Francis was immediately captured and initially abused by the Muslim soldiers. Francis demanded to see the *sultan* in order to preach the Gospel to him. Francis greeted the *sultan* with a greeting of "God give you peace." Ironically Francis himself had devised this greeting, which happened to correlate wonderfully with the standard greeting used by Muslims: *As-salamu Alaikum* (Peace be upon you).

Christine Mallouhi in her wonderful book, *Waging Peace on Islam,* walks through the various stories and legends that surround this meeting between Francis and Kaamil. While there are differing accounts, there are some things that we can know for sure about this meeting. We know that Francis was well received by the *sultan*. Most traditions support that Kaamil was so taken aback by Francis that he invited him to stay for a prolonged period with the Muslims. The record also shows that Francis accepted this invitation. We even know that the *sultan* gave written permission to Francis and his men to freely preach the Gospel in Muslim lands.

But what exactly happened to the two men as a result of their meeting? Based on interviews with Brother Illuminato, the *sultan* was quoted as saying to Francis, "I believe your faith is good and true," and upon parting ways, he asked Francis to pray that he would be able to find the correct path. Whether or not the *sultan* converted is in question, but even the Muslim accounts mention that Kaamil indeed changed after his encounter with Francis. But here's the interesting part and a lesson for us as well. Francis also changed. Francis was so impacted by the Muslims, that upon returning home to Europe he adapted some elements of Muslim practice into his religious life. For instance in accordance with the Muslim call to prayer five times a day, Francis declared to the superiors of the Franciscan Order that they were to "announce and preach to all the people…tell them about the glory that is due to him, so that at every hour when bells are rung, praise and honor may be offered to Almighty God by everyone all over the world." It is also said that Francis began bowing down with his head to the ground as the Muslims do when praying. He wrote to the general Chapter: "At the sound of his name you should fall to the ground and adore him with fear and reverence. Give hearing with all your ears and obey the Son of God. This is the very reason he has sent you all over the world, so that by word and deed you might bear witness to his message and convince everyone that there is no other Almighty God besides him." This last part of course, is very similar to the Muslim credo, "There is no god but God (Allah)."

So in the final assessment, we learn that both the *sultan* and Francis changed as a result of their meeting. The reason for this is that in every encounter, Francis did not look to merely convert "the other" but himself as well. Francis did not see the greatest enemy in others, but rather in his own "self."

The purpose of pointing out this story of Francis is that today, as then, we live in a time when Christian/Muslim tensions, misunderstandings, and fears are strong. How much more will such feelings reach their full peak in the last days? Francis is a wonderful model for us as he reached out to Muslims. He came to Muslims in confidence, without fear, yet humble, teachable, and in an absolute spirit of peace. Francis did not go to the antichrist/infidel enemy with a spirit of prejudice, but rather simply to a people who needed Jesus. Likewise Francis did not go to defend the Gospel, but to die for it. We will discuss this issue in the next chapter.

PERSONAL BENEFITS

While the primary purpose of outreach is of course to offer the message of salvation and life abundant to our Muslim brothers and sisters, there are also some very powerful benefits that we receive as well when reaching out to Muslims. Regardless of how mature a believer you are, anyone who enters into deep religious dialogue with Muslims will be challenged. You see, most Muslims spend a lot of time training themselves to argue with Christians. Eventually, you will find your core beliefs challenged. The good news, however, is that through challenge comes strengthening. My personal encounters with Muslims have caused immense growth in terms of my personal revelation and understanding of my own faith. I have never meditated more on the wonders of the incarnation, the Trinity, or the cross than I have during the periods that I am engaged with Muslims who vehemently oppose all of these doctrines. Is it at all surprising then that many of those who have reached out to Muslims have walked in a powerful revelation of the very issues that Islam denies? A wonderful example is Samuel Zwemer. Zwemer was a forerunner in ministry to Muslims who lived through the turn of the last century. One of Zwemer's books, *The Glory of the Cross*, is a classic that should read by every Christian. Its title says it all — as a result of his encounter with Muslims, Zwemer walked in a deeper revelation of the glory of the cross. And thus it will be with us as well. As we approach Muslims, the purpose is not only to introduce them to the real Jesus in order that they can be "converted," but equally in order that we might find ourselves in an ongoing and continual state of "conversion" and transformation as well.

CHAPTER TWENTY-THREE

PREPARING FOR MARTYRDOM

BECOMING PART OF THE PERSECUTED CHRISTIAN WORLD

While most of us in the West may not live in an atmosphere where martyrdom is a present threat or reality, I believe that it is very important for all of us to remain connected to our brothers and sisters who do. Presently there are numerous countries throughout the world where persecution and martyrdom are common. I believe that we can all take practical steps to connect our hearts to those who live on the front lines. Surely the Christian church on the earth needs to strive to build stronger bonds of unity, mutual support, and connectedness. And of course, we in the West, who presently "dwell securely in the coastlands," can certainly benefit from regular reality checks.

Jesus explained the principle to us that where our treasure is, there our hearts would be also. Our "treasure" may be defined by more than just our money. Beyond our finances, our time and our energies are also equally our treasures. So if we wish to begin building heart connections with those in lands of persecution, then there are some very simple things that we can do. Of course, to start, we can get to know who they are and where they are, and we can begin to regularly pray for them. If you are a leader or a pastor, then I encourage you to take a brief moment during every church service to pray for our persecuted brothers and sisters around the world.

By doing this you will facilitate the development of a bond between your entire congregation and the persecuted church. This is a good reality check for those of us who live in such a state of comfort in the West.

Second, we can begin to develop relationships with real people who live under the threat of persecution. Letter writing, e-mails, or even visits are all very simple ways to build bonds of mutual support. If you have a young family with children, then "adopt" a family in a land of persecution. Your families can exchange letters and the children can draw pictures and make small gifts for each other, etc. As a family, you can regularly pray together for your friends in Pakistan, China, Iraq, or wherever they might live.

And lastly, of course, you can send money. Do not feel as though you necessarily need to send large amounts, but simply choose an amount, and set it aside each month and send it wherever you feel led to give. Even if you sent only five dollars a month, you would sow a seed and build a bridge.

How do you begin to get acquainted with the persecuted church? First, there are various organizations that minister directly to the persecuted church throughout the world. Each ministry has its own special emphasis. I refer you here to four very good ministries: Voice of the Martyrs at www.persecution.com; Operation Nehemiah at www.operationsnehemiah.org; the Barnabas Fund at www.barnabasfund.org; Open Doors Ministries at www.opendoorsusa.org.

Each ministry has a newsletter that provides updates about current events as well as prayer points and practical ways to support their efforts. They also have e-mail reports that they send out with day-to-day updates and prayer requests. Contact one of these organizations and ask them to help you in establishing a contact such as we discussed above.

PREPARING FOR MARTYRDOM IS NOT OPTIONAL

But martyrdom is not merely something for those in some far far-off lands to think about. Everyone who claims the name "Christian" should be preparing his or her heart for potential martyrdom. This is not an optional preparation for only those who live in Third World countries or those who live at certain times in world history. Preparing for martyrdom has always been part of what it means to be a true Christian. Christianity is the only religion that has as its highest example a man who was tortured and put to death publicly. As Christians, we are his followers. Yet the concept of martyrdom is essentially a foreign one to most of us in our Western Christian culture. But in many parts of the world today, such as China, Pakistan, or the Middle East, those who choose to follow Jesus likewise all realize that they are saying yes to potential martyrdom. This was also the case for Christians for the first three hundred years of church history. Persecutions and martyrdom were common, especially among those who assumed positions of leadership.

MARTYRDOM AND MIRACLES

Yet during the periods of the early church and since the communist takeover of China, when martyrdom has been commonplace, the church has thrived. Not only does the church grow in such an atmosphere, but it is also experiences the greatest measure of power. Miracles, prophecy, angelic encounters, visions: these are the experiences that we read about as common in such an atmosphere of heavy persecution. Not surprisingly, then, the Bible likewise says that in the last days, when persecution will have peaked on a worldwide scale, the greater church will experience that same measure of power:

> In the last days, God says, I will pour out my Spirit on all people. Your sons and daughters will prophesy, your young men will see visions, your old men will dream dreams. Even on my servants, both men and women, I

213

> will pour out my Spirit in those days, and they will
> prophesy. I will show wonders in the heaven above and
> signs on the earth below, blood and fire and billows of
> smoke. The sun will be turned to darkness and the moon
> to blood before the coming of the great and glorious day
> of the Lord (Acts 2:17-20).

The Bible makes it clear that the last days will be a period not only marked by severe persecution and martyrdom, but also by perhaps the greatest measure of corporate anointing by the Holy Spirit for miracles and demonstrations of God's power. God will show mighty signs and wonders not only in the heavens but also "on the earth below." During the last days, the church will simultaneously shine the brightest and experience its darkest defeat.

OVERCOMING BY BEING OVERCOME

In the Book of Daniel and the Book of Revelation, we see the clearest articulation of this paradox. As the Lord revealed images of the last days to Daniel, he was totally confused and utterly devastated. Daniel actually says that after seeing these things he was sickened and remained so for days afterward. What did Daniel see? As the Lord visited Daniel with visions of the last days, he saw the mystery and the paradox of the Cross lived out by the church. Daniel saw the very means by which the last days church would overcome Satan and his hoards and ultimately receive its reward — the kingdom of God:

> As I watched, this horn [the Antichrist] *was waging war against*
> *the saints and defeating them,* until the Ancient of Days came
> and pronounced judgment in favor of the saints of the Most
> High, and the time came when they possessed the kingdom.
> He gave me this explanation: "The fourth beast is a fourth
> kingdom that will appear on earth. It will be different from
> all the other kingdoms and will devour the whole earth,
> trampling it down and crushing it. The ten horns are ten
> kings who will come from this kingdom. After them another
> king will arise, different from the earlier ones; he will subdue

three kings. *He will speak against the Most High and oppress his saints* and try to change the set times and the laws. *The saints will be handed over to him for a time, times and half a time.* But the court will sit, and his power will be taken away and completely destroyed forever. *Then the sovereignty, power and greatness of the kingdoms under the whole heaven will be handed over to the saints, the people of the Most High.* His kingdom will be an everlasting kingdom, and all rulers will worship and obey him." This is the end of the matter. I, Daniel, was deeply troubled by my thoughts, and my face turned pale, but I kept the matter to myself (Daniel 7:21-28, emphasis mine).

This very passage is reflected in the Book of Revelation:

The beast was given a mouth to utter proud words and blasphemies and to exercise his authority for forty-two months. He opened his mouth to blaspheme God, and to slander his name and his dwelling place and those who live in heaven. *He was given power to make war against the saints and to conquer them.* And he was given authority over every tribe, people, language, and nation. All inhabitants of the earth will worship the beast—all whose names have not been written in the Book of Life belonging to the Lamb that was slain from the creation of the world. *He who has an ear, let him hear. If anyone is to go into captivity, into captivity he will go. If anyone is to be killed with the sword, with the sword he will be killed. This calls for patient endurance and faithfulness on the part of the saints* (Revelation 13:5-10, emphasis mine).

The saints at the end of this age will be "conquered." They will fall by the edge of the sword. The armies of the Antichrist will take the saints as captives and martyr multitudes. The Book of Revelation says that those who come through the tribulation will be a vast multitude "that no one could count":

After this I looked and there before me was a *great multitude that no one could count, from every nation, tribe, people, and language,* standing before the throne and in front of the Lamb. They were wearing white robes and were holding palm branches in their hands. And they cried out in a loud voice: "Salvation belongs to our God, who sits on the throne, and to the Lamb." Then one of the

> elders...said, *"These are they who have come out of the great*
> *tribulation*; they have washed their robes and made them
> white in the blood of the Lamb. Therefore, they are before
> the throne of God and serve him day and night in his
> temple; and he who sits on the throne will spread his tent
> over them. Never again will they hunger; never again will
> they thirst" (Revelation 7:9-16, emphasis mine).

In these verses, we see the paradigm that defines the last days church. It is the paradox of the Cross: Like their Lord and Master, those who are defeated and overcome *are the actual overcomers.* While those in the army of the Antichrist will think that by defeating their detractors physically and militarily, they will gain the victory, they will actually set their own snares. Instead, in the wisdom of God, even as it was at the Cross, the very ones who appear humiliated, beat down, and defeated crush Satan under their feet (Romans 16:20). But how do they overcome him? "They overcame him by the blood of the Lamb and by the word of their testimony; they did not love their lives so much as to shrink from death" (Revelation 12:11).

The overcomers will fix their eyes on Jesus, Who is not only the author and perfecter of our faith (Hebrews 12:2), but also our example. Jesus set the bar. Martyrdom for those who have chosen to follow Jesus fills the pages of Christianity's history books. Every apostle except one is believed by church historians to have died the death of a martyr for preaching the Christian message.

THE DEATHS OF STEPHEN AND ANDREW

If you've read the Book of Acts, then you've read the story of Stephen, one of the early leaders in the church. Like the believers in the last days, Stephen was "full of God's grace and power, [he] did great wonders and miraculous signs among the people." Stephen was also martyred for his bold declaration of the Gospel message. And like his Master, as Stephen died, he prayed for those killing him: "While they were stoning him,

Stephen prayed, "Lord Jesus, receive my spirit." Then he fell on his knees and cried out, "Lord, do not hold this sin against them." When he had said this, he fell asleep (Acts 7:59-60).

Stephen was just a regular guy. But Stephen was an overcomer. While Jesus is our ultimate example, Stephen is proof that it is possible for all of us to also be overcomers.

Andrew was the brother of Peter and one of the twelve apostles. Andrew also died the death of a martyr. The account of his death is recorded in church history. I have never been able to read the story of Andrew's death without crying:

> Peter's brother was crucified by Aegeas, a Roman governor, in the city of Sebastopolis. Andrew had brought so many to faith in Christ that the governor came to the province to compel the new Christians to sacrifice to idols and renounce their faith. Andrew challenged Aegeas to his face, told him to renounce his false gods and idols, and declared that the gods and idols of the Romans were not gods but devils and the enemies of mankind. In a rage, the proconsul ordered Andrew not to teach and preach, and warned him that if he did he would be fastened to a cross. Andrew replied, "I would not have preached the honor and glory of the cross, if I feared the death of the cross." He was immediately condemned. As Andrew was taken to the place of his execution, he saw the cross in the distance and cried out, "O cross, most welcome and looked for! With a willing mind, joyfully and desirously, I come to thee, being the scholar of him who did hang on thee: because I have always been thy lover, and have coveted to embrace thee."[1]

Whenever I read this, I pray that if and when my one opportunity arrives, I will likewise possess such a willing spirit. It is clear that Andrew had actually anticipated and looked forward to that moment. Andrew had not ignored the possibility of martyrdom until it was upon him; he actually had meditated on the idea. Church history records countless stories of those who died glorious deaths in the grace of God. I encourage you to occasionally read such accounts and talk to the Lord about your feelings regarding martyrdom. Many such accounts are available in books like *the Foxes Book of Martyrs* or the more modern *Jesus Freaks* published by the Voice of the Martyrs.

IS MARTYDOM GLORIOUS? EMBRACING THE SHAME OF THE CROSS

While it is encouraging to hear stories of those who died with such a spirit of courage and grace, seemingly without any fear and in some cases without any pain, I do not personally believe that every martyrdom is this way. While we like to read about valiant stories of martyrs throughout church history, I do not personally think that every martyrdom is necessarily glorious. Reality rarely is as it is described in books. My mind flashes to the recent martyrdom of Kim Sun-il, a Korean Christian beheaded by Muslim extremists in Iraq. Few news reports mentioned that Kim Sun-il died specifically because he actively shared his Christian faith with Iraqis.

Kim Sun-il had always dreamed of bringing the Gospel to Muslims. He had learned Arabic for this purpose and worked in Iraq as an interpreter. All the while he shared the Gospel message with those he met. After Kim's death, the group that claimed responsibility, Tawhid wa al-Jihad, made this statement on their Web site: "We have killed an infidel who tried to propagate Christianity in Iraq.... This infidel studied theology and was preparing to become a missionary in the Islamic world."[2] So while most people probably assumed that Kim was merely another political beheading, to those who killed him, it was because he spoke about Jesus to the Iraqi people.

While Kim had obviously heard the call of God on his life and had been preparing for some years, when he found himself in the hands of evil men who intended to kill him, he broke down. He wept and begged for his life. Recordings of this were played on newscasts all over the world. Three days later he was beheaded and the videotape was sent to news organizations all over the world. Those who saw the footage said that Kim did not weep or beg or fight as his captors read their message to the world and then beheaded him. Instead Kim died with a solid resolve and without any protest—courageously.

Why do I recall this horrific event? Because it is reality. While, by the grace of God, when Kim Sun-il died, he seemed to have accepted his fate and met it with a solid resolve, the reality is that, just days before his death, he was weeping and pleading for his life. And the straight truth is most of us would probably do the same thing.

In preparing our hearts for martyrdom, I think it is important that we shed our false notions that martyrdom is purely a valiant, glorious, and honorable event like we read about in the pages of some Christian history books. We need to remember the very important fact that martyrdom is not intended to make the martyr look good. Martyrdom is not about the glory of Christians, but the glory of God.

I want to be very frank here for a moment. The point that I am trying to convey is that I suspect that to a degree we Christians—particularly men—might have a rather macho or idealistic image of martyrdom in our minds. I fear that many young men in the church tend to think of martyrdom as a means to essentially "look awesome." We imagine how we would be remembered if we were to die as a martyr. It is the means by which we might achieve the status of Christian *legend*.

But if martyrdom is identification with the death of our Lord— the death of Jesus on the Cross, then isn't martyrdom also a shameful event? Is martyrdom limited merely to a quick death? Or does martyrdom also include immense suffering, torture, and utter humiliation? Again, what was Jesus subjected to? Jesus endured not only pain but also great shame and humiliation during his trial and crucifixion. And not only shame and humiliation but an utter turmoil gripped his soul until he actually began to sweat blood. I think of the many stories that came out of Iraq after the war ended. I hear stories of people given the option of confessing to a crime that they never committed or watch as members of their families endured rape, torture, and murder.

What if you were given the option of renouncing Jesus or seeing your children abused and slowly tortured to death? Which would you choose? I understand that this is a nightmare even to think about. Please forgive me for even going here, but this is a point that needs to be made. Martyrdom is not macho. Martyrdom is not glorious. Martyrdom is not merely enduring great amounts of pain. Martyrdom is also not merely dying gracefully. Martyrdom is utter embarrassment, shame, confusion, and turmoil beyond what most have ever experienced. For me personally, it does not take very long before even the mildest of difficult circumstances in my life move me to begin complaining to God and giving myself over to sinful attitudes. So how does one prepare his or her heart for martyrdom? We begin today. Martyrdom is not a one-time event. Martyrdom is identification with Jesus on the Cross. And taking up our cross is supposed to be a *daily* exercise. "Then Jesus said to them all: "If anyone would come after me, he must deny himself and take up his cross daily and follow me" (Luke 9:23).

Isn't that what we signed up for? A lifelong exercise of daily dying to ourselves, living for God's glory and not our own? We cannot expect to walk according to our own ways today and yet expect to die for God tomorrow. Martyrdom is something that we need to begin living now. "To him who overcomes, I will give the right to sit with me on my throne, just as I overcame and sat down with my Father on his throne. He who has an ear, let him hear what the Spirit says to the churches (Revelation 3:21, 22).

social skills. If you are the kind of person that doesn't alienate people now, then you won't alienate people after you become familiar with eschatology. And besides, what other people might think certainly shouldn't be anyone's basis for decision-making (Proverbs 29:25). Paul once said that if his actions and behavior were motivated by a concern for what people thought of him, then he was no longer a servant of Christ (Galatians 1:10). I hope we are in agreement on this point.

REASON TWO: ESCHATOLOGY IS IMPOSSIBLE TO UNDERSTAND

Another reason that people do not study eschatology is that they feel as though it is so confusing it is impossible to understand, so why bother? Let me say very clearly, without any qualifications, that that assumption is a blatant lie. I agree that the world of eschatology can be confusing. But it has really only become such because of the interference of people who don't like what the Bible clearly says regarding these events and therefore try to devise systems of interpretation to get around the clear meanings. But the speculative theological contortionism of such systems is apparent to anyone who tries to follow such lines of reasoning. There are several very different perspectives regarding the end times. Some positions take an allegorical or symbolic view of the eschatological portions (and even entire books!) of Scripture while other positions attempt to simply understand the Bible at face value. This is to say that if we read a portion of the Bible that is, for instance, historical narrative, we read it as such. If it is poetry, we read it as poetry. If it is a parable, we read it as a parable. But if it is history, we do not read it as allegory. This is only common sense. The book in your hands is not an allegory. It doesn't take a theologian to explain this to you. God did not put information in His Bible that is impossible to understand. Yes, some things are hard to understand, but difficulty cannot be an excuse to avoid trying. With some diligent study and a prayerful attitude (more on this later) the Scriptures will be

EMBRACING BIBLICAL ESCHATOLOGY

In this section the question is addressed: Why study eschatology? But before we address this question, I want to bat around a couple of the reasons why people *do not* study eschatology.

REASON ONE: PEOPLE WHO STUDY ESCHATOLOGY ARE WEIRD

I don't know about you, but I think one of the reasons that a lot of people do not study eschatology is that many of the people that I know who do study eschatology seem weird. Have you personally ever noticed that? Over the years, I have attended several "home groups," which are basically small weekly gatherings of Christians that usually meet in people's homes for the purpose of community and mutual edification. And it seems like it never fails—there is always one person in each group obsessed with the end times. No matter what the discussion is about, they always seem to want to talk about the end times. It can certainly be a real party killer. It can really make people uncomfortable. Have you experienced this? Personally part of my fear in writing this book is that I didn't want to be viewed as "one of those guys." Maybe you are like me and you likewise don't want to be viewed as an odd bird, and for that reason have shied away from the study of eschatology. That's understandable. But can I assure you of something? The type of person that we are talking about was not a bit different *before* they started studying eschatology. Eschatology is not responsible for any person's oddness or poor opened up to you and even the more complex issues will become completely understandable.

REASON THREE: ESCHATOLOGY IS IRRELEVANT; THERE ARE OTHER FAR MORE RELEVANT ISSUES TO ATTEND TO

Some people feel as though there are more pertinent and more relevant issues to attend to than studying eschatology. They think that we should be about the work of ministering to the immediate needs of the people around us rather than staring at the clouds, dwelling on some future events, perpetually on the horizon. Some might say that the Gospel message is about the good news of salvation, not about the bad news of the Antichrist and false prophets and persecutions, etc. Again, I certainly understand these kinds of feelings. But if we just boil down "biblical eschatology" into its simplest function, what we have is essentially the study of the return of Jesus. The study of such odd and frightening concepts as the Antichrist and the False Prophet are not the primary reasons to study eschatology, but are rather simply one of the signs that happen to precede the true focus of a healthy eschatology, namely, "the return of the King." While Jesus and the apostles did spend plenty of time talking about everyday issues such as healthy relationships and giving thanks and speaking in tongues and choosing deacons, etc., it cannot be denied that eschatology also featured very prominently in their preaching and teaching. And these men lived two thousand years before us. I remember a particular preacher who made the goofy yet very true comment that we are closer to the last days than anyone before us. So if Jesus and the apostles didn't think that eschatology was irrelevant two thousand years ago, then why should we think any different? If they made these distant future events an integral part of their preaching, then why do we fail to do so? What did they understand that we might be missing?

POSITIVE REASONS TO STUDY ESCHATOLOGY

Reason One: Eschatology and Hellfire Preaching Saved Me

The first Christian book I ever read was by John Walvoord, a prominent end times teacher. I can't remember exactly what motivated me to buy the book. For whatever reason many people who are not Christians are fascinated by eschatology, and I was one of them. When I committed my life to the Lord a few months later, the eschatological/wrath of God type of verses in the Bible that I first encountered in Walvoord's book spoke strongly to me and weighed on my thoughts as I made that most important of all decisions: to repent of my former patterns of thinking and live in exchange for something far better. The verses that influenced me to do so were not the type of verses that most Christians today would use when attempting to share the Gospel message with someone in a sensitive manner. In many Christian circles today, if a preacher said something to the effect of, "Be saved from this perverse generation!" (Acts 2:40), he might be viewed as a radical or an old-fashioned hellfire-and-brimstone sort of preacher. What I am trying to say here is that eschatology is part of the Gospel message. It was part of the Gospel message in the New Testament and it should remain part of today's Gospel message as well. If it doesn't seem seeker-sensitive enough, then so be it. We have our example in the New Testament. Many pastors need to ask themselves: Why have I strayed from the New Testament model? As Christians, do we really think we can do better than John the Baptist, Jesus, and the apostles? So while I understand that there are numerous relevant issues to study and understand within the context of the normal, everyday, healthy Christian life—such as relationships and giving and gathering together and so much more—biblically speaking, eschatology cannot be excluded. To eliminate eschatology from evangelism or discipleship or the regular spiritual diet of any believer is to water down the complete New Testament/Apostolic Gospel message. Following are six more very basic reasons to commit to a healthy embrace of biblical eschatology.

Reason Two: Jesus, Our Example, Studied Eschatology. (What Would Jesus Do?)

This may sound a bit too obvious, but please do think about this simple fact: Jesus studied eschatology. Of course the eschatological portions of Scripture were not the only portions of Scripture that Jesus studied, but nevertheless He did study them. If you are a Christian, then you have decided to be a follower of Jesus (Matthew 28:19, 20). In the Gospels we often see Jesus quoting from the eschatological portions of Scripture. It was clear that Jesus not only knew the eschatological portions of Scripture but that He also understood and rightly interpreted the rich prophetic meanings of them. At the onset of his earthly ministry we see Jesus rising in the synagogue to read from the scroll of the Prophet Isaiah:

> He went to Nazareth, where he had been brought up, and on the Sabbath day he went into the synagogue, as was his custom. And he stood up to read. The scroll of the prophet Isaiah was handed to him. Unrolling it, he found the place where it is written: "The Spirit of the Lord is on me, because he has anointed me to preach good news to the poor. He has sent me to proclaim freedom for the prisoners and recovery of sight for the blind, to release the oppressed, to proclaim the year of the Lord's favor." Then he rolled up the scroll, gave it back to the attendant, and sat down. The eyes of everyone in the synagogue were fastened on him, and he began by saying to them, "Today this scripture is fulfilled in your hearing" (Luke 4:16-21).[1]

In one of Jesus' final messages to His disciples, He answered their questions, "when will this (destruction of the Temple) happen, and what will be the sign of your coming and of the end of the age?" (Matthew 24:3). In answering their questions, Jesus makes direct references to the Book of Daniel the Prophet, one of the most thoroughly eschatological books in the Bible:

> So when you see standing in the holy place the abomination that causes desolation spoken of through the prophet Daniel—let the reader understand—then let those who are in Judea flee to the mountains (Matthew 24:15, 16).

In the same chapter Jesus also quotes from Isaiah again and makes allusions to the Prophet Jonah as well, the simple point being that Jesus had a thorough command of the eschatological portions of Scripture. Let me repeat my point: Jesus studied eschatology. Yet many believers today disregard the eschatological portions of Scripture for various reasons. Unless we think we are somehow more advanced or more in touch with reality than Jesus, then surely we as His followers should likewise earnestly pursue a solid command of biblical eschatology.

Reason Three: God Put It in the Bible

Again, I don't mean to sound like a wise guy here, but hopefully the strength of this point is its obviousness. If the Holy Spirit saw fit to fill the pages of the Bible with abundant (and I do mean abundant) references to the last days, then why do the vast majority of Christians pass over these portions of Scripture? Why do so many Christians tend to be a bit cynical or dismissive when it comes to, for instance, the Book of Revelation? While God never said explicitly, "thou shall study eschatology," he may as well have said it by simple virtue of the fact that he gave it such a place of prominence in the Bible. We must ask ourselves, "If God doesn't want me to study and understand this stuff, then what is it there for?" Think about this fact: Over twenty-five percent of the verses in the Bible contain predictive/prophetic content.[2] If we disregard that twenty-five percent (along with, of course, those infamous and pesky genealogies) then we can significantly whittle the Bible down quite a bit. But before we do that, I suppose we'll have to first toss out that verse that says, "All Scripture is inspired by God and profitable for teaching, for reproof, for correction, for training in righteousness" (2 Timothy 3:16). Sorry, I guess I was trying to be a wise guy after all…my apologies.

Reason Four: This Stuff Is Just Too Serious to Ignore

Anyone who has read the Book of Revelation knows that the events that many of us may live to see are serious. There is the description of literally half of the inhabitants of the earth dying (Revelation 9:18). We read about plagues, wars, and earthquakes (Revelation 6). There is very little in the way of "your worst nightmare imaginable" that the book of Revelation does not contain. But we don't have to even venture into the Book of Revelation to realize the gravity of these events. When we read the twenty-fourth and twenty-fifth chapters of the Gospel of Matthew, we see Jesus making one of the most terrifying and tragic statements in all of Scripture. Consider for a minute, the reality and the weight of what is being stated by Jesus here:

> Then you will be handed over to be persecuted and put to death, and you will be hated by all nations because of me. At that time many will turn away from the faith and will betray and hate each other, and many false prophets will appear and deceive many people. Because of the increase of wickedness, the love of most will grow cold, but he who stands firm to the end will be saved (Matthew 24:9-13).

If that doesn't sadden and scare you to no end, then I simply cannot relate to you. I am firmly secure in the love of God. I am confident that Jesus died for my sins. I have no question that there is nothing in the universe that can separate me from the love of God. But I am also fully aware of my sin. I am aware of my propensity to slip into a self-deluded state that can indeed be compared to a state of drunkenness. The expression above does not say "many will fall away from going to church," but rather "many will fall away from the faith," and "the love of most will grow cold." This is absolutely terrifying. These are people that we know. These are people that we have experienced sweet fellowship with. These are our brothers and our sisters. This stuff is real and it is deadly serious and we simply cannot afford to ignore it.

Reason Five: We Very Well May Live to See These Events

This point cannot be underscored enough. The events that the Bible outlines are real. Many of us who read this material may quite possibly live to see the return of Jesus. Now, you may say that every generation has believed that they were living in the last generation. While many may argue that this universal feeling of the anticipation of Jesus' return has always been the case in the church, I completely reject that notion. There have, of course, been numerous groups, many of them fringe, that have anticipated Jesus' return in their generation, but far more did not anticipate Christ's imminent return. In fact a fair argument could be made that this generation is the first generation since the apostolic generation which has had such a universal witness to the imminence of the final hour. Personally, whenever I hear someone emphasize the idea that every generation of the church has universally believed that Christ would return in their generation, I listen to see what they are about to excuse themselves and others from. It never fails that whenever that point is emphasized, it is done for the purpose of making an excuse for a life lived in a manner that does not anticipate His return. Again, the question that we all need to ask ourselves, especially those who are leaders in the church, is: Are our attitudes the same as those of the members of the early church? Or have we adopted an attitude that looks less like the example that we see in the New Testament and more like the spirit of the age that we now live in?

Reason Six: To Give Us Understanding and Prepare Our Hearts

One of the primary reasons that we all need to make eschatology part of our regular spiritual diet is that through such, we become prepared. This preparation is not primarily a physical preparation.

It is not about the stockpiling of food or finding a safe route of escape from your city (although, to a degree, it certainly could be). It is primarily a spiritual preparation. This preparation or "readiness" occurs for two reasons and neither should be ignored.

The first and most important reason is based on the spiritual effects that the study of eschatology has on our hearts. These spiritual effects affect our actions and the way we live. One of these effects is a desire for personal holiness (Hebrews 12:14). When we read about the events as described in the Bible and the terrible and fearful events that will occur, followed by the glorious appearing of Jesus from heaven, we find ourselves desiring to throw off all sin and focus on the hope of one day seeing him face to face. Indeed, "everyone who has this hope fixed on him purifies himself, just as he (Jesus) is pure" (1 John 3:3). When we read the description of us as the bride of Christ we desire to purify ourselves and maintain our chastity for our future husband:

> Christ loved the church and gave himself up for her to make her holy, cleansing her by the washing with water through the word, and to present her to himself as a radiant church, without stain or wrinkle or any other blemish, but holy and blameless (Ephesians 5:27).

> For I am jealous for you with a godly jealousy; for I betrothed you to one husband, so that to Christ I might present you as a pure virgin (2 Corinthians 11:2).

We will also most certainly develop a deep urgency for prayer and evangelism and maybe even church planting. We may find a deeper felt need for communion and community with fellow followers of Jesus (Hebrews 10:25). And there are many other positive spiritual benefits of studying eschatology as well. All of these effects are part of the greater cumulative effect that will make us "ready" through the great and terrible days ahead, and until the day when Jesus finally returns.

The second way that eschatology makes us prepared is through the foreknowledge and understanding that it imparts. Simply stated, to be forewarned is to be forearmed. If indeed we are the generation living just prior to the return of Jesus, then this factor could not be more crucial. The study of eschatology not only prepares our hearts but it also gives us specific descriptions of future events to watch for. Things will occur on the earth that we will need to understand mentally in order to escape or avoid them (Matthew 24:15, 16; Revelations 14:9). True readiness comes through both a prayerful, continual communion with Him and an informed response to the external unfolding of the signs and events all around us. It is the communion that is the "One Thing" that takes priority over all other issues in the Christian life (Mark 12:29, 30; Psalm 27:4; Luke 10:42), but He also expects us to not be ignorant. Again, that is why He shared so much information with us. Jesus said, "Behold, I have told you in advance" (Matthew 24:25).

So both understanding and spiritual readiness combine in our hearts and lives to make us truly "ready." This state of readiness is described in the Bible with terms like "sobriety," "alertness," "watchfulness," etc. And we are warned abundantly to always remain in such a state. In Matthew 24 and 25, we find Jesus repeatedly saying such things as "Be on the alert" (Matthew 24:42, 25:13), "See to it that no one misleads you" (24:4). Whenever we approach the eschatological portions of Scripture we find these types of warnings/exhortations.

We are commanded to remain in a spirit of watchfulness:

> But as for me, I will watch expectantly for the LORD; I will wait for the God of my salvation. My God will hear me (Micah 7:7).

> For many deceivers have gone out into the world, those who do not acknowledge Jesus Christ as coming in the flesh. This is the deceiver and the antichrist. Watch yourselves, that you do not lose what we have accomplished, but that you may receive a full reward (2 John 1:7, 8).

We are commanded to always be alert:

> Therefore, be on the alert—for you do not know when the master of the house is coming, whether in the evening, at midnight, or when the rooster crows, or in the morning...What I say to you I say to all, *Be on the alert!'* (Mark 13:35, 37, emphasis mine).

> *But keep on the alert at all times,* praying that you may have strength to escape all these things that are about to take place, and to stand before the Son of Man (Luke 21:36).

> [A]nd from among your own selves men will arise, speaking perverse things, to draw away the disciples after them. *Therefore be on the alert...* (Acts 20:30, 31, emphasis mine).

> With all prayer and petition pray at all times in the Spirit, and with this in view, *be on the alert* with all perseverance and petition for all the saints (Ephesians 6:18, emphasis mine).

Indeed, the Scriptures compare living in ignorance of the last days to being asleep or drunk:

> So then let us not sleep as others do, *but let us be alert and sober* (1 Thessalonians 5:6, emphasis mine).

> *Be of sober spirit, be on the alert.* Your adversary, the devil, prowls around like a roaring lion, seeking someone to devour (1 Peter 5:8, emphasis mine).

In fact, drunkenness is the specific state that describes those who have compromised with the "Babylonian Harlot" of the Book of Revelation: "Fallen! Fallen is Babylon the Great! For all the nations have drunk the maddening wine of her adulteries (Revelation 17:1-3). These expressions: "be sober," "be watchful," "be on your guard," "be aware," "be careful" all speak of very deliberate activity. So let us all heed these warnings. Let us all pursue a deeper love relationship and daily communion with our beautiful King, and let us not neglect the information that He has shown us ahead of time in His awesome Word.

Reason Seven: As A Basis For Any Prophetic Office.

Another reason that has, in my opinion, been highly overlooked by most prophetic ministers in the church is that a proper grasp of biblical eschatology is the essential foundation of any truly prophetic ministry. I say this in reference to any individual called to the specific office of prophet as well as to any church that feels called corporately to be a prophetic people. What I mean by prophetic in this case is not merely the gifting or ability from God to speak an encouraging, edifying or even a directional word to another individual. I am speaking of those prophetic ministers or churches that feel called to prophesy to and about specific events from God's perspective. I am speaking about individuals and churches that feel called to become a relevant force on the earth or in their cities and communities. It is my conviction that as a result of a lack of a clear vision of the future, founded on a proper understanding of biblical eschatology, the church suffers and tends to be far less effective as a truly prophetic people. The same can be said regarding any individual called to a prophetic ministry.

Let me try to restate this a bit more clearly. The Bible gives us very specific and detailed information about the future of this world. These events will have unparalleled social, economic, religious, and most importantly, spiritual implications for the entire earth. If someone believes himself or herself called to be a prophetic voice that speaks with relevance and power from God to the world and the greater lukewarm Western church, (a majority of the Old Testament's prophecies were directed at the lukewarm Israelites), then it is absolutely necessary to first understand the clear prophetic word already written.

A good contemporary example to demonstrate my point here is the fact that God Himself has reestablished the Jewish people in the land of Israel. He made it clear thousands of years ago that He would do so. The return of the Jewish people to their homeland is unquestionably part of the clear unfolding of biblical prophecy. The rebirth of Israel is a necessary step in God's plans to fulfill all of His good promises and covenants with the Jewish people. Presently a massive renewed surge of anti-Semitism is spreading all over the world. This time around, however, anti-Semitism is not called anti-Semitism, but rather disguised under the euphemism "anti-Zionism."[3] As a result of a lack of understanding of God's clear purposes for the nation of Israel and the Jewish people as laid out in Scripture, many Christians have unknowingly (or even completely knowingly) supported anti-Semitic causes and theologies. This is a grievous error. Throughout history the church has made this same mistake over and over. As a matter of fact, it was precisely due to a lack of understanding of the nature of the future eschatological kingdom of God and Israel's part in it that the Christian church made, arguably, the most significant errors in its history. The establishment of the church state under Constantine and the Crusades were both the direct results of bad theology regarding the Kingdom of God and the status of the Jewish people based on a false eschatology. Think of how the world might have been different if the church had not fallen into these errors. The nation of Israel is far from perfect and certainly not beyond criticism; the same can be said of any nation. But without the foundation of the clear prophetic Word in the Bible regarding Israel, many Christians do not know how to properly discern the nature or source of many events that revolve around the State of Israel and the Jewish people today.

This is especially true in light of the growing cloud of misinformation and blatant propaganda that seeks to demonize Israel. This is just one example of how a lack of understanding of the biblical prophetic timeline of events in the last days can cause well-meaning, intelligent Christians to miss what is unfolding right before their eyes. Rather than being a relevant force in the world, in tune with God's mind, such a person may instead actually be aiding the plans of those whose inspiration is from Satan. I understand this issue to be very controversial, but I stand very firmly on it.

The revelation that any prophet delivers needs to be built on the solid foundation of the established (capital P), Prophetic

Word in the Bible. Those who wish to be prophetic (lower case p) without first having ingested and assimilated the Prophetic Eschatological Gospel into their being will be significantly stunted in the effectiveness of their ministry. People who believe they can be truly effective prophetic voices without actually understanding the Gospel message would be regarded as delusional by most Christians.

But the Gospel message is the prophetic eschatological message. The Gospel message is not merely that Jesus died on the Cross for our sins. The Cross of Jesus is the foundation of the Gospel message, but the conclusion of the Gospel message is His return. The central crowning element of biblical eschatology is the return of Jesus to literally reign over the earth from Jerusalem! The Gospel message of Jesus dying for our sins, without His return, is not the full Gospel. Biblical eschatology completes the Gospel message. "For the testimony of Jesus is the spirit of prophecy." (Revelation 19:10). Or paraphrased; the message about Jesus to the world (the Kingdom Gospel message) and biblical eschatology (the spirit of prophecy) are one and the same thing. In order to flow in the spirit of prophecy, God expects His prophets to understand the full Gospel message that is nothing short of the full "testimony of Jesus."

HOW TO STUDY ESCHATOLOGY: A BIBLICAL PATTERN

Like His contemporaries, Jesus studied the Scriptures from an early age, but I also believe that He regularly came before the Father in humility and in prayer and asked the Father to open the Scriptures to Him (Mark 1:35; Luke 5:16; Matthew 14:23). I think it is safe to say that Jesus came to understand His calling to the world and ultimately to His death on the Cross, not solely by virtue of the fact that He was the Word of God incarnate, but also by diligently studying the Scriptures combined with the discipline of spending time with the Father through the Holy Spirit in prayer. And while the Bible does not explicitly state exactly how often Jesus fasted, I am confident that He fasted regularly (John

4:32, Matthew 17:21, Hebrews 5:7). Jesus lived His life on the earth in full dependence upon the Holy Spirit (Luke 4:1). If we desire to be true followers of Jesus, and understand what the Scriptures have to say about the future of our world, our country, our cities, our lives, and the lives of our families, we need to diligently study the Scriptures with prayer and consistent, regular fasting. It is as simple as that. There are no shortcuts. God promises us that if we will diligently seek Him, He will respond:

> Call to Me and I will answer you, and I will tell you great and mighty things, which you do not know (Jeremiah 3:33).
>
> So I say to you, ask, and it will be given to you; seek, and you will find; knock, and it will be opened to you (Luke 11:9).
>
> You will seek me and find me when you seek me with all your heart (Jeremiah 29:13).

Prayer and fasting combined with an attitude of desperation will move God's heart to respond. I believe that in regard to the last days, this is the pattern we need to follow. We find this pattern in the life of Daniel the Prophet. Let's look at what it says in Daniel 9:1-4:

> In the first year of Darius the son of Ahasuerus, of Median descent, who was made king over the kingdom of the Chaldeans—in the first year of his reign, I, Daniel, observed in the books the number of the years which was revealed as the word of the LORD to Jeremiah the prophet for the completion of the desolations of Jerusalem, namely, seventy years. So I gave my attention to the Lord God to seek Him by prayer and supplications, with fasting, sackcloth, and ashes. I prayed to the LORD my God and confessed...

Notice the pattern. Daniel reads from the Scripture of the former Prophet Jeremiah and discerns that he is living in the times that are spoken of prophetically. His response is our mandate: "So I turned to the Lord God and pleaded with him in prayer and petition, in fasting, and in sackcloth and ashes. I prayed to the LORD my God and confessed..."

Daniel had not finished praying when the angel Gabriel appeared to him:

> Now while I was speaking and praying, and confessing my sin and the sin of my people Israel, and presenting my supplication before the LORD my God in behalf of the holy mountain of my God, while I was still speaking in prayer, then the man Gabriel, whom I had seen in the vision previously, came to me in my extreme weariness about the time of the evening offering. He gave me instruction and talked with me and said, "O Daniel, I have now come forth to give you insight with understanding. At the beginning of your supplications the command was issued, and I have come to tell you, for you are highly esteemed; so give heed to the message and gain understanding of the vision" (Daniel 9:20-23).

Awesome! If you feel confused or hopeless about understanding the last days, take heart at this story and this pattern. When we do our part by studying, praying, and fasting; asking for insight, understanding and revelation; then God has promised to do His part and answers with supernatural assistance. He will come and open up the Scriptures and even enlighten us concerning world events. And it is specifically this type of supernatural enlightenment that we will need in the days to come. But take heart—while the future may look scary, we do not have to face it alone. Jesus has promised that He would be with us (Matthew 28:19, 20). He has promised not to leave us as orphans; that He would be with us to help us:

> I will ask the Father, and He will give you another Helper, that He may be with you forever; that is the Spirit of truth, whom the world cannot receive, because it does not see Him or know Him, but you know Him because He abides with you and will be in you. I will not leave you as orphans; I will come to you" (John 14:18).

He has promised very specifically that in the last days there would be those who would shine with His radiance and give understanding and light to others:

> Those who have insight will shine brightly like the brightness of the expanse of heaven, and those who lead the many to righteousness, like the stars forever and ever (Daniel 12:3).

> Those who have insight among the people will give understanding to the many; yet they will fall by sword and by flame, by captivity and by plunder for many days (Daniel 11:33).

> He said, "Go your way, Daniel, for these words are concealed and sealed up until the end time. Many will be purged, purified, and refined, but the wicked will act wickedly; and none of the wicked will understand, but those who have insight will understand" (Daniel 12:9, 10).

Now unfortunately there is the obvious downside also mentioned here that many will fall and be refined through "purging" and tribulation, but the point here is that in the last days, God has stated that He will raise up those who will "shine brightly." They will lead "many to righteousness" and will "give understanding to the many." We have already discussed the biblical pattern for gaining such understanding: Communion with God, prayer and fasting, and a humble diligent studying of God's Word. Through this pattern, God will allow many to avoid being overcome or confused by the darkness. Instead, they will "shine brightly like the brightness of the expanse of heaven, and lead the many to righteousness, like the stars forever and ever..."

AN E-MAIL FROM AN AMERICAN MUSLIM

From: Tamim
Subject: Give it up. UR losing to us.
Wa'laikum,

I perused your pathetic little attempt to discredit the Religion of God and his Great Prophet. Truly sad. i am not an apologist. Yes, the Prophet Muhammad (pbuh) committed acts of violence. i have no problems with this. We are muslims, not passivists. Sometimes in life you have to fight. you dont have to stand tall, but you do have to stand up.I do not rectify the violence of terrorists, nor do i rectify the acts of violence made by 2000 years of Christian tyranny and violence. Its destruction of polytheist cultures, its 1000 years of genocidal mission toward jews, and its persecution of free thinkers such as Galileo, Bruno, and Capurnicus. The Eurpoean and American Witch trials, and the "Christian terrorism" of the Irish, the KKK (a Whitye Anglo-Saxon CHRISTIAN terrorist organzation). We should ask the nomadic Avars how much they love the religion of the "Prince of Peace"....oh wait, we cant. They were completely wiped out in a genocidal effort by Charlemagne because they refused to convert to the Paulian Blood Cult you laughingly call "The Way." Christianity has been the scourge of this planet. It has caused more pain, torture, and death than any other fanatical movement ever invented. So take a look in the mirror the next time you start to criticise us. Islam DOES condone violence under the right conditions. If you threaten our community, our faith, or our home and way of life, then we are ORDERED by God to defend what is ours. We do not turn the other cheek, we kick your ass—and all in the name of God. But Islam gives us very stiff guidelines; rules of engagement if you will. You may not kill a non-combatant, a woman, child, or elderly person. You may not destroy trees, buildings, or burn fields. And under no circumstance are you to kill a muslim. This is all in black and white and not up to "interpretation." Anyone who violates them is going to Hellfire and in violation of Islam. Your evaluation is correct. We muslims do not play PC games. God gave us laws and rules, just like the jews and we follow them no matter what a group of "enlightenment" philosophers think. That is man-made, not divine law. In Islam to blaspheme the Prophet Muhammad (or any prophet) is to be put to death. Period. As it should be. Unfortunately, we cannot do this in America, or you people would get the just reward you have coming through your Internet efforts. But we still amnage to teach you some respect and manners on occassion. The last man who blasphemed the Holy Prophet to my face swallowed both his front teeth about three seconds later. I took great pleasure in the fact that the next time he spoke blsphemy,it would be with a lisp. Pagans are to convert or die. Period. As it should be. People such as wiccans, New Agers, and Hindus are parasites to gods planet. Either they should change their ways or accept their just punishment. Christians and jews are People of the Book,and should be tolerated and even protected. But they are misguided, and should be taxed in our countries for having to put up with them. If they speak out against Islam in our countries, they should be punished. Homosexuals. In this country of my birth they are shamefully allowed to parade up and down the streets in front of our children. Some states even try to allow them to marry. The sentence for homosexuality in Islam is death. As it should be. Calipha Omar ibn Kattaub(ra) used to have them thrown off the top of minarets. Do that in San Francisco with 25% of their popuilation off some of those sky scrapers and this nation will drastically improve. Thieves should have their hands cut off and murderers their heads, as it used to be in our country, when we hung and shot *horsethieves and killers. Not lock them up and feed them at our expense for the rest of their lives. Run this country with those frontier laws and crime will diminish. And perhaps someday soon it will. You see, silly Paulian zealots, your religion is about to be outnumbered. By 2025 we will be the majority religion in the world. We have doubled our number in the last 20 years, and in America we now outnumber the jews. Where one mosques wre only found in a few cities just ten years ago, now they are popping up in almost all towns and suburbs. The call to Prayer can be heard over loudspeakers in most large cities now, where in 1980 it would have been unheard of. We are the fastest growing religion in the world, with 20,000 converts in this country a year. 8 out of ten are women, who will marry muslim men, and have muslim children, thus elevating our numbers in this country double or triple in the next 20 years. Islam, whether you like it or not, is the future of this planet, and a future fast approaching. May Allah be praised! This was inevitable. Christianity is a false religion that idolizes Jesus as a Herculean God in some bizzare and morbid blood sacrifice that has pagan overtones. It comes not from Jesus or God but from a false prophet named Paul who violated the Law of Moses and made a man equal to God. Your Bible is a corrupted text that has been rewritten, added to, and re-edited from the very beginning to match your sick beliefs. This is blasphemy and all who believe it are doomed to hellfire. It has taken us 1425 years to start to overcome this blood cults stranglehold on mankind, but at last we near making it a minority opinion. God is finally having his true way prevail. So you dont like us? You want us "controlled in America" you say? Too bad. We have fredom of religion in this country, and are protected by the 2nd Amendment and the Title 7 of the Civil Rights Act of 1964. Fire us, we sue. Persecute us, we get sympathy and thus more converts. Burn down our mosques, we build a new one with the sympathetic donation (often from church groups) and the guilty go to prison. And all the time, we get larger, richer, and become more of an influence in this country. We are your police, your grocers, your secretaries, doctors, lawyers, schoolteachers, and neighbors. Your children go to school with our children. Omar and Muhammad are now almost as common in a school roster as Brendan and Michael. We are here. We are getting larger by the minute. We are taking over this planet. And theres NOTHING you can do about it. So go ahead and whine; i will enjoy watching your pathetic tantrums as we rule your future. Or join us. Accept islam for your salvation. Because your children and/or grandchildren probably will.*

Peace Be With You, Tamim

INTERVIEW WITH HARUN YAHYA
JANUARY 10, 2009

Do you consider Christianity a system of disbelief that will be eliminated under the rule of the Mahdi and Jesus?

Genuine Christians are people who believe in Allah (God), have a great love of the Prophet Jesus (peace be upon him), and believe in the angels and the Hereafter. It is impossible for a Muslim to regard a Christian as an unbeliever. According to the Qur'an, Christians and Jews are the People of the Book. In the Qur'an, Muslims are encouraged to establish civilized relations based on respect and compassion with the People of the Book. It is lawful for the People of the Book and Muslims to eat food prepared by the other, and Muslim men can marry women from the People of the Book (Surat al-Ma'ida, 5). These provisions show that friendly, neighborly, and familial relations can be established between Muslims, Christians, and Jews, and that they should therefore enjoy sincere, lively, loving, and affectionate social relations. Devout Muslims regard the People of the Book as a legacy from the prophets Abraham, Moses, and Jesus (peace be upon them all). They protect and watch over them and provide an environment in which they can worship as they wish and live at ease. The Prophet Muhammad (may Allah bless him and grant him peace) is Muslims' role model here. He always treated Jews and Christians with great justice and compassion and sought a climate based on love and agreement between members of the Abrahamic faiths and Muslims.

At the Prophet Muhammad's (may Allah bless him and grant him peace) advice, some Muslims exposed to oppression and intimidation from the idolaters of Mecca sought shelter with King Najashi of Ethiopia. They developed a model of co-existence with Jews living in Medina that would represent a model for all subsequent generations. There are accounts of the Messenger of Allah (may Allah bless him and grant him peace) attending wedding feasts of the People of the Book and extending hospitality to them. When the Najran Christians visited, the Prophet Muhammad (may Allah bless him and grant him peace) spread his woolen garment out for them to sit on. Our Prophet's (may Allah bless him and grant him peace) marriage with Mariye (or Maryam), an Egyptian Christian, is another example of that attitude. Following the death of the Prophet (may Allah bless him and grant him peace), Muslims' virtuous attitudes toward the People of the Book were based on the stipulations in the Qur'an and the tolerance that the Prophet Muhammad (may Allah bless him and grant him peace) extended to these communities throughout his life.

The Christian belief in the Trinity needs to be changed. There is one God. And the Prophet Jesus (pbuh) is Allah's servant. His moral values make him a superior and holy servant, but one who still has to eat, drink, and sleep, and who has other physical, humanly needs. According to the idea of the Trinity, there is God the Father, the Prophet Jesus (pbuh), and the Holy Ghost. But Christians only pray to Jesus (pbuh). Why do they avoid praying to Allah? Why do they not pray to the Holy Ghost? If there are three deities (surely Allah is beyond that), why do they not pray to them all at once? There is obviously an error and illogicality in this belief. But it is the Prophet Jesus (pbuh) who will correct that error. When the Prophet Jesus (pbuh) returns to Earth, he will tell Christians the truth and direct them towards the true faith.

Do you agree with these other Muslim authors, jurists, and scholars that under the rule of the Mahdi and Jesus, Christians and Jews will face the option of converting to Islam or death?

The system of Hazrat Mahdi (as) is a well-intentioned and rational one based on human love, respect, and compassion. There are hundreds of completely trustworthy *hadiths* about the coming of Hazrat Mahdi (pbuh) and the return of the Prophet Jesus (pbuh), but not a single one says that blood will be shed during the time of the Mahdi. If anyone suggests such a thing, they are in error and have misinterpreted the *hadiths* and other accounts. One of Hazrat Mahdi's (pbuh) distinguishing characteristics is that he will cause religious morals to prevail by means of peace and love. The *hadiths* say that in the time of the Mahdi, nobody's nose will even bleed, and that the sleeper will not be wakened:

> Those who swear allegience to him (Hazrat Mahdi) will do so between the Pilar and the Rock (near the Kaaba). He will not waken the sleeper, and will never shed blood (al-Haytamî, Al-Qawl Mukhtasar fi Alamat-al Mahdi al-Muntazar, p. 24).

> People will swarm around Hazrat Mahdi (pbuh) like bees round their keeper. He will fill the world with justice, where before it was full of oppression. So great will be his justice that nobody who is sleeping will be awakened, and not even a drop of blood will be spilled... (Al-Qawl Mukhtasar fi Alamat-al Mahdi al-Muntazar, pp. 29 and 48).

It is also narrated that justice, peace, and love will rule the world after the coming of Hazrat Mahdi (pbuh) and the Prophet Jesus (pbuh):

> He will eliminate hatred and enmity...he will fill the world with peace like a bowl with water. There will be religious unity and none but Allah will be worshipped. War will set aside its burden (Sunan Ibn Majah, 10/334).

No enmity will remain between anyone. And all enmity, conflict and disputes will vanish (Imam Sha'rani, *Death-Doomsday—The Hereafter and the Portents of the End Times*, 496).

As noted in the expression "war will set aside its burden," all forms of violence, oppression, tyranny, and conflict will come to an end in his time.

If the day ever comes that the Mahdi and Jesus are here on earth, I will not convert to Islam. Will there be any other option for myself other than death? And what would be the purpose of abolishing the jizyah, if not to eliminate the option of being a protected dhimmi?

When Hazrat Mahdi and the Prophet Jesus (peace be upon them) come, they will tell people of the existing errors in Christianity. If someone comes and says, "I am the son of Allah" (Allah is beyond that), we must follow the course of that person's destiny. It is impossible for him to be successful in his destiny. Only someone who says, "There is one God and I am His servant" can be successful. Otherwise, they will obviously fail, because the Prophet Jesus (pbuh) also says there is one God and he prays to Him. Allah (God) cannot pray to Allah (God). The Bible contains various instances of Jesus (pbuh) praying to Allah (God):

Now during those days he went out to the mountain to pray; and he spent the night in prayer to God (Luke 6:12).

In the morning, while it was still very dark, he got up and went out to a deserted place, and there he prayed (Mark 1:35).

And after he had dismissed the crowds, he went up the mountain by himself to pray. When evening came, he was there alone (Matthew 14:23).

Why do Christians pray only to Jesus (pbuh) and not to the Holy Ghost? If they also consider them to be God, (Allah is beyond that) there is clearly an error here. Since they regard all three as Allah (God) (Allah is beyond that), why do they only pray to Jesus (pbuh), when they should pray directly to

Allah (God)? The Bible says there is only one Allah (God) and that believers must serve Him on many occasions:

> Jesus answered, "The first is, 'Hear, O Israel: the Lord our God, the Lord is one; you shall love the Lord your God with all your heart, and with all your soul, and with all your mind, and with all your strength'" (Mark 12: 29-32).

> "Worship the Lord your God, and serve only Him" (Matthew 4: 10).

> To the King of the ages, immortal, invisible, the only God, be honour and glory for ever and ever... (Timothy 11:17).

> Because they exchanged the truth about God for a lie and worshipped and served the creature rather than the Creator, Who is blessed for ever... (Romans 1: 25).

Hazrat Mahdi (pbuh) will clarify all this when he appears, and when he comes, the Prophet Jesus (pbuh) will teach the truth.

At this time, Christians and Jews will become Muslims through the marvelous nature of a miracle. In the Qur'an, Allah says that none will fail to believe in the Prophet Jesus (pbuh) before they die:

> There is not one of the People of the Book who will not believe in him before he dies; and on the Day of Rising he will be a witness against them (Surat an-Nisa, 159).

Allah is referring to genuine believers here. There is no reference here to a hypocritical belief imposed under duress. *Hypocrite* is the word for someone who believes under force, and Allah reveals that hypocrites are the most despicable people in the world and will be cast into the lowest, most humiliating, and violent circle of Hell. Allah does not want people to be hypocrites. But if someone describes himself as a Muslim when he is not, then he is a hypocrite. Islam strongly opposes that. As verse 256 of Surat al-Baqara says, "There is no compulsion where the religion is concerned..."

Everyone at that time will be true believers by means of their devotion to the Prophet Jesus and Hazrat Mahdi (peace be upon them) and under their influence. All people will believe willingly, happily, and knowingly, out of their love for the Prophet Jesus and Hazrat Mahdi (peace be upon them). Allah will cause everyone to believe, as a miracle.

As for the capitation tax on non-Muslims, it is not a compulsory matter. If someone wants to live under the protection of an Islamic state, then it is perfectly normal and essential for him to contribute to the state's expenses. Like every citizen, he must contribute to state spending. But if he does not want the state's help and protection, then there is of course no need to pay. In the same way that the countries joining the EU set up a common fund, in the same way that any citizen in any country pays something toward municipal expenses and costs such as roads, water, and electricity and the like, this is a similar kind of requirement, but not compulsory.

How often do you receive reports that Christians or Jews have read your books and converted to Islam as a result?

I know there are hundreds of people all over the world who have become Muslims after reading my works. You can even see this from a brief research on the Internet. There has been huge progress in Russia, Britain, China, America, Germany, and France in particular. It is also reflected in the press from time to time, but many people contact us every day via the www.harunyahya.com Web site and send messages saying they have converted to Islam.

Many of the Shi'a believe that through the emergence of al-Mahdi Muntadhzar, that all Sunnis will convert to Shi'a Islam. How do you perceive that the Mahdi will unify the Sunni and Shi'a? What will this look like? Do you believe that the Shi'a will become Sunni?

What is being referred to here is an increase in love of the *alh al-bayt* [line of descent of the Prophet Muhammad] in the time of Hazrat Mahdi (pbuh). There will be a strong love for the desendants of the Prophet Muhammad (may Allah bless him and grant him peace). And this is already happening. Muslims increasing their love of the blessed Ali, Hasan, and Hussein, the line of the Prophet Muhammad (may Allah bless him and grant him peace), in other words, does not necessarily mean being Shiite, of course. Shiites and Sunis are two separate schools. When Hazrat Mahdi (pbuh) comes, both Shiites and Sunnis will swear allegiance to Hazrat Mahdi (pbuh) alone. In other words, it is not a matter of Shiites becoming Sunni or Sunnis becoming Shiite.

According to Islamic tradition, ad-Dajjal is said to be blind in one eye and have the word KUFR written on his forehead. Do you believe that this is to be taken literally or do you believe that these descriptions should be understood in a symbolic and spiritualized manner?

It is true he will have one blind eye, and will claim to be divine (surely Allah is beyond that) despite being blind in one eye, but the word *kafir* (unbeliever) may not be written on his forehead.

Imagine if a man appeared in Israel who claimed to be divine and the Son of God, who claimed to be Jesus Christ and had the ability to do powerful miracles. If this man claimed that Islam was not the truth and instead taught that the Bible was not corrupted and that Christianity was the true religion, would this man, in your opinion, fulfill the necessary requirements to be viewed as ad-Dajjal?

For one thing, by Allah's leave, when the Prophet Jesus (pbuh) comes nobody will confuse him with anyone else, due to his extraordinary beauty, radiance, luminosity of faith, cleanliness, majesty, modesty, and honesty. We will immediately know and recognize him. At the time of the coming of the Prophet Jesus (pbuh), there will also appear someone who claims to be Jesus and even, surely Allah is beyond that, works miracles and claims to be Allah (God) Himself. This person will cause terrible strife and corruption on Earth but, by Allah's leave, the Prophet Jesus (pbuh) will destroy his false miracles and corruption. He will dissolve away and vanish like salt in water. If this person were the real Jesus (pbuh) he would prevent the eradication of his marvels. The real Jesus (pbuh) would be strong enough to prevent that. It will therefore be seen that he is not the true Jesus. The false Jesus will not have the strength of the real Jesus (pbuh). And it will immediately be obvious which is the real Jesus (pbuh).

The false Jesus will in any case be abnormal-looking. You will feel no love for him. Allah will create him with one blind eye for identification purposes. One will tell that he is an imposter, unbalanced and aggressive, from his face. The true Jesus is beautiful and with two healthy eyes. He is tall, red-haired, narrow-waisted, with an innocent expression, polite-looking, and highly logical and rational. He will imediately be recognized as the true Jesus (pbuh) from his honest language, cleanliness, human love, warmth, extraordinary intelligence, and peaceful nature. And he will do away with all the false marvels of the false Jesus.

In short, there will be no difficulty or confusion when it comes to recognizing the real Jesus (pbuh). There will be no difficulty in recognizing either. In verse 185 of Surat al-Baqara, Almighty Allah says, **"Allah desires ease for you. He does not desire difficulty for you."** In another verse (Surat al-Baqara, 286) He states, **"Allah does not impose on any self more than it can stand."** Therefore, it will be very easy for true believers to recognize the real Jesus, *insha'Allah*.

Islamic tradition holds that Jesus will descend by the White Mosque in Damascus. Do you believe that this is also not to be taken literally, but rather symbolically?

Jesus (pbuh) may descend in Damascus, or Jerusalem, or in Istanbul. Various places are mentioned in the *hadiths*. It may even be in the USA. When the Prophet Jesus (pbuh) returns, he will do so as a very delightful person who has no memory of his own past, wearing the clothing and footwear of that time. He will subsequently learn foreign languages, the Qur'an, the Torah, and the Gospels. He will appear in a Christian community reminiscent of Islam. He will be a Muslim and will call the whole Christian world to Islam.

Could you share a bit about how you believe the Islamic Union will emerge in the years to come?

The Turkish-Islamic Union is a union of love, a union of hearts, in which every state will maintain its own identity. It will have a democratic and secular nature. It will respect human rights. It will establish an environment in which people of all beliefs—Christians, Jews, Buddhists, and atheists—can freely express those beliefs. Its foundations will be love, altruism, mutual aid, compassion, tolerance, understanding, and reconciliation. The Turkish-Islamic Union will oppose all movements that incite war and conflict and represent a power that opposes all developments that provoke war. **With the founding of the Turkish-Islamic Union, America, Europe, China, Russia, Israel, and in short the whole world, will be able to relax.** The problem of terror will come to an end, access to raw materials will be guaranteed, economic and social order will be protected, and cultural conflict will be entirely eradicated. America will have no need to send its troops thousands of kilometers away, Israel will no longer live behind walls, the nations of the EU will encounter no economic obstacles, Russia will have no security concerns, and China will have no difficulties over raw materials. **With the founding of the union, the Western world's defense spending will decline.** The USA heads the list of military spending with a budget of some $400 billion. Then comes Russia with $60 billion and China with $42 billion. The Turkish-Islamic Union will establish an environment of global peace and security that will eliminate all conflict and tension regarding the Islamic world. It will enable many countries of the world, not just Muslim countries, to reduce their military spending. Investment on the military and armaments development will thus be diverted to such fields as education, medicine, science, and culture. **The Turkish-Islamic Union will reinvigorate commerce and strengthen the economy.** The single entity formed by Muslim countries in the political, economic, and cultural spheres will allow the more backward to progress rapidly and those with the necessary means and infrasructure to use them in the most productive manner. Economic growth will increase investment in science and technology. With economic growth, education levels in the union will naturally rise and society will develop in many directions.

How do you suspect that Turkey will emerge as the leader of this Union?

There is much information in the *hadiths* of our Prophet (saas) to the effect that the Turkish nation will undertake a very special task in the end times. Istanbul is much noted in the *hadiths*. The Turkish nation is the best suited, in terms of moral values and nature, to the task, and whoever you may ask is agreed on that. The characteristic of the Turkish nation is this: it is a virtuous and religious one. It has always been the standard bearer of Islam. Such a nation has the right to be a leader. It will justly discharge that function and be an excellent leader. But this is not a claim of any kind of racial superiority. It is impossible for a Muslim to make such a claim. We are servants of Allah. Superiority lies in *taqwa* (awe or fear of Allah, which inspires a person to be on guard against wrong action and eager for actions which please Him). Anything else leads to fascism, infertility, and evilness. Allah will respond to anyone who thinks like that, and the result will be catastrophic for them.

When I talk about a Turkish-Islamic Union under Turkish leadership and supported by the Turkic states, I am referring to the moral values of the Turkish nation. Allah has created this nation to be very excellent and charged it with spreading justice to mankind and the world. It is a natural leader, resistant to suffering, troubles, and hunger; loyal, courageous, religious, morally virtuous, and honest. Anatolian people are very virtuous. Go to the Black Sea region and you will be amazed at their moral values, or to Anatolia. Go to the South East and you will be amazed. Words canot describe their hospitality, affection, respect, kindness, and honor. You cannot find that anywhere else in the world. To sum up, first, Turkey will undertake this duty as a legacy from the Ottoman Empire. Second, the model of Islam as is lived by in Turkey is an exemplary one. The rational, enlightened, and honest conception of Islam in Turkey, warm, tolerant, and not at all radical, is of the greatest importance. This is both an excellent example for the Muslim world and also an ideal model that will eliminate all doubts in Western minds. Third, all the sacred and holy relics are in Turkey. Fourth, we are at the center. We are at a key point for connecting the Turkic states and Islamic countries to Europe. We have a very-well educated and enlightened potential and are eager to assume the job. We are highly enthusiastic for it. Nobody else is as keen as us.

How do you perceive that both the people and the leaders in Iran would respond to an Islamic Union led by Turkey? Do you believe that they would willingly go along with such an arrangement?

Our Iranian brothers are completely willing. If Turkey proposed it today they would agree at once. Iran will never be concerned over Turkish leadership, and that is clear from recent developments. As you know, President Ahmadinejad recently visited Istanbul, during which he prayed behind a Sunni *imam* at the Sultanahmad Mosque. In his statement he said, "The political message I am sending here is very significant." What does a Shiite leader praying behind a Sunni *imam* mean? It means, "If the Turkish-Islamic Union is established I will go along with the Sunnis, I will pray behind the Sunnis and accept their leadership." And it means, "I support the Turkish-Islamic Union." Another important event was Iranian and U.S. officials meeting together in Ankara under Turkish mediation. Iran has stated it wants Turkey to act as an intermediary and has expressed its pleasure at that. That means they trust Turkey's justice, honesty, sincerity, and neutrality. People who trust in those will also trust in Turkish leadership and want it to be to the fore. Because the foundation of the Turkish-Islamic Union will mean the salvation of Iran, too. It will bring security and well-being to Islam and totally eliminate all tensions.

Once the **caliphate** *is established, will it be acceptable for the* **ummah** *to wage war against any nations that refuse to accept Islam?*

The leadership that will emerge with the establishment of the Turkish-Islamic Union is a spiritual one, one that will provide a spiritual leader for the whole Islamic world. There is no question of establishing a *caliphate* in the historic sense. Islam is not a religion of war and violence. It is a religion of peace. Allah states in one verse of the Qur'an as:

> You who believe! Enter Islam totally. Do not follow in the footsteps of Satan. He is an outright enemy to you (Surat al-Baqara, 208).

There is no compulsion in Islam. It invites people to adopt moral virtues using love, compassion, and kind words alone. Muslims have to extend invitations, not force people to embrace the faith. Everyone is responsible for his or her own self desires. Qur'anic moral values require Muslims to avoid war and all forms of conflict and to be reconciliatory, resolving disputes by negotiation and discussion. War, according to the Qur'an, is only to be resorted to when obligatory, and is an "undesired obligation" to be waged within human and ethical bounds. Believers always prefer peace and reconciliation when problems arise, and have a responsibility only to wage war for the purpose of self-defense if attacked by the other side.

Another verse describes how there are evil people who start wars, and how Allah does not like such corrupt types:

> Each time they kindle the fire of war, Allah extinguishes it. They rush about the earth corrupting it. Allah does not love corrupters (Surat al-Ma'ida, 64).

The distinguishing feature of Islamic communities is that they are moderate and well-balanced, and use kind words to command people to do good and avoid evil. The founding aim of the Turkish-Islamic Union is to establish a climate of peace in which disagreements can be resolved by reconciliation and rational means. When the Turkish-Islamic Union is established, terror and conflict will come to an end in a matter of moments, and all the world will live in peace.

Do you perceive the present global economic meltdown as contributing positively to the rise of global Islamic power?

A great economic crisis is one of the portents of the coming of Hazrat Mahdi (pbuh). This is revealed in the *hadiths* of our Prophet (saas):

> (Before the coming of Hazrat Mahdi [pbuh]) THE MARKET WILL FREEZE AND EARNINGS WILL DECLINE (*Portents of Doomsday*, 148).

> Before the coming of Hazrat Mahdi (pbuh), TRADE AND ROADS BETWEEN NATIONS WILL BE CUT, and strife among people will grow (*Al-Qawl Mukhtasar fi Alamat-al Mahdi al-Muntazar*, 39).

> Everyone will complain of LOW EARNINGS and the rich will be respected for their money (*Portents of Doomsday*, 146).

> Business will be bad. Everyone will complain, "I cannot sell anything, I cannot buy or earn anything" (*Portents of Doomsday*, 152).

This economic crisis is one of the most important signs of the end times and, according to the *hadiths* and the Qur'an, will be long-lasting. There are many references to the end times in Surah Yusuf in the Qur'an. The way the Prophet Yusuf (pbuh) attached great importance to agriculture and livestock raising also has a figurative sense. It also stresses the number seven. The crisis began in 2007, a year ending in seven, and may continue for seven years, ending in 2014. At the heart of the crisis lie high interest rates, lack of trust in Allah, fear—in other words the idea that bad things will happen tomorrow, saving money and goods away, not spending, not helping the poor, not distributing money, and general parsimony. If money is distributed, the money supply is activated and production is stimulated. But when money is held back, so are goods, and production is stalled, and the system as a whole dies. This stems from the selfishness of some people. Interest must be abolished, and interest rates have indeed fallen to nearly zero percent in the world as a whole. The Bank of England has announced it is thinking of moving to a no interest system. Taxes must also be reduced. We need high demand in the markets and people need to be freed from this state of panic. In other words, they must spend the money they have saved up, and that has to be encouraged. In that event, the market will automatically be reinvigorated, production will be easier because interest rates have fallen, and manufacturing will be easier with low taxes. Such troubles and difficulties are of course means whereby people turn to religious moral values. They bring about a climate of solidarity, love, and altruism. There is good in everything that Allah creates, and there is also much wisdom in this crisis. One of them may be that people will turn to religious moral values. Allah knows the truth, *insha'Allah*.

What changes do you perceive the United States will undergo within the next ten years?

I expect America to become more religious in the next ten years. Love for the Prophet Jesus (pbuh) will grow. Belief in creation will dominate the USA. There may be a contraction in industrialization. Economic difficulties may continue, but there is also good in this, *insha'Allah*.

Presently, there are various peace deals that seem to be in the works involving Israel and other parties. Do you think that Turkey will be the nation that is finally able to make such a peace treaty take place?

Turkey has recently been following a very active and successful policy, *masha'Allah*. It is a sign that Turkey will be an important element, a leader, in future world politics. The meetings between Syria and Israel, the steps taken for the foundation of the Caucasian Alliance, the bringing together in Istanbul of the leaders of Pakistan and Afghanistan, and all such developments are proof that Turkey will lead the way to love and peace. But the salvation of Syria, Israel, and Palestine will basically be enabled by the foundation of the Turkish-Islamic Union. And that is what they want, too. Leading Israelis say, "In Ottoman times you governed the region with ten privates and a sergeant, while we are unable to with all our troops." They look back to the old Ottoman times. Syria openly wants to join with Turkey, and if an official proposal were made, Syria would sign up within a week. Iraq is already a river of blood. But if Turkey assumed the role of older brother it would immediately become a truly heavenly place. The problem would be totally resolved. Everyone can see that. Delegations coming from Palestine always propose it and they all demand it. Turkey's playing the role of older brother has become of crucial importance to the region. There is a vacuum in the region, one that only Turkey is in a position to fill. And that is a human, ethical, and religious duty. It is a duty that Turkey wants. When the Turkish-Islamic Union is founded, the whole Middle East will be a paradise; Israel and Palestine will be at ease and as free as possible. It will be a salvation for the peoples of Palestine and Israel. Everyone will be freed from the problem of terror and violence. An age of total peace and security will dawn. That is why I can say that the foundation of the Turkish-Islamic Union is the most urgent issue facing the world.

Have you ever had the chance to discuss your beliefs about the Mahdi, Jesus, and the Islamic Union with fellow Turkish intellectual Fethullah Gulen? As far as you know, do you and Gulen share similar beliefs on most of these issues?

I do not know Fethullah Gülen personally, so we have had no chance to talk face-to-face. But he is a highly respectable, gentle, virtuous, modest, polite, and immaculate person. Like all the people of the Sunna, Fethullah Gülen refers to Hazrat

Mahdi (pbuh) in terms of love and joy in his works and addresses. He describes how the Mahdi will appear and how the Prophet Jesus (pbuh) will return to Earth. He educates and encourages Muslims. He is also instrumental in very good works, *masha'Allah.*

How do you think that Prime Minister Erdogan would respond to these ideas concerning an Islamic Union with Turkey in a leadership role?

The prime minister and the current government are striving with all their might for the establishment of the Turkish-Islamic Union. The initiative for the establishment of the Caucasian Union, the pipeline projects, railway projects, Turkey's adopting an active role in the Middle East, and problems being resolved under Turkish leadership are all initiatives being taken for the establishment of the Turkish-Islamic Union. These are all very excellent, very successful initiatives. They will pick up further pace in the future and, by Allah's leave, a Turkish-Islamic Union under Turkish leadership will be founded in the next ten to twenty years.

According to certain hadiths, *Muhammad once said that Turkey would be conquered a second time for Islam through peaceful means. Are you aware of any within the Turkish Islamic community that believe that this prophecy has been or is being fulfilled through the rise of the AKP Islamist party in Turkey?*

The *hadiths* describe how Hazrat Mahdi (pbuh) will capture Istanbul with the *taqbir,* that is to say, by reciting the name of Allah. This once again shows that Hazrat Mahdi (pbuh) will strengthen belief in Allah through cultural and intellectual activities, that he will be instrumental in a rise in spiritual matters and people turning to religious moral values, and that religious moral values will prevail over the world in that way. You know, when Fatih Sultan Mehmet captured Istanbul he was initially unwilling to undertake the campaign since the *hadiths* say that he who captures Istanbul will be Hazrat Mahdi (pbuh). He then consulted with his teacher, Akshemsettin, who told him, *"First Mehmet will capture Istanbul, and the Mahdi will subsequently capture it spiritually."* In other words, he says that the physical capture of Istanbul will be by Fatih, and its spiritual conquest by the Mahdi. Fatih then set out on his campaign. The Turkish nation has always been loyal to spiritual values, a religious nation. But there has been a very evident strengthening in that context in recent times. Intellectual work that has demolished Darwinism and materialism has of course played a major role in this. In the 1970s, the level of belief in Darwinism was very high, around 80 percent. Today it is the exact opposite. Turkey is the country with the lowest level of belief in Darwinism. More than 90 percent believe in creation.

You have stated that you believe that both the Mahdi and Jesus are present now on the earth. What makes you believe this exactly?

Allah promises in verse 55 of Surat an-Nur that Islamic moral values will prevail over the world. Many other verses also impart these welcome tidings. There are some three hundred portents in the *hadiths* regarding the coming of Hazrat Mahdi (pbuh). Our Prophet (may Allah bless him and grant him peace) says these will happen one by one, "like beads on a necklace." And these really have happened one after the other since 1400 (*hegira*-style, AD 1979). A great many portents have come about. Our Prophet (saas) says that Afghanistan will be invaded, and that happened. He says that Iraq will be occupied, and that has happened. He says blood will be spilled in the Kaaba, and that happened. He says the waters of the Euphrates will be cut, and that happened. He says there will be eclipses of the sun and moon at fifteen-day intervals in the month of Ramadan, and that happened. He says there will be a sign in the sun, and that happened. He speaks of the devastation of Baghdad, and that has happened. He reveals the economic crisis, and that is happening. Many other things have happened, but what really matters is that they have all taken place in the space of twenty to thirty years.

Afghanistan may have been invaded or Baghdad devastated at their times in history, but this is the first time that all these events have happened in the same period as described by the Prophet (may Allah bless him and grant him peace). That means there is something extraordinary going on.

I think that the coming of the Prophet Jesus (pbuh) is also very close. The Prophet Jesus (pbuh) will return, and we will welcome, love and embrace him in ten to twenty years, *insha'Allah*. After that, *insha'Allah*, the world will be very delightful, bright, and prosperous.

According to Islamic tradition, in the last days the beast will emerge from Mecca. He will mark the foreheads of all true believers. What do you understand this "mark of the beast" to be?

The Dabbat al-Ardh [the beast coming out of the earth] is one of the portents that will appear in the end times, and there are a great many *hadiths* concerning the Dabbat al-Ardh, although some are confused and they may not all be true. I do not think this is a completely sound *hadith*. But the subject does appear in the *Qur'an*. In verse 82 of Surat an-Naml Allah says: **"When the Word is justly carried out against them, we will produce a Beast from the earth which will speak to them. Truly mankind had no certainty about our signs."**

The verse reveals that the Dabbat al-Ardh will appear from the earth, in other words that it is a product of the earth. It describes an entity that will talk to people. The *hadiths* refer to him being able to cross large distances in a single step, talking to people, and travelling everywhere. Since it is a product of the earth, it will be something made up of such minerals and metals extracted from underground as iron, copper, zinc, cobalt, and chrome. These substances are the basic components of present-day computers. Talking to people and covering large distances in a short space of time is a reference to the Internet. Thanks to the Internet it is very easy to access or transfer information, to speak to people, and establish communications with them. And thanks to the Internet, people will be told about the Qur'an even more quickly. In the end times, the Internet will be an important means whereby Islamic moral values come to prevail the world.

Will the Mahdi be able to bring together all religions, and if so, how will he do this?

The Mahdi will bring together with love people from all faiths and holding all kinds of ideas, will enable them to see one another's good sides by strengthening their feelings of friendship and brotherhood, and will ensure they treat one another with understanding. When Hazrat Mahdi (pbuh) appears, love will rule the world and people will abandon all fellings of hatred and anger. So much so that, the *hadiths* describe how even the fish in the sea and the birds in the air will be content with the environment of beauty and love of which Hazrat Mahdi (pbuh) will be instrumental, and that love for Hazrat Mahdi (pbuh) will descend on everyone's hearts. The sincere love that people feel for Hazrat Mahdi (pbuh) will be instrumental in them trusting each other with love, affection, and compassion.

The career and life of Muhammad as well as that of his earliest followers is undeniably one that involves much bloodshed, assassinations, and wars of aggression. Your vision of the Mahdi is one of a peaceful and violent rise to power as well as a peaceful rule. Yet one must ask how the Mahdi would be able to do that which Muhammad was not able to accomplish? Does the Mahdi rule in a superior manner than even Muhammad?

The revelation of the Qur'an to our Prophet (saas) took twenty-three years. During the first thirteen years, Muslims lived as a minority in the idolatrous system in Mecca and were subjected to enormous oppression. Many Muslims were physically tortured, some were killed, most had their goods and homes plundered and were constantly exposed to insults and slander. Nonetheless, Muslims did not turn to war but always invited the idolators to peace. When the pressure they were exposed to from the idolators became intolerable the Muslims migrated to the city of Yathrib (later to be known as Medina), where there was a freer and more friendly climate, and established their own administration there. Even after establishing their own political order in that way, they still did not wage war against the idolators of Mecca. When they did fight, it was always for reasons of self-defense. The superior moral values demonstrated by the Prophet (may Allah bless him and grant him peace) and his companions during these unavoidable wars have gone down in history as highly exemplary.

For example, Arab custom dictated that anyone taken prisoner in battle should be killed. Because of the commandments revealed by Allah, however, our Prophet (may Allah bless him and grant him peace) ordered that captives be treated well and that Muslims should share their food with them. These characteristics of believers in revealed in verse 8 of Surat al-Insan, **"They give food, despite their love for it, to the poor and orphans and captives."** All that was asked of people taken captive was, if they were able, for them to teach those Muslims who could not read and write to do so. Muslims' justice, courage, and determination was instrumental in many Arab tribes converting to Islam; in other words, Islam was spread, not through war, but by the moral virtues and *taqwa* exhibited by Muslims. Another example of this took place during the capture of Mecca. The army of Islam set out for Mecca in AD 630. The Meccan idolators were terrified that the Muslims would wreak revenge for their previous oppression of them. According to Arab custom, the males of a tribe defeated in war would be put to the sword, and the women and children enslaved. The idolators of Mecca were convinced that was what would happen to them. But our Prophet (may Allah bless him and grant him peace) declared that no vengeance would be extracted from the people of Mecca and that nobody would be forced to become a Muslim. This great forgiveness and tolerance has also attracted the attention of Western historians. For instance, the Haverford

University academic Micheal Sells describes this superior moral virtue of the Prophet (saas) and says that when he arrived to Mecca, let alone taking a bloody vengeance, he embraced Meccans who were making war with him and struggling to kill him for three years. He further adds that this attitude evoked great admiration in the people of that time. Sells concludes that for that reason in the foundation of a religion, there existed great benevolence, an extraordinary civility and compassion (*Islam Empire of Faith; An Empires Special*, PBS Home Video).

A Christian author named Dr. David Reagan has just released a very critical review of some of the things that I have written. In his criticism, he claims that I am "very misleading" when I claim that belief in the Mahdi is not exclusively held by the Shi'a belief but is also held by a wide range of Sunnis as well. Dr. Reagan then states that Sunnis are not looking for the Mahdi. What would you say to Dr. Reagan? In your experience, what percentage of Sunnis generally believe in the Mahdi?

According to Sunni belief (in the Hanafi, Hanbali, Shafi'I, and Maliki schools), it is an absolute and unanimous article of faith that Hazrat Mahdi (pbuh) will come, that the Prophet Jesus (pbuh) will descend from the sky, and will insist that Hazrat Mahdi (pbuh) act as his *imam*. It is perfectly normal for people who are not Sunni and who reject the *hadiths* also to deny the coming of the Prophet Jesus (pbuh) and belief in Hazrat Mahdi (pbuh). But none of the Sunni *ulama* (scholars) have ever rejected the coming of the Prophet Jesus and Hazrat Mahdi (peace be upon them), but have all been unanimously agreed on the subject for hundreds of years. Our scholars are in "full agreement" in imparting this truth to Muslims. For example, the great Imam Abu Hanifa, the founder of my school, reveals that the coming of the Prophet Jesus and the appearance of Hazrat Mahdi (peace be upon them) are matters "which cannot possibly be denied."

The appearance of the Dajjal and of Gog and Magog, the sun rising in the West, the Prophet Jesus (pbuh) descending from the sky and all the other trustworthy reports of the portents of Doomsday are true and inevitable. There are other great portents of Doomsday. Such as the coming of Hazrat Mahdi (pbuh). All these events reported in trustworthy accounts are true and will happen (Fiqhi Aqbar Translation, *The Great Imam Abu Hanifa*, edited by Ali Rıza Kaşeli, 99).

The great Imam Abu Hanifa, the founder of my school; Imam Hanbal, founder of the Hanbali school; Imam Malik, founder of the Maliki school; and Imam Shafi, founder of the Shafi'i school, have all stated that the Prophet Jesus (pbuh) will return to earth and that Hazrat Mahdi (pbuh) will appear. These *imams* of the four great Sunni schools are all expounders of Islamic law. In addition to them, all great Islamic scholars have said that Islamic moral values will prevail in the world in the end times, that the Prophet Jesus (pbuh) will return, and that Hazrat Mahdi (pbuh) will appear. Sunni Muslims following in the path of these great scholars naturally believe in the coming of Hazrat Mahdi and the Prophet Jesus (peace be upon them). It is impossible for any Sunni to believe or say anything else.

INTRODUCTION

1. Zwemer, *Islam and the Cross*, 56.

CHAPTER ONE: WHY THIS BOOK? WAKING UP TO THE ISLAMIC REVIVAL

1. Pawson, *Challenge of Islam*, 11.

2. Ibid.

3. McDowell and Zaka, *Muslims and Christians*, 6.

4. Ibid.

5. Wilgoren, "Islam Attracts Converts."

6. *Al-Hayam* (London), November 12, 2001, as quoted in Middle East Media & Research Institute, *Muslim American Leaders: A Wave of Conversion to Islam in the U.S. Following September 11*, November 16, 2001.

7. *Al-Ahram Al-Arabi* (Egypt), October 20, 2001, as quoted in Middle East Media & Research Institute, *Muslim American Leaders: A Wave of Conversion to Islam in the U.S. Following September 11*, November 16, 2001.

8. Whittell, "Allah Came Knocking at My Heart."

9. McDowell and Zaka, 6.

10. Ibid., 6.

11. Ibid., 7.

12. Middle East Media & Research Institute, *Muslim American Leaders: A Wave of Conversion to Islam in the U.S. Following September 11*, November 16, 2001.

13. Wilgoren, "Islam Attracts Converts."

14. Hogan, "Drawn to Islam."

15. Pawson, *Challenge of Islam*, 36.

16. Ibid., 6, 7.

17. Al-Jazeera, *Christianization in Africa*, December 12, 2001, http://www.aljazeera.net/programs/shareea/articles/2000/

12/12-12-6.htm. For the English translation see:
http://www.islamreview.com/articles/fastdemiseprint.htm.

18. "Who is Isa Al-Masih—The Man in White?" http://isaalmasih.net/.

19. Brother Andrew, *Light Force*, 140.

CHAPTER TWO: THE SACRED TEXTS OF ISLAM

1. There is, however, a very small Islamic cult that adheres only to the Qur'an as its source of religious belief and practice. They are known as "The Submitters."

2. Malik's Muwatta Book 9, Number 9.7.27.

CHAPTER FOUR THE MAHDI: ISLAM'S AWAITED MESSIAH

1. Kabbani, *Approach of Armageddon?*, 228.

2. Kathir, *Signs Before the Day of Judgement*, 18.

3. Izzat and 'Arif, *Al Mahdi and the End of Time*, 18.

4. Kabbani, *Approach of Armageddon?*, 228.

5. Al-Sadr and Mutahhari, *The Awaited Savior*, 1.

6. Sachedina, *Islamic Messianism*, 2.

7. Kabbani, *Approach of Armageddon?*, 229.

8. Tirmidhi Sahih, Sunan Abu Dawud, (Sahih), vol. 5, p. 207; also narrated by Ali b. Abi Talib, Abu Sa'id, Umm Salma, Abu Hurayra.

9. Sunan Abu Dawud, Book 36, Number 4271, narrated by Umm Salamah, Ummul Mu'minin.

10. Ibn Maja, *Kitab al-Fitan* #4084 as quoted in Kabbani, *Approach of Armageddon?*, 231.

11. *Sunan Abu Dawud,* narrated by Umm Salamah, Ummul Mu'minin.

12. Veliankode, *Doomsday Portents and Prophecies*, 277.

13. Al-Sadr and Mutahhari, *The Awaited Savior*, prologue, 4, 5.

14. Izzat and Arif, *Al Mahdi and the End of Time*, 4.

15. Kelani, *The Last Apocalypse*, 34-35.

16. Ibn Hajar al-Haythami, Al-Qawl al-Mukhtasar fi'Alamat al-Mahdi al-Muntazar, 50 as quoted in Yahya, *The End Times and the Mahdi*, 96.

17. Kabbani, *Approach of Armageddon?*, 231.

18. Abu Nu'aym and As-Suyuti, related by Thawban, as quoted in Izzat and Arif, *Al Mahdi and the End of Time*, 44.

19. "Flags of the Islamic State," www.islamic-state.org/resources/

flags-of-the-islamic-state.html.

20. Ibn Kathir, *The Beginning and the End*, vol.2, pt. 3, p.288 as quoted in Gabriel, *Jesus and Muhammad*, 60.

21. Tirmidhi as quoted in Zubair, *Signs of Qiyamah*, 42 and Abdullah, *Islam, Jesus, Mehdi, Qadiyanis and Doomsday*, 54.

22. Izzat and Arif, *Al Mahdi and the End of Time*, 40.

23. Sahih Muslim Book 041, Number 6985.

24. Sahih Hakim Mustadrak, related by Abu Sa'id al-Khudri (4:557 and 558), as quoted in Kabbani, *Approach of Armageddon?*, 233.

25. At-Tabarani, Related by Abu Hurayra, as quoted in Izzat and 'Arif, *Al Mahdi and the End of Time*, 9.

26. El-Kavlu'l Muhtasar Fi Alamet-il Mehdiyy-il Muntazar, as quoted by Yahya, http://www.endoftimes.net/08mahdiandtheendtimes.html.

27. Al-Burhan fi Alamat al-Mahdi Akhir al-Zaman, as quoted by Yahya, http://www.endoftimes.net/08mahdiandtheendtimes.html.

28. Tabarani, as related by Hadrat Abu Umamah, as quoted in Zubair, *Signs of Qiyamah*, 43 and Abduallah, *Islam, Jesus, Mehdi, Qadiyanis and Doomsday*, 55.

29. Ibid.

30. Sunan Abu Dawud, Book 36, Number 4273, narrated by Umm Salamah, Ummul Mu'minin.

31. Sunan Abu Dawud, Book 36, Number 4272, narrated by Abu Sa'id al-Khudri.

32. M S M Saifullah, Muhammad Ghoniem, Abu Hudhayfah & Khalid al-Khazraji, *On the Transmitters of Isra'iliyyat (Judeo-Christian Material)* http://www.islamic-awareness.org/Hadith/Ulum/israel.html.

33. Izzat and Arif, *Al Mahdi and the End of Time*, 15.

34. Ibid, 15.

35. Michael Elliot, "The Semiotics of Saddam."

36. Izzat and Arif, *Al Mahdi and the End of Time*, 40.

37. Ibid., 16.

CHAPTER FIVE: COMPARING THE BIBLICAL ANTICHRIST AND THE MAHDI

1. Al-Sadr and Mutahhari, *The Awaited Savior*, 4, 5.

2. Sunan Abu Dawud, Book 36, Number 4273, narrated by Umm Salamah, Ummul Mu'minin.

3. Al-Sadr and Mutahhari, *The Awaited Savior*, prologue, 4, 5.

4. Amini, *Al-Imam Al-Mahdi*.

5. Sahih Muslim, Book 041, Number 6985.

6. Tirmidhi as quoted in Zubair, *Signs of Qiyamah*, 42 and Abdullah, *Islam, Jesus, Mehdi, Qadiyanis and Doomsday*, , 54.

7. Izzat and'Arif, *Al Mahdi and the End of Time*, 40.

8. Ibid.

9. Tabarani as quoted by Mufti A.H. Elias and Muhammad Ali ibn Zubair Ali, Imam Mahdi, online article from: http://www.islam.tc/prophecies/imam.html.

10. Dr. Waleed A. Muhanna, "A Brief Introduction to the Islamic (Hijri) Calendar," available online at http://fisher.osu.edu/~muhanna_1/hijri-intro.html.

11. Izzat and 'Arif, *Al Mahdi and the End of Time*, 15, 19.

CHAPTER SIX: THE MUSLIM JESUS

1. Sahih Muslim Book 041, Number 7015.

2. Veliankode, *Doomsday Portents and Prophecies*, 351.

3. Sahih Muslim, Book 001, Number 0293, narrated by Jabir bin 'Abdullah.

4. Veliankode, *Doomsday Portents and Prophecies*, 350.

5. Sais I-Nursi, "The Fifth Ray," in *The Rays*, 493, quoted in Yahya, *Jesus Will Return*, 66.

6. Al-Sadr and Mutahhari, *The Awaited Savior*, prologue, 3.

7. Hakim Mustadrak (2:651) # 4162 as related by Abu Harayra, quoted in Kabbani, *Approach of Armageddon?*, 237.

8. Sahih Ashrat as-Sa'at, quoted in Kabbani, *Approach of Armageddon?*, 236.

9. Veliankode, *Doomsday Portents and Prophecies*, 351.

10. Shafi and Usmani, *Signs of the Qiyama and the Arrival of the Maseeh*, 60.

11. Kabbani, *Approach of Armageddon?*, 237.

12. Al-Sadr and Mutahhari, *The Awaited Savior*, prologue, 3.

13. Sunan Abu Dawud, Book 37, Number 4310, narrated by Abu Hurayrah. See also Sahih Bukhari Volume 3, Book 43, Number 656.

14. Shafi and Usmani, *Signs of the Qiyama and the Arrival of the Maseeh*, 59.

15. Veliankode, *Doomsday Portents and Prophecies*, 358.

16. Yahya, *Jesus Will Return*, 52.

17. Al-Misri, *Reliance of the Traveller*, 603.

18. Muhammad Ali Ibn Zubair, "Who Is the Evil Dajjal (the "anti-Christ")?" Online article from http://www.islam.tc/prophecies/masdaj.html.

19. Veliankode, *Doomsday Portents and Prophecies*, 360; Sahih Bukhari Volume 3, Book 43, Number 656.

20. Zubair, *Signs of Qiyama*.

21. Sunan Abu Dawood, Book 37, Number 4310, narrated by Abu Hurayrah.

22. Tirmidhi, quoted in "Jesus (Isa) A.S. in Islam, and his Second Coming" by Mufti A.H. Elias at http://www.islam.tc/prophecies/jesus.html.

CHAPTER SEVEN: COMPARING THE FALSE PROPHET AND THE MUSLIM JESUS

1. Ibn Maja, Kitab al-Fitan #4084, quoted in Kabbani, *The Approach of Armageddon?*, 231.

2. Al-Sadr and Mutahhari, *The Awaited Savior*, prologue, 3.

3. Sais I-Nursi, "The Fifth Ray," in *The Rays*, 493, quoted in Yahya, *Jesus Will Return*, 66.

4. Kabbani, *The Approach of Armageddon?*, 237.

5. Shafi and Usmani, *Signs of the Qiyama and the Arrival of the Maseeh*, 59.

6. Veliankode, *Doomsday Portents and Prophecies*, 358.

7. Al-Misri, *Reliance of the Traveller*, 603.

8. Zubair, "Who Is the Evil Dajjal (the "anti-Christ")?"

9. Zubair, *Signs of Qiyama*.

10. Veliankode, *Doomsday Portents and Prophecies*, 218.

CHAPTER EIGHT: THE DAJJAL: ISLAM'S ANTICHRIST

1. Kabbani, *The Approach of Armageddon?* 223.

2. Sahih Muslim Book 041, Number 7005, reported by Ibn Umar.

3. Sahih Muslim Book 041, Number 7010, reported by Hudhalfa.

4. Sahih Muslim Book 041, Number 7009, reported by Anas b. Malik.

5. R'ad, *Freemasons and Dajjal*, 173.

6. Kabbani, *The Approach of Armageddon?* 223-4.

7. Sunan Ibn Majah #4067, related by Abu Umamam Al-Bahili, quoted in Kabbani, *The Approach of Armageddon?*, 225.

8. Philips, *Ad-Dajjal, the Antichrist*.

9. Zubair, *Signs Of Qiyama*, 17.

10. Sahih Bukhari, Volume 9, Book 88, Number 248, narrated by Anas bin Malik.

11. Kabbani, *The Approach of Armageddon?* 226.

12. Philips, *Ad-Dajjal, the Antichrist*.

13. Suyuti, Durr al-Manthur, as quoted in Kabbani, *The Approach of Armageddon?* 227.

14. Excerpts from a Friday sermon delivered by Palestinian Authority *imam* Sheikh Ibrahim Madhi at the Sheikh 'Ijlin Mosque in Gaza City, broadcast live on April 12, 2002 by Palestinian Authority television http://memri.org/bin/articles.cgi?Page=archives&Area=sd&ID=SP37002.

15. Shahid, *The Last Trumpet*, 254.

16. Veinakode, *Doomsday Portents and Prophecies*, 312.

17. Sahih Muslim, Book 041, Number 6924, reported by Abu Huraira.

CHAPTER NINE: COMPARING THE BIBLICAL JESUS AND THE DAJJAL

1. http://www.answering-christianity.com/que5.htm.

CHAPTER TEN: THE REVIVED ISLAMIC EMPIRE OF THE ANTICHRIST

1. Unger, *Beyond The Crystal Ball*, 81.

2. Hitchcock, *The Coming Islamic Invasion of Israel*, 44, 45.

3. Roger Hardy, "Islamic affairs analyst: Islam in Turkey: Odd One Out," BBC, September, 26. 2003.

4. *Matthew Henry Complete Commentary on the Whole Bible*, Ezekiel 38 http://bible.crosswalk.com/Commentaries.

5. Hitchcock, *The Coming Islamic Invasion of Israel*, 31.

6. Shoebat, *Why I Left Jihad*, www.shoebat.com; *Islam and the Final Beast*, http://www.answering-islam.org/Walid/gog.htm.

7. Mostaghim, "Ruling Shiites' Influence Eroded by Other Faiths."

8. http://www.blueletterbible.org

9. Fred G. Zaspel, "The Nations of Ezekiel 38-39 Who Will Participate in the Battle?" http://www.biblicalstudies.com/bstudy/eschatology/ezekiel.htm

10. ibid.

11. See for instance, Robert Van Kampen, *The Sign* (Crossway, Wheaton, Illinios, 1992).

12. http://www.worldhistory.com/ancientrome.htm.

CHAPTER ELEVEN: THE DARK NATURE OF MUHAMMAD'S REVELATIONS

1. W.H.T. Gairdner, *The Reproach of Islam*, (Foreign Mission Committee of the Church of Scotland, 1911), 158.

2. Armstrong, *Muhammad*, 46.

3. Guillaume, *Life of Muhammad*, 106.

4. At-Tabari, *The History of at-Tabari*, Vol. 9, page 167, note 1151.

5. Sahih Bukhari Volume 6, Book 60, Number 478.

6. Gilcrest, *Jesus to the Muslims*. An online version entitled *Muhammad and the Religion of Islam* is also available at http://answering-islam.org.uk/Gilchrist/Vol1/3b.html Also, for a good discussion of the demonic activity in Muhammad's life see the article "Muhammad and the Demons," by Silas: http://www.answering-islam.org/Silas/demons.htm.

7. Ibid. (Gilcrest).

8. Sahih Buhkari Volume 7, Book 71, Number 660.

CHAPTER TWELVE: THE ANTICHRIST SPIRIT OF ISLAM

1. http://www.troid.org/articles/islaamicinfo/Islaamingeneral/shirk/theultimatecrime.htm.

CHAPTER THIRTEEN: ISLAM'S ANCIENT HATRED FOR THE JEWS

1. Walid Shoebat radio interview with Joseph Farah., available online at www.shoebat.com.

2. Gabriel, *Islam and the Jews*, 46-49.

3. Sahih Muslim Book 041, Number 6985.

4. Palestinian Media Watch, Studies on Palestinian Culture and Society by Itamar Marcus, available online at www.pmw.org.il.

5. Middle East Media Research, Friday Sermon on Palestinian Authority TV, April 17, 2002 Palestinian Authority Imam Sheikh Ibrahim Madhi at the Sheikh 'Ijlin Mosque in Gaza City, www.memri.org/bin/articles.cgi?Page=archives&Area=sd&ID=SP37002.

6. Josephus, *Wars of the Jews*, Book VI, Chapter V, Section 3.

CHAPTER FOURTEEN: END TIME MARTYRDOM

1. CBS News, "Saudia Arabia's Beheading Culture," June 27, 2004.

2. Duin, "Beheadings Allowed by Islam."

3. Ali Sina, "The Examples of Muhammad," available online at http://www.faithfreedom.org/Articles/sinaawa40621.htm.

4. Guillaume, *Life of Muhammad*, 464.

5. Ibid., 752.

6. Gabriel, *Jesus and Muhammad*, 60.

7. At-Tabari, *The Challenge to the Empires*.

8. http://www.muhammadanism.com/Islam/islam_beheading.pdf.

9. Ibid.

10. Taheri, "Chopping Heads."

11. Thacktson, *The Baburnama*, 188.

12. Taheri, "Chopping Heads."

13. Ibid.

14. Ibid.

15. Ibid.

16. CBS News, "Saudia Arabia's Beheading Culture."

17. Sahih Bukhari Volume 1, Book 3, Number 111.

18. http://forums.gawaher.com/index.php?showtopic=415.

19. Tasfsir Ibn Kathir Surah 9:5 available at: http://www.tafsir.com/Default.asp.

20. Ibid. -Surah 47:4.

21. Farah, "IslamicTerror.com?"

22. Sahih Muslim Book 20, Number 4546.

23. Saudi Arabian Islamic Affairs Department Web site: "Rights Dictated by Nature—The Rights of the Rulers and the Ruled Ones." http://www.iad.org/The Royal Embassy of Saudi Arabia.

CHAPTER FIFTEEN: ISLAM AND THE GOAL OF WORLD DOMINATION

1. Sahih Bukhari Volume 9, Book 84, Number 59, narrated by Abu Huraira.

2. Farah, "IslamicTerror.com?"

3. http://iisca.org/knowledge/jihad/jihad_for_allah.htm.

4. Tafsir Ibn Kathir Surah 9:123, available online at Tafsir.com.

5. Khaldun, *The Muqaddimah*, Vol. 1:473.

6. Al-Buti, *Jurisprudence in Muhammad's Biography.*

7. Tyan, "Jihad."

8. Gabriel, *Islam and Terrorism*, 81.

9. Ibid.

10. Al-Araby, *The Islamization of America*, 8.

11. Pipes, "CAIR: Moderate' Friends of Terror."

12. Report in the *San Ramon Valley Herald* of a speech to California Muslims in July 1998; quoted in Pipes, "CAIR: 'Moderate' Friends of Terror."

13. Ahmed Reza, "CAIR' Responds to Reverend Franklin Graham," Shia News.com, August 5, 2002.

14. Pipes, "The Danger Within: Militant Islam in America."

15. Jenkins, *The Next Christendom*, 180.

16. http://answering-islam.org.uk/Terrorism/agenda.html.

17. Patrick E. and Van Natta, Jr., "Militants in Europe Openly Call for Jihad and the Rule of Islam."

18. Ibid.

19. Massie, "Peaceful Religion Is Not Spelled I-s-l-a-m."

CHAPTER SIXTEEN: UNDERSTANDING DISHONESTY AND DECEIT IN ISLAM

1. Sunan Abu Dawood Book 14, Number 2631, narrated by Ka'b ibn Malik.

2. Hadith Imam Jafar Sadiq Footnote. #1 Usool al Kafi, 88.

3. Ibid., Ft. #2, Ibid., 522.

4. *A Shiite Encyclopedia*, October 1995, revised January 2001, available online at http://www.al-islam.org/encyclopedia/chapter6b/1.html.

5. Ibn Kathir's Tafsir -Surah 16:106, available online at www.tafsir.com.

6. Confirmed by At-Tabari and narrated by Abd al-Razak, Ibn Sa'd, Ibn Jarir, Ibn Abi Hatim, Ibn Mardawayh, al-Bayhaqi in his book *Al-Dala-il*, http://www.al-islam.org/encyclopedia/chapter6b/1.html.

7. Sunan al-Bayhaqi and Mustadrak al-Hakim, available online at http://www.al-islam.org/encyclopedia/chapter6b/1.html.

8. Ibn Kathir's Tafsir -Surah 3:28, available online at www.tafsir.com.

9. Taymiyah, *The Sword on the Neck of the Accuser of Muhammad*, 221, quoted in Gabriel, *Islam And Terrorism*, 91.

10. Al-Sirah al-Halabiyyah, vol. 3, 61, http://www.al-islam.org/encyclopedia/chapter6b/1.html.

11. Bukhari Volume 5, Book 59, Number 369, narrated by Jabir bin 'Abdullah.

12. Abdullah Al Araby, "Lying in Islam."

13. Al-Misri, *Reliance of the Traveller*, 745.

14. Ulum id Din, 3,137, quoted in Gabriel, *Islam and Terrorism*, 95.

15. Abdullah Al Araby, "Lying in Islam."

CHAPTER SEVENTEEN: THE GREAT APOSTASY, TERROR, AND ISLAM'S CONVERSION RATES

1. Amini, *Al-Imam Al-Mahdi: The Just Leader of Humanity*.

2. Graham, Rawlings, and Rimini, *The Stockholm Syndrome*.

3. Rubin, "Letters."

4. Aharon Megged, Israeli novelist, The Center for Ethnic Jewish Studies http://www.yahoodi.com/peace/stockholm.html#howwel.

5. Wilgoren, "Islam Attracts Converts by the Thousands."

CHAPTER NINETEEN: POTENTIAL PROBLEMS WITH THE THESIS

1. Boyer, *When Time Shall Be No More*.

CHAPTER TWENTY: FURTHER THOUGHTS

1. Oswald Chambers, *My Utmost for His Highest*.

2. Ahmed, "Islam Under Seige."

3. An essential read in this regard is an article from *Inside Report* at: http://www.insiderreport.net/clash_1-2.html.

CHAPTER TWENTY-ONE: HOW SHOULD WE RESPOND?

1. Francis Frangipane, "This Day We Fight!" http://www.elijahlist.com/words/display_word.html?ID=2294.

CHAPTER TWENTY-TWO: RESPONDING WITH OUTREACH

1. McDowell and Zaka, *Muslims and Christians at the Table*, 26.

2. Mallouhi, *Waging Peace on Islam*, 263-287 (Note from the author: I highly recommend this book).

CHAPTER TWENTY-THREE: PREPARING FOR MARYRDOM

1. Rick Joyner, *Shadows of Things to Come*, 116.

2. Dhimmi Watch, *Muslim, Christian Leaders Condemn `Religious Killing' of Kim Sun-il*, http://www.jihadwatch.org/dhimmiwatch/archives/002526.php.

APPENDICES

1. Or even better, try John the Baptist's approach: "So he began saying to the crowds who were going out to be baptized by him, 'You brood of vipers, who warned you to flee from the wrath to come? Therefore bear fruits in keeping with repentance, and do not begin to say to yourselves, "We have Abraham for our father," for I say to you that from these stones God is able to raise up children to Abraham. Indeed the axe is already laid at the root of the trees; so every tree that does not bear good fruit is cut down and thrown into the fire'" (Luke 3:7-9).

2. Pawson, *When Jesus Returns*, 2, 3.

3. Chesler, *The New Anti-Semitism*, 4, 87, (and most of what is in between).

Abdullah, Professor M. *Islam, Jesus, Mehdi, Qadiyanis and Doomsday.* New Delhi: Adam, 2004.

Ahmed, Akbar. "Islam Under Seige," *The Globalist*, July 20, 2003, http://www.theglobalist.com/DBWeb/printStoryId.aspx? StoryId=3319.

Al-Araby, Abduallah. *The Islamization of America.* Los Angeles: The Pen vs. the Sword, 2003.

-----. "Lying in Islam." *Islam Review*, available online at http://www.islamreview.com/articles/lying.shtml.

Al-Buti, Dr. Muhammad Sa'id Ramadan. *Jurisprudence in Muhammad's Biography*, 7th ed., 134, http://www.secularislam.org/jihad/exegesis.htm

Al-Misri, Ahmad ibn Naqib. *The Reliance of the Traveller and Tools of the Worshipper, a Classic Manuel of Islamic Sacred Law.* Translated by Noah Ha Mim Keller. Beltsville, Maryland: Amana Publications, revised 1994.

Al-Sadr, Ayatullah Baqir, and Ayatullah Muratda Mutahhari. *The Awaited Savior.* Karachi: Islamic Seminary Publications.

Armstrong, Karen. *Muhammad: A Biography of the Prophet.* New York: Harper Collins Books, 1993.

Amini, Ayatollah Ibrahim. *Al-Imam Al-Mahdi: The Just Leader of Humanity.* Translated by Dr. Abdulaziz Abdulhussein Sachedina. Qum, Iran: Anasaryan Publications, 1997, available online at: http://al-islam.org/mahdi/nontl/Toc.htm.

At-Tabari. *The History of at-Tabari (Ta'rikh al-rasul wa'l-muluk).* Vol 11, *The Challenge to the Empires.* Translated by K.Y. Blankkinship. SUNY series in near Eastern Studies, Bibliotheca Persica. Albany: State University of New York Press, 1993, p.44-45 as quoted in http://www.muhammadanism.com/Islam/islam_beheading.pdf.

Boyer, Paul. *When Time Shall Be No More: Prophecy Belief in Modern American Culture.* Cambridge: Belknap Press, 1994.

Brother Andrew. *Light Force*. Grand Rapids: Fleming H. Revell, 2004.

Chesler, Phyllis. *The New Anti-Semitism*. Jossey Bass, 2003.

Duin, Julia. "Beheadings Allowed by Islam but Only in Extreme Situation." *Washington Times*, June 24, 2004.

Elliot, Michael. "The Semiotics of Saddam." *Time Magazine*, December 29, 2003.

Farah, Joseph. "IslamicTerror.com? Muslim Web sites in West Defend Bin Laden, Call for '5th Column." *WorldNetDaily*, November 13, 2001.

Gabriel, Mark A. *Islam and the Jews, The Unfinished Battle*. Lake Mary, Florida: Charisma House, 2003.

-----. *Jesus and Muhammad*. Lake Mary, Florida: Charisma House, 2004.

Gilcrest, John. *Jesus to the Muslims*. Benoni, Republic of South Africa, 1986.

Graham, Dee L.R., Edna Rawlings, and Nelly Rimini. "The Stockholm Syndrome: Not Just For Hostages." Available at http://www.yahoodi.com/peace/stockholm.html#howwel.

Guillaume, A. *The Life of Muhammad*. Oxford University Press, 2001.

Henry, Matthew. *Matthew Henry Complete Commentary on the Whole Bible*. Henrickson, 1991.

Hitchcock, Mark. *The Coming Islamic Invasion of Israel*. Sisters, Oregon: Multnomah, 2002.

Hogan, Susan. "Drawn to Islam." *Dallas Morning News*, November 3, 2001.

Izzat, Muhammad ibn and Muhammad 'Arif. *Al Mahdi and the End of Time*. London: Dar Al-Taqwa, 1997.

Jenkins, Phillip. *The Next Christendom, The Coming of Global Christianity*. New York: Oxford University Press, 2002.

Josephus, Flavius. *Wars of the Jews, The New Complete Works of Josephus*. Translated by William Whiston. Paul L. Maier, Kregel Academic & Professional, 1999.

Joyner, Rick. *Shadows of Things to Come*. Nashville: Thomas Nelson, 2001.

Kabbani, Shaykh Muhammad Hisham. *The Approach of Armageddon? An Islamic Perspective*. Canada: Supreme Muslim Council of America, 2003.

Kathir, Ibn. *The Signs Before the Day of Judgement*. London: Dar Al-Taqwa, 1991.

Khaldun, Ibn. *The Muqaddimah*. Translated by Franz Rosenthal. New York: Pantheon Books, Inc., 1958.

Kelani, Abdulrahman. *The Last Apocalypse, An Islamic Perspective*. Fustat, 2003.

Mallouhi, Christine A. *Waging Peace on Islam*. Dowers Grove: Intervarsity, 2000.

Massie, Mychal. "Peaceful Religion Is Not Spelled I-s-l-a-m." *WorldNetDaily*, May 25, 2004.

McDowell, Bruce A. and Anees Zaka. *Muslims and Christians at the Table*. Phillipsburg, New Jersey: P& R Publishing, 1999.

Mostaghim, Ramin. "Ruling Shiites' Influence Eroded by Other Faiths." Inter Press Service News Agency, May 5, 2004

Pawson, David. *The Challenge of Islam to Christians*. London: Hodder and Stoughton, 2003.

-----. *When Jesus Returns*. London: Hodder and Stoughton, 1995.

Philips, Abu Ameenah Bilal Ph.D. *Ad-Dajjal, the Antichrist*. Alexandria: Soundknowledge Audio Publishers, 2001.

Pipes, Daniel. "CAIR: Moderate' Friends of Terror." *New York Post*, April 22, 2002.

-----. "The Danger Within: Militant Islam in America." *Commentary Magazine*, November 2001.

R'ad, Kamran. *Freemasons and Dajjal*. London: Islamic Academy, 2003.

Rubin, George E. "Letters." *Commentary Magazine*, May 2000.

Sachedina, Abdulaziz Abdhulhussein. *Islamic Messianism, The Idea of the Mahdi in Twelver Shi'ism*. Albany: State University of New York, 1981.

Shafi, Mufti Mohammad and Mufti Mohammad Rafi Usmani. *Signs of the Qiyama and the Arrival of the Maseeh*. Karachi: Darul Ishat, 2000.

Shahid, Samuel. *The Last Trumpet: A Comparative Study of Christian-Islamic Eschatology*. U.S.: Xulon Press, 2005.

Shoebat, Walid. *Why I Left Jihad*. U.S.: Top Executive Media, 2005.

Taheri, Amir. "Chopping Heads." *New York Post*, May 14, 2004.

Thacktson, Wheeler M., ed. and trans. *The Baburnama—Memoirs of Babur, Prince and Emperor*, Oxford University Press, 1996, 188; quoted in Bostom, Andrew. "The Sacred Muslim Practice of Beheading." *FrontPageMagazine.com*, May 13, 2004.

Tyan, E. "Jihad." *Encyclopaedia of Islam*. 2nd ed. Leiden: Brill, 1965.

Unger, Merrill F. *Beyond The Crystal Ball*. Chicago: Moody Press, 1974.

Van Kampen, Robert. *The Sign*. Wheaton, Illinois: Crossway, 1992.

Patrick E. and Don Van Natta Jr. "Militants in Europe Openly Call for Jihad and the Rule of Islam." *New York Times*, April 26, 2004.

Veliankode, Sideeque M.A. *Doomsday Portents and Prophecies*. Scarborough, Canada, 1999.

Whittell, Giles, "Allah Came Knocking at My Heart," *Times*, January 7, 2002.

Wilgoren, Jodi. "Islam Attracts Converts by the Thousands, Drawn Before and After Attacks." *New York Times*, October 22, 2001.

Yahya, Harun. *Jesus Will Return*. London: Ta Ha, 2001.

-----. *The End Times and the Mahdii*. Clarkesville: Katoons, 2003.

Zwemer, Samuel S. *Islam and the Cross: Selections from "The Apostle to Islam."* Edited by Roger S. Greenway. Phillipsburg: P&R Publishing, 2002.

Zubair Ali, Mohammed Ali Ibn. *Signs of Qiyamah*. Translated by M. Afzal Hoosein Elias. New Delhi: Abdul Naeem, 2004. Available online at http://members.cox.net/arshad/qiyaama.html.

For more information, please visit the author's web site at:

www.Joels-Trumpet.com